The Cowboy

At Work

All about his job and how he does it,

with 600 detail drawings by the author

by

FAY E. WARD

Foreword by

John R. Erickson

UNIVERSITY OF OKLAHOMA PRESS
Norman and London

ISBN: 0-8061-2051-7

Copyright © 1958 by Hastings House, Publishers, Inc. All rights reserved. Paperback edition published by the University of Oklahoma Press, Norman, Publishing Division of the University. Manufactured in the U.S.A. First printing of the paperback edition, 1987; second printing, 1989.

To my friend, Bill Simpson, and all other old-time cowhands who rode the open range in those days. May they never be forgotten.

FOREWORD
BY
JOHN R ERICKSON

Every now and then I run into someone who can tell firsthand stories about J. Frank Dobie, Walter Webb, Ben K. Green, and other major writers in our literature of the West.

But I have never met anyone who knew Fay Ward, and not many who were even aware of his work.

That's odd, because I would rank *The Cowboy at Work* among the best books ever written about the American cowboy, maybe *the* best. It's strange that we should know so little about the man who wrote it.

In his Preface, Ward offers only this general bit of information about himself: "The author worked as a horse wrangler, cowhand, bronc breaker and rough-string rider for cow outfits in Canada, and for outfits extending from there to the border of Mexico, for a period of over forty years. He feels somewhat qualified, therefore, to speak with authority about the methods and equipment employed by cowhands in their work."

There is no question that Ward was "somewhat qualified" to write about the cowboy of his day, but I can't help wondering about the man himself. From the jacket and an interview that he gave to the Grand Junction, Colorado, *Daily Sentinel* on June 16, 1968, we learn that he was born in Ackley, Iowa, in 1888 to a family who traveled to rodeos and fairs with an exhibition of Roman riding. Placed in an orphans' home in Des Moines, he was later adopted by a pioneer rancher near Crow Lake, South Dakota. After three unsuccessful attempts he ran away from the rancher's home at age fourteen. Heading westward across the Missouri River, he made it to the Black Hills afoot. His first job was with the "Reversed D 4 P Connected" cow outfit of "Prusho" (Presho?), South Dakota. From there he migrated northward and lived with the Sioux Indians while he worked for the Dupree outfit that owned the Circle D buffalo herd.

But most of all I would like to know where Fay Ward acquired the skills that enabled him to write and illustrate this book. Acquiring knowledge is one thing; turning it into a book is another. And producing a book as good as this one requires gifts that can only be described as extraordinary.

The *Daily Sentinel* interviewed Ward when he was participating in the 1968 Colorado Stampede activities. Describing Ward, who was then nearing eighty-one years of age, as "quiet yet extremely alert," the *Sentinel* quoted him as saying, "I'm not a writer; just a cowboy telling what he knows." Nevertheless, at that time Ward, who was living with his wife in Prescott, Arizona, was looking forward to the publication of three books besides *The Cowboy at Work:* a history of rodeos, a rodeo manual that he hoped would be called "Rodeo and How," and a book telling "some of the unusual predicaments a man and a horse can get into."

The *Sentinel* reported that Ward had won the Grand Junction Frontier Days, the predecessor of the Colorado Stampede, in 1915—fifty-three years before. With seemingly characteristic modesty, Ward said that he had won it "accidentally." The same cowboys had beaten him earlier, at the Cheyenne Frontier Days.

Although Ward didn't think of himself as a particularly good writer, he wrote a kind of prose that sparkles in its clarity and simplicity. He stated his business, didn't waste the reader's time, and didn't try to impress anyone with his vocabulary.

In the process of being who he was, he succeeded in doing what writers are supposed to do: communicate information and emotion. Somehow he managed to avoid the most common error made by novice writers, overwriting. Instead of pushing for style and effect, he built page after page of good, solid sentences. He also illustrated the book with six hundred of his own drawings. In the Preface he writes, "The illustrations are examples of my first efforts at serious drawing, for which I make due Apology."

Apology for what? His drawing, like his prose, is a tool of communication: simple, unadorned, honest, and accurate. He illustrates the point he's describing extremely well, and the reader with a good eye for detail will search in vain for evidence of shoddy work. The tiny details of hands, feet, horse ears, cow horns, loops in the air, calves under stress—they all serve as character witnesses for the fellow who drew them.

Ward's scholarship was the rarest kind, that which came from his own observation and experience, and he wrote for the very best of reasons: he had something to say.

There lies the strength of Fay Ward. He very definitely *did* have something to say, and every word he wrote can pass the tests and cross-examinations of the severest critics in his field: the saddlemakers, horse trainers, ranchers, and cowboys who have an uncanny knack for smelling out a fraud.

It's a pity these people don't write reviews and compile lists of the most important books about the West. If they did, we would hear a good deal more about Fay Ward and a good deal less about many of his contemporaries—and a good deal less about the writers of the following generation who have borrowed from the Ward treasure without leaving any IOU's behind.

I think it would be safe to say that no one has ever compiled more good raw information on the working cowboy than Fay Ward. A more worldly author would have rationed out the experiences of a lifetime and stretched them into three or four books. Ward put them all into one.

From his essay on the evolution of the cowboy to his final chapter on firearms, he covered every piece of equipment used by the cowboys of his time: quirts, saddles, stirrups, saddle horns, chaps, spurs, brands, bridles, bits, boots, and clothes.

Even the lowly cinch webbing, perhaps the least-noticed part of the cowboy's gear, gets a four-page treatment. I doubt there has ever been another author who could think of that much to say about the cinch.

He gives detailed explanations on rounding up cattle, holding herd, packing and camping, judging the age of horses and cattle, trapping wild stock, breaking horses, roping, and braiding rawhide.

His section on roping technique is especially impressive. Most cowboy memoirs contain references to roping such as, "We roped the big steer and tied him down." But they don't give any detailed information on the type of loop or how it was thrown. Perhaps the authors thought that roping styles would never change, but they were wrong. Pasture roping techniques have changed so much in the past thirty years that many of the old-time loops known to Ward and his contemporaries have all but disappeared.

Ward's chapters on roping are the best single source of information we have on old-time ranch roping techniques. With his descriptions and illustrations, a young cowboy today can go to his roping dummy and reconstruct throws that he has never seen in the arena or even on a ranch.

Ward's knowledge of cowboying and the cattle industry came out of the first half of this century, and cowboying has changed a great deal since this book first appeared in 1958 (the index has an entry for "horse wrangler" but none for "horse trailer," which pretty well dates the material to before 1950). Still, the core of Ward's knowledge is as timely and accurate today as it was fifty or seventy-five years ago.

I am delighted that the University of Oklahoma Press has brought out this masterpiece in paperback and made it available to a wider audience. If I were a young cowboy today, I would read it and study it and keep it beside my bed. No one has ever written a better manual on cowboying, and I doubt that anyone ever will.

PREFACE

In presenting this book for public consideration, my purpose is to make available to all those who happen to be interested the facts pertaining to the history of the cowhand, the type of equipment he used in his everyday work, and how he used it. I have tried to present a clear and useful outline of the methods an experienced cowhand employed in his work on the open range.

I must confess that in the beginning this book was designed to be a complete cowboy's manual—not, indeed, purporting to tell the experienced cowhand how to go about getting his job done, but as an authoritative reference work for all those interested in the cowhand as he functioned in his job during the period when there was still plenty of open range for him to circulate in. The illustrations are examples of my first efforts at serious drawing, for which I make due apology; but it is hoped that they will be a useful supplement to the text for which they were drawn originally, more than twenty years ago.

The author worked as a horse wrangler, cowhand, bronc breaker and rough-string rider for cow outfits in Canada, and for outfits extending from there to the border of Mexico, for a period of over forty years. He feels somewhat qualified, therefore, to speak with authority about the methods and equipment employed by cowhands in their work.

'Nuff said, *amigos!*

ACKNOWLEDGMENTS

Acknowledgment is due many friends and advisors for assistance in the preparation of this book, most particularly to Edmund Collier who found a publisher for it and helped prepare the manuscript; to Nick Eggenhofer who checked technicalities in some of the drawings and drew the handsome illustration on the dust jacket; to Katherine Field for her drawing on page 60; to the late "Coteau" Gene Stebbings for his text on the handling of guns; and to the editors at Hastings House.

F. E. W.

CONTENTS

LIST OF
ILLUSTRATIONS

Circles or drives; working a roundup herd; cows and
calves cut, stray cut; checking a milling herd; moving a
herd. Bending a herd; counting cattle; moving wild stock;
stopping a stampede; crossing bridges.

Southern outfit; the *remuda.* Northern outfit; the
rope corral.

THE
COWBOY
AT WORK

PLATE 1

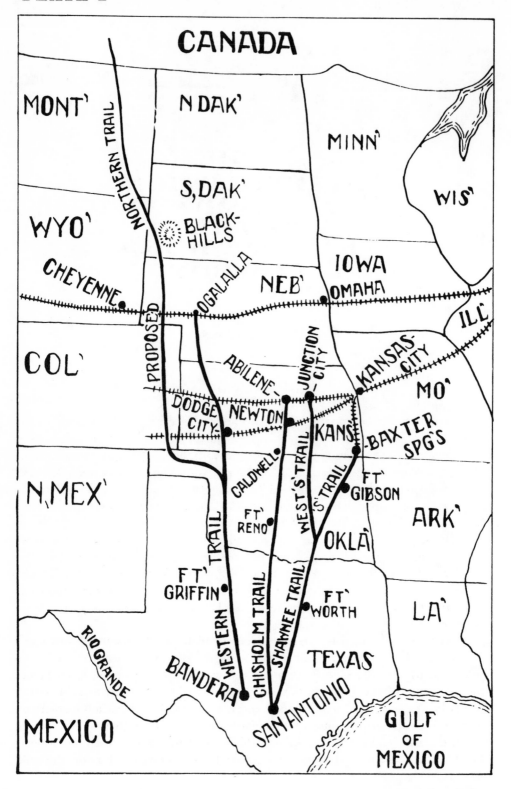

The Old Cattle Trails

1

EVOLUTION
OF THE
COWBOY

The evolution of the American cowboy and his equipment dates back to the Spanish conquest of Mexico in 1519 by Cortes and his conquistadors. The descendants of these same adventurous conquistadors settled in Mexico. Some of them became owners of large estates and were known as *hacendados,* and their extensive ranches were called *haciendas.* Eventually they drifted northward with their great herds of longhorn cattle and mustang horses and crossed the Rio Bravo, now called the Rio Grande.

The stock industry thrived and spread from Texas to California, and there naturally came into being a great number of stockmen who operated on a smaller scale than the *hacendados.* They were known as rancheros, or small ranch owners. The men who were employed to handle the range stock were known as *vaqueros,* meaning cowboys. The term "buckaroo" in common use in the West is derived from this Spanish word.

When Texas gained her independence in 1836, the American cowboy came into being. The Mexican ranchers abandoned their ranches and drifted *muy pronto* across the Rio Grande to avoid the wrath of the *Tehanos.* Even before the departure of the Mexican ranchers, and as early as the first Spanish settlements in Texas, a great many horses and a large number of cattle escaped and went wild in the brush. Since the Spaniards did not castrate their animals, these escaped horses and cattle multiplied rapidly, so that, together with the animals the Mexicans abandoned when they trekked back across the Border, the wild herds became incredibly numerous. The great number of horses and cattle running wild tempted many a buffalo hunter and Indian scout to go into the cattle business, for cattle and horses were to be had for the taking.

Naturally the Americans adopted the equipment and methods used by the Mexican rancheros and *vaqueros*. Therefore, the style of equipment used by the early-day buffalo hunters and scouts had its influence, to a certain extent, upon the outfits used by the old-time cowhand that followed. The illustrations on Plates 2 and 3 show the various stages of development of the cowhand's equipment.

During the Civil War many of the ranchers and cowhands deserted the ranches and enlisted in the service of the Confederate army. As a consequence, the cattle and horses that were left to range unmolested increased to even greater numbers and ran wild over a vast territory. When the war was over, many of the former cowmen returned to their old occupation and with them came ex-soldiers, their friends and friends of their friends who saw that here was a great opportunity to build up independent stock businesses. When the northern trails were opened, the Texas cowhand came into his own. It is estimated that fully ninety per cent of the old-time Texas cowhands were former Confederate soldiers.

During the period from 1865 to 1895, the cowhand and his equipment changed materially. In California the Spanish methods and equipment retained their influence upon the outfits of the cowhand much longer than in any other part of the cow country north of the Mexican Border.

When the northern trails were closed, the northern cowhand became an important factor in the cattle businesses, and the equipment and methods he used were the result of Texas and California influences. But these influences, when fused with and then modified by conditions of climate and locale, produced a distinct type, as easily distinguishable and recognizable as its Texas or California counterparts.

However, Texas, California and Montana cowhands are the same kind of guys under the skin; they differ, actually, only in the style of their equipment and in the methods used in their work which are largely shaped by the kind of country they operate in and the sort of weather they have to face.

The species "cowhand" is no special breed of human; but he is a special type created by his special way of life. Perhaps, though, it does take a special kind of guy to choose to be a cowhand. The cowhand is possessed by a sort of pioneering spirit; he likes nature—that is, nature in the raw. He doesn't mind taking a chance, win or lose. He can take it on the chin and keep coming back for more.

The cowhand and the stock range are as closely identified with each other as the cowhand and his horse. Anything written about the evolution of the cowboy assumes that the reader has some knowledge of the history of the cow country and the stock business. The author realizes that the short outline presented above does not cover the subject adequately. However, he hopes it will help in

PLATE 2 *Evolution of the Cowboy*

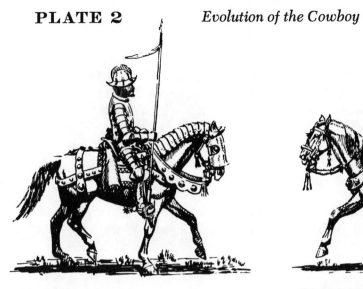

CONQUISTADOR

HACENDADO

RANCHERO

VAQUERO

BUFFALO HUNTER

SCOUT

PLATE 3   *Evolution of the Cowboy*

TEXAS COWHAND OF 1870

EARLY CALIFORNIA-NEVADA HAND

MONTANA OR NORTHERN COWHAND

SOUTHWESTERN TYPE OF RIDER

MODERN RODEO ROPER

MODERN RODEO BRONC RIDER

the understanding of the pages that follow which have, moreover, been made as self-explanatory as possible.

The professional rodeo° hand is also a product of the cow country, generally speaking, and is of the same type as the average cowhand. As a rule he is a "top-hand" and was schooled in the actual work of riding and roping out where skyscrapers seldom grow. Because of the inducements offered in cash prizes to the winners of the various roping and riding events and the thrill of winning over the best men in the game, some of the finest riders and ropers have become professional rodeo contestants and have made history which will long be remembered. The rodeo or frontier-contest hand has become a popular figure wherever he is seen in action.

Rodeo work is highly specialized and every move that a contestant makes is carefully planned to save time. The equipment used is designed and arranged to promote speed and efficiency. The element of chance, which may stand between the rodeo artist and the winning of the contest, is far greater than in any other line of sport. And there are always many keen competitors for the prizes. Rodeo work is more dangerous, too, than any other sport at present featured before the American public.

° Pronounced ródeo by the cowhand, cattleman and others identified with the cattle business; and rodéo by some outsiders who have adopted the Spanish pronunciation.

PLATE 4   *Types of Range Stock*

MUSTANG

LONGHORN

CROSSBRED   **BRAHMA**   **HEREFORD**

COW HORSE

RODEO ROPE HORSE

2

TYPES OF
RANGE STOCK

The different breeds of horses and cattle which have been predominant in the cow country since the beginning of the stock industry are shown to some extent in the illustrations on Plate 4.

The mustang and the longhorn are of Spanish origin; they are the descendants of the cattle and horses which Cortes and the other conquistadors brought over from Spain 1519 (the date of the conquest of Mexico) and during the years that followed. The Spanish horse was of Moorish and Arabian origin. The original Arab strain had great endurance and certainly many of the Indian horses in the early 1800's showed this quality. The cattle were for the most part of the Andalusian breed.

The mustang evolved from a process of inbreeding that went on among the horses that escaped from the Spaniards and lapsed into a wild state. Very few of them ever made good cow horses because they lacked the great stamina and endurance needed for cow work. Generally speaking, they were narrow-chested, light-boned and droop-rumped. This deterioration of the mustang can be ascribed to the fact that many of the best stallions were killed or badly injured in the fights between them during the mating season. What brought the wild mustangs of the Navajo country down in size more than anything else was probably the fact that they suffered from undernourishment. Also, the screw-worm's ravages contributed to the decimation of the best sires. So, for the most part, only the weaker specimens were left to propagate the species.

The Mexican horse, which is often referred to as the Spanish pony, and the Indian pony are descendants of the mustang; they are distinct breeds even though they have this common ancestry. Generally the Mexican or Spanish pony shows certain marked characteristics such as black stripes running down the length of the back and across the shoulders; frequently there are also black or dark-colored stripes or bars on the forelegs. The prevailing colorings are *grulla* (gru-ya), smoky blue or mouse color; *palomina*, a golden cream color; *appalusa*, a sort of bluish or red-roan color with spots of pure color juxtaposed in striking contrasts. Browns or buckskins are common colors, too. These Mexican or Spanish ponies are capable of great endurance and make good saddle horses.

The Indian pony is a decided improvement over the Mexican horse, both as to conformation and disposition. He is a blocky, well-proportioned horse, and because of the Indians' partiality for the pinto (paint), this type of horse has, through selection, been widely propagated among Indian ponies. The colors of the "paint" are generally white and black or white and bay, each color in its purity, so that there is a strong contrast between them.

The modern range horse and cow horse is the result of crossbreeding the Mexican or Spanish pony mares with the saddle horse—Thoroughbred, standard-bred and purebred sires. In the northern sections of the cow country the breeding trend is toward a large-boned, blocky and clean-limbed type of horse. The Percheron sire is the type of horse used. In the southwest, the qualities mostly favored in a good cow horse are conformation, endurance and speed. The Thoroughbred and the quarter-horse types of sire are much in evidence.

The rodeo roping horse and the horses generally used for bulldogging purposes are of the quarter-horse type. They are very compact, clean-limbed and powerful. For short distances of up to one quarter of a mile, this type of horse has no equal for speed. This is a desirable quality for a roping horse.

The longhorn breed of cattle is also the outcome of inbreeding among the animals in their wild state. These cattle that escaped from the Spaniards were of Andalusian strain, the same breed that provides the famous bulls of the Spanish bull ring. Longhorns are of many colors, including *appalusas, grullas,* browns and duns, as well as blues and red-roans and blacks. They are among the sturdiest of all the cattle breeds; they can go farther to water and grass, and still thrive, than any other type of cattle to be found on the North American continent. The longhorn dominated the range until the late 19th century. By crossing the Durham and the Hereford with the longhorn, a crossbred type of range cattle was produced which proved to be a good "rustler" and a good beef producer. The crossbred cattle are high-horned and easier to handle than the longhorns.

The Texas Brahma is also a crossbred type of range critter. It has been experimented with in the coastal regions of south Texas and in some parts of the southwest. It is the result of a cross between the longhorn and the Brahma cattle of India, and the Hereford. Texas Brahmas are very thrifty and are immune to ticks. They are wild-natured and difficult to handle in rough country and, because of their color, they have been widely discriminated against by cattle buyers. The colors are mixtures of brown and light cream which have been hard to erase in crossbreeding, but a fixed, blood-red color has been obtained by a few breeders. They are high-withered, because of the hump on the Brahma, and they are also droop-rumped and droop-eared. Because of their wild disposition and their ability to jump high and crooked, they are used extensively in rodeos and frontier contests for riding purposes. Their horns curve vertically above their heads, which helps to give them a wild and scary expression.

The Hereford, or white-face, has become the standard breed of range cattle because of qualities which make for a better type of beef carcass and because of their general adaptability to range conditions in the different sections of the cow country. They are light-boned and lower in stature than the other types of cattle mentioned herein, and though they are not as thrifty as the other types, their color and uniformity are more important qualities.

3

RANCH WORK

A brief summary of the different kinds of work that a cowboy is called upon to do in different seasons of the year, in the north and in the south, is outlined in the following paragraphs.

Northern ranch work: In the spring, riding bog is the job of keeping weak stock pulled out of the mud or bog holes. Stock which has become weak by springtime, especially the old cows, is easily bogged down. While crowding around some small water hole, weak stock is often knocked down by the stronger animals and is not able to get up. It is then necessary to pull 'em out at the end of a catch rope. The best way to pull a bogged critter out of a hole is to pitch a loop over its horns—not around its neck—and then pull it straight out on its back. This is better than to try to pull the animal out sideways or straight ahead with its legs under it. It is often necessary, if the animal has been bogged down for some time, for the rider to wade in and pull the critter's legs out of the mud before a horse can haul it out. Once the critter is out, it is generally necessary for the rider to tail the animal up (pull it up by the tail) to get it on its feet. Generally, once it is standing, it will try to turn and charge its rescuer. By watching his chance, the rider can get away from the critter by going off directly behind it. Sometimes it is necessary for two riders to lift an animal to its feet; one gets ahold of its horns and the other gets a tail hold. The man in front makes his get-away while the man behind holds the critter back. When the front man is safe, the other man high-tails it for *his* horse which is off at a safe distance where the steer can't easily charge him right away, and so both hands escape the irate animal.

Gathering weak stock is another job which the cowhand is often required to do in early spring when feed is scarce and it is necessary to feed the animals. Cows with early calves often need feeding to keep 'em going and those that have been weakened from being bogged down have to be gathered and fed. Weak stock has to be handled easy. Give 'em plenty of time and don't crowd 'em and then they will travel better.

Cleaning out water holes is sometimes necessary, though not often. A team and slip (scraper) are generally used to do the work which may take as much as a week, or only a day, depending on the country and the water supply.

Riding fence is sometimes part of the job of working for a barbwire outfit. Here is where a pair of wire-plyers takes the place of a six-shooter.

Breaking horses is generally done by a professional bronc snapper, but often a cowhand breaks out three or four head that look good to him for his own personal use; these horses he is then allowed to ride as part of his string. Young horses are generally easily broken. If plenty of time is taken in handling them and they are given good treatment, they will seldom make a jump. Details on breaking horses are given in another chapter of this work.

Calf work is spring wagon work (roundup), and consists of gathering and branding calves. This work is described in detail elsewhere. The interval between the spring and fall roundup work is often filled by two or three weeks of haying or fence riding and a number of other jobs that have nothing to do with handlin' a rope or a gun. Some cowhands have been known to take a short vacation during this season until the fall work is ready to start.

Fall work generally starts with beef work, that is, the job of rounding up and gathering beef cattle and other stock for shipment to market. At the same time, calves that were dropped after the spring calf work and any that may have been overlooked are branded and marked. Big outfits may make from two to four shipments during the season and keep a wagon busy gathering stock until snow falls.

Bulls are often gathered after beef work is ended so they can be fed during the winter. Calves are gathered and weaned in order to give their mothers a better chance to pull through the winter.

Winter work does not require as many hands as are needed in other seasons. The old hands—men who have made good—are the ones who are generally given a winter job. Gathering poor cows, cutting ice to open up water holes, feeding bulls and poor stock, hauling firewood, and riding line to keep stock from drifting off their range are the things which keep a stockhand from getting lonesome through the winter.

Line-camp work is practically the same as that done at the headquarters or home ranch. A line camp is located on the outer edge of an outfit's range and a couple of riders are posted there to look after poor stock and feed 'em, and to keep the water holes open by cutting the ice. They also ride line on the stock to keep it from drifting off its range. During storms cattle drift with the storm, and by cutting sign after a storm the line riders can generally tell whether any of the stock has drifted beyond the boundary of its range. If so, the riders locate 'em, drive 'em back and turn 'em loose where they belong.

A cowhand's mount in the winter consists of two horses which he calls his winter horses and which are kept up and fed grain. They are generally horses that a hand can pack a calf on if necessary and drive an old, poor cow with at the same time.

Southern ranch work: In presenting a brief outline of the work which a cowhand is expected to do in the southwestern range country, it must be borne in mind that ranching conditions vary greatly and that the methods of handling range stock and the kind of ranch work required depend on the type of country being worked and on the conditions of climate. Much of present-day ranch work is in fenced range territory; ranch work is different under these conditions from that in open range country. However, there is far more open range than the average individual realizes. It should be remembered that the general outline given in this book of the work that is done by cowhands covers the range country as a whole, closed or open.

Spring work is the gathering and feeding of weak stock, generally cows either with their calves or heavy with calf. The condition of the stock depends on whether there has been an early or late spring, as well as on the range conditions during the winter. If the cattle winter well, very few will require feeding, but if they need it, they are given cotton-seed cake, sotol, burned prickly pear (cactus leaves with the spines burned off) and sometimes hay. Where local range conditions are poor, stock is often moved to another range until the grazing improves and the cattle can be brought back.

Riding fence is necessary where the range is enclosed. The job of keeping up a fence around a hundred-section* ranch will keep a stockhand from loafin' when other work is scarce.

Range riding is generally for picking up any calves that have not been branded and marked and to keep cases on the activities of any *hombres* who happen to be handy with a long rope and an outlaw hot iron. Then there is crippled or injured stock that screwworms have started to work on. These animals it is necessary to rope and bed down so that someone can doctor 'em.

Screwworms are a constant source of trouble for the cowmen in the southwest during the warm months from the first of June until the end of September. Blowflies will blow (lay their eggs in) a freshly exposed injury and a horde of screwworms will attack the area the same day the wound is blown. And if the animal attacked is not caught and doped (doctored) within a day or so, the worms will do great damage. Calves freshly branded and marked have to be closely watched and looked after until the wounds have healed because of the danger of screwworms getting into the exposed places, especially in the bag of a calf that has been cut (castrated). Riders pack a screwworm remedy in a little bottle attached to the saddle so it will always be handy when wanted. When the range rider finds a case of worms that needs doctoring, he ropes the animal, ties

* A section is a square mile.

it down, and proceeds to shoot the dope into the affected part. The medicine used for this purpose exterminates the worms. It is generally a fly repellant and a healing antiseptic all in one. If there is no special worm medicine at hand when a case of worms has been found, the next best thing to do is to fill the wound with dry, pulverized cow chips or something similar that is locally available. This sort of substitute has proved effective at times when the wound is deep enough to hold the powdered material. Whatever is used should be tamped in closely in order to shut off the air from the worms. If the air can be cut off the worms will suffocate. This may not seem practical to some who have never tried such an emergency remedy, but it can work. (In the northern section of the range country the blowfly is not so prevalent as in the southern states, and consequently the danger from screwworms is minor compared to what it is in warmer climates.)

Water is always a problem that demands attention in the southwest and is often looked after by a rider while doing general ranch work. Where there are no running streams or natural water holes, windmills or dirt-tank reservoirs are depended upon to supply the water for the stock. If the water supply fails on some part of the outfit's range, it will become necessary to move the stock to some other locality. Windmills must be kept in operation, the outlet of the water supply source must be carefully watched to prevent loss of water, and so forth.

Roundup work, gathering yearlings for shipment, and branding and marking calves is a part of the spring work.

Summer work generally keeps a hand busy shootin' the dope to screwworms. Motherless calves are picked up and packed or driven to camp where they can be looked after. Bulls are scattered to different parts of the range wherever they are needed.

Fall work is practically the same as summer work; the same job of doctoring stock is continued until late in the season. During range branding, a rider must keep his eye peeled for sleepers (calves that have been earmarked by a rustler, but not branded; the rustler intends to return later to brand the calves with his own brand; see Section entitled "How Brands and Marks are Worked"); it is necessary to look over every calf that is earmarked to make sure that it is packing a brand. Salt grounds must be watched and salt put out when the supply gets low. Breaking horses is a job often done in the fall when there is plenty of grass to keep them in shape while they are being handled.

Fall roundup work includes gathering calves for shipment to feeders who fatten them for baby beef. Old cows and dry or barren she-stuff are also gathered and shipped for slaughter.

Water problems, range riding, and fence riding occupy the stockhand's time during the winter months. Roundup work and the gathering of calves for shipment is done in the winter by those outfits that did not ship calves in the fall. Also, bulls are gathered and placed in a separate pasture. Many of the big outfits have the hands break in horses during the winter. The horses are kept up and fed and this helps to gentle them so that when spring comes they are in good shape.

Telling the age of cattle by the horns and teeth: There are two ways by which the experienced cowhand can determine the age of range cattle, to wit, by reading the teeth and the horns. The diagrams on Plate 5 illustrate how the ages of cattle can be determined by both horns and teeth, though it is seldom necessary for a cowman to tooth a critter to determine its age, as most all range cattle have horns and the horn rings which are easily noted reveal the critter's years of growth.

The diagrams on the left of Plate 5 illustrate the growth and wear of the front teeth of the lower jaw of cattle. (Cattle have teeth only on the lower jaw.) The first set of teeth shown at the top of the Plate are those of a month-old calf. At birth the calf has two or more temporary or first sets of incisor teeth. With the first month the entire set of eight incisors has appeared as shown.

The diagram entitled "18 to 20 Months" shows how the temporary teeth have worn down; they will soon be replaced by permanent teeth.

The drawing entitled "2 Years" shows the third set of teeth with two permanent center pinchers which have replaced the two temporary incisors.

PLATE 5   *Telling the Age of Cattle by the Horns and Teeth*

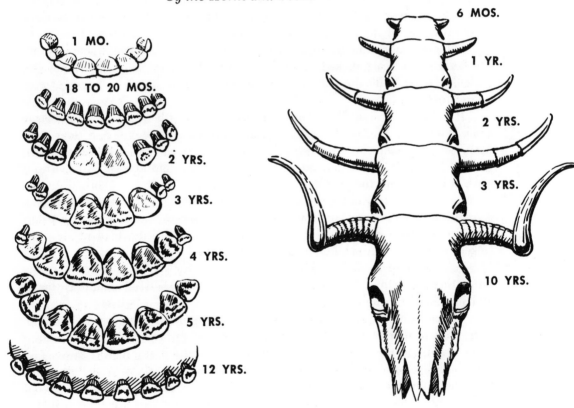

Now note the diagram entitled "3 Years." At two and a half to three years the permanent first intermediates are cut and are usually fully developed at the end of three years.

In the diagram "4 Years," the internal faces of the incisors as they look at four years are shown. At three and a half years the second teeth will have been cut and will be on a level with the first intermediates which will begin to wear at four years.

"5 Years": This diagram shows the teeth as they appear when the critter has reached maturity and is full mouthed. At four and a half to five years the corner teeth are replaced and the animal has a full complement of incisors with the corners fully developed.

At five to six years there is a leveling of the permanent pinchers and the corner incisors show wear. At seven to eight years the pinchers are noticeably worn, and at eight to nine years the middle pairs are worn. By ten years the corner teeth are worn.

After six years the arch or curve of the teeth gradually loses its rounded contour, and it becomes nearly straight by the twelfth year, as can be seen in the diagrams. In the meantime the teeth have become triangular in shape and distinctly separated, showing a progressive wearing down to stubs.

It is not difficult to tell the age of range cattle by their horns, as can be seen from the diagrams on the right of Plate 5. These diagrams show the development of the horns of a cow from the time she is eight months old until her tenth year. The way a critter's horns develop can be summed up as follows:

Two small, hard, rounded buttons, or points, emerge from the skin when the calf is eight to ten days old. At three weeks a little flexible horn has appeared. At five or six months the horn begins to curve and to assume a little of the shape it will eventually have. Up to this time, and during the first year, the horn is covered with an epidermic prolongation of the skin similar to that seen on a foal's hoof at birth. This covering dries and scales off by the twelfth or fifteenth month. Then the horn grows its permanent, natural, shining, tough surface and has the shape indicated in the diagram at "1 Year."

In the second year the horns start a second growth and a small groove is seen encircling the horn between the substance secreted the first year and that developed in the second. A second ring appears during the third year. These two rings, or grooves, around the horn are not well marked and all traces of them disappear as the animal becomes older. From three years on, the growth of the horns is marked by a groove or ring that is much deeper and shows clearly as an elevation of horny substance around the horn. These rings provide an accurate basis for estimating the age of the animal. After the animal is three years old, the outer part of the horn plus the first ring or groove are counted as representing three years, and each subsequent ring toward the base of the horn is counted as representing one year. At the part of the diagram marked "10 Years," the horn is shown as having seven rings, with an eighth ring about to appear. The first ring represents three years, the six other rings indicate nine years in all, and the growth from the last ring shows that the animal is really ten years old. The rings are more distinct on the concave or front part of the horns. After an animal has reached nine years the horns have a tendency to become smaller at the base. To make *certain* of an animal's age, the teeth should also be taken into consideration.

Fighting prairie fires: In the states where the range is heavily sodded and covered with buffalo and other grasses, prairie fires are a menace to the cowmen who have constantly to keep a good eye peeled for any indication of smoke appearing on the horizon. In hot, dry seasons, when the grass is withered and dry, the danger of fire is perhaps greater than at any other time. A big fire sweeping across an outfit's range may cause untold damage and loss of stock.

The causes of fire are many; a fire may be started by a piece of glass, a dropped match, lightning, and so forth. At night a fire can be spotted a long way off by the reflection of light in the sky. By the direction the wind is blowing, one can tell which way the fire is traveling. If the fire is headed for an outfit's range, then all hands get busy and proceed to gather old slickers, sacks, pieces of saddle blankets, etc., to fight the fire with. Sometimes a wagon with several barrels of water is taken along if the country to be crossed is not too rough. The sacks and blankets are soaked in the water, but often water is not available and the fire is whipped out with dry sacks and blankets.

Where the fire is running in heavy grass and is fanned by a strong wind, more effective measures are necessary to battle and check the devastating flames. A very effective technique often employed by cowmen is the following: A cow or horse is killed, the head is cut off and the carcass is split in half lengthwise. The two halves make two fire drags. Each half-carcass is turned so the inside will be down and ropes are attached to the forelegs and hind legs. These ropes are grasped by riders, two to each carcass section, and they drag the carcass over the flames on each side of the fire. Meanwhile the other men extinguish the sparks and small flames that may be left behind the drags with their sacks and slickers. Sometimes the riders haul the drags in opposite directions, depending upon the direction in which the fire is traveling. The riders who are handling the drags ride on a trot in order to put the fire out as quickly as possible.

Back firing is a device often resorted to to check an approaching fire. The idea is to burn over a strip about thirty to forty feet wide to serve as a fire guard. With a burning sack or a bunch of flaming weeds a man goes along setting fire to the grass while the other fire fighters stand watch and whip the blaze out when it has gone far enough. When the approaching fire reaches the burned-over fire guard, it will die out; but the fire fighters will have to watch out and see to it that the flames do not leap over the guard barrier. This often happens if a strong wind is blowing. Blazing embers of grass and dry cow chips are generally blown for some distance and if they are not put out, they are apt to set another fire to charging across the country.

4

ROUNDUP WORK

The map on Plate 6 will give some idea of how a range, or territory, is worked. The endless dotted line is the trail of the chuck wagon which has its beginning and ending at the spot designated as ⌐ (T L Connected) on the upper part of the map. Ranches are designated by large spots and the brand of each outfit is beside them. Such brands as I X, P-Cross, T L, T U, Horseshoe, Fiddle-Back, Circle-C, Frying-Pan, F, P N, R-Bar, and Turkey-Track are shown. Some stock-hands will recognize the country, located in Montana and shown as it actually is except for some of the names of creeks, etc. It is a territory which has produced some of the most outstanding western writers and artists, such as Charles M. Russell, B. M. Bower, Bertrand Sinclair (The Fiddle-Back Kid), Walt Coburn and others. These are names of men who have immortalized the history and traditions of the cow country.

The moves made by the chuck wagon each day are indicated by stars along the trail, and between the stars are black circular spots where the wagon camps. Each camp is the roundup ground for each drive, or circle, made. In making drives from one camp to another, the riders are split up into two groups. One group works the left side of the circle, and the other works the right side, as shown in the diagram at the top of Plate 7.* Though a drive is not always made on each side of the wagon trail in this way, and many a circle is made off to one

* The place names shown in the diagram at the top of Plate 7 will not be found on the map on Plate 6; the Plate 7 diagram is used simply to demonstrate the method of making circles during a drive.

PLATE 6   *Working a Range*

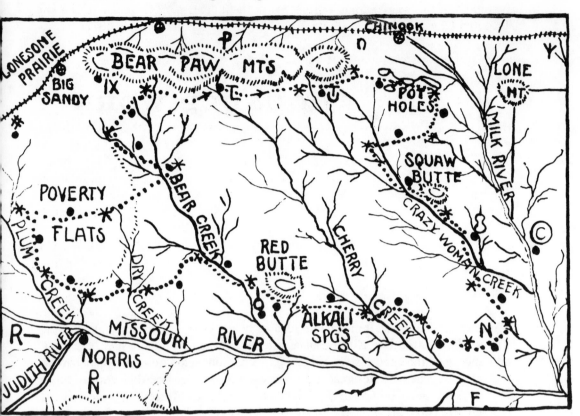

side only, the drives generally are made on each side of the trail traveled by the chuck wagon. A wagon may camp in one place for a couple of days and circles may be made and roundups worked several miles from camp. Much depends on the type of country and the number of cattle in the territory. Water and feed influence the selection of a camp and roundup ground, as well as the type of country which is being worked. The country to be worked that is shown in the map on Plate 6 extends to Milk River on the east, the Missouri River on the south, Plum Creek on the west, and to the Bear Paw Mountains on the north.

General roundups: These are a series of roundups which are planned and mapped out by the stock associations of each state. The wagons are numbered and those having consecutive numbers work adjoining territories. Thus the entire range will be thoroughly covered, or worked. The cow outfits in the country worked generally have their reps (representatives) or "stray men" with the wagons to help work the range and to gather and brand their own stock. The itinerary given below is the general plan of roundup work which was outlined by the Wyoming Stock Growers Association in 1884. It will be noted that the range was divided into specific districts with numbers corresponding to the numbers of the wagons that were to work them. This plan is similar to the one adopted by the Texas & Southwestern Cattle Raisers Association in 1877:

No. 1.   To commence at Big Crow Springs, June 1st, and work up Crow Creek to Ullman's ranch, thence across to Terry's ranch on Lone Tree; up Duck Creek to Twin Mountain; thence to the head of Crow; down Crow to Whitcomb's; thence to Arnold's ranch; down Pole Creek to Stage Road; up Horse Creek to the Lakes; thence down Bear Creek to the road; across to Kelley's and up Chug to its head; down Reishaw and Hunton Creeks, working the country West of Chug to Ft. Laramie; thence up the Laramie and Sabylle Creek to its head, working its branches. Fall roundup to begin September 20th. J. Preston, foreman; William Booker, assistant foreman.

No. 2.   Meet at Durbins crossing on Pole Creek, May 25th; work down Pole Creek to Julesburg; meet Cheyenne County roundup and South Platte roundup there; thence, in connection with the Cheyenne County roundup, work north to Rush Creek; thence up the North Platte to mouth of Pumpkin Creek; thence up Pumpkin Creek to its head. Fall roundup to begin September 20th. William H. Ashby, foreman; Chris Streaks, assistant foreman.

No. 3.   Shall commence May 20th, at Camp Clarke, on south side of North Platte; shall work the river up to Fort Laramie, then Cherry Creek and Box Elder, the Fox, Bear and Horse Creeks, from the telegraph road to their mouths. Fall roundup to begin October 1st. E. M. Tucker, foreman; Thomas McShane, assistant foreman.

No. 4.   Commence at Sidney Bridge, May 25th, work up the Platte in two divisions; first division working the head of Red Willow; thence up Snake Creek at the Sidney Crossing; then up Snake Creek to the head, taking in all the country west, and tributary to Snake Creek; thence across to the Platte at Godfry Bottom, and join the second division working up the Platte River; then both divisions work up the Platte River, taking in Sheep Creek, then up to the mouth of Rawhide, working country between Rawhide and Fort Laramie, then up Rawhide to its head, then to Fort Laramie and up the Platte to Broom Creek. Fall roundup to begin on Wyoming line, October 1st. Tom Snow, foreman of roundup in Wyoming; foreman of ranges in Nebraska, acting as foreman of roundup.

This schedule of the roundup work was drawn up by an association which comprised some thirty-one districts, covering the greater part of the state of Wyoming of those days. It will be noted that spring work started about the first of June and the fall work about the 20th of September. There is a foreman and an assistant foreman.

Big cow outfits which ran roundup wagons often blackballed small outfits that were accused of crooked work. The outfit blackballed was barred from working with the big outfit's wagon. Being barred from using a wagon which worked his range placed the owner of the small outfit under a handicap; it was unprofitable for him to run a wagon of his own, and under such circumstances he was generally forced to go out of business. However, there were times when neighboring outfits didn't approve of the decision of the big outfit to blackball the small one out, and then they would get together and form a roundup outfit of their own which was called a pool outfit or shotgun outfit.

Pool outfits, or shotgun outfits, are made up of a number of small cow outfits in a territory where no general roundup wagon is being run, or where the cow outfit which runs a wagon will not permit these other outfits, in the territory being worked, to have reps with its wagon. Each outfit furnishes a part of the roundup equipment, such as wagons, teams, etc. The grub bill and the expense of hiring a wagon cook, horse wrangler and night-hawk (see p. 34) are divided equally among the participating outfits. Otherwise, the pool outfit is handled in much the same way as in any other roundup.

This outline, together with the map on Plate 6, should give the reader a good idea of how a range is worked.

Working cattle: Methods for working mountain country differ from those suitable for open or prairie country. In open country the work is like that described in the map (Plate 6) of working a range, and in the diagram (Plate 7) of handling a herd. In mountain work, drives and circles are generally made from camp; that is, a camp is established and the surrounding country is worked from there. The territory may require several days to cover and pack outfits are generally used, as the country is too rough to run a wagon in.

Making a drive, riding circle and rounding up are all the same thing and the procedure is as shown in the diagrams on Plate 7. The large diagram at the top of the Plate shows how two drives or circles are made. These represent a day's work in open country. The two large ovals are each a circle, or drive. The trail of the chuck wagon is shown running through them. The circles shown near Hot Springs and Dry Lake are the roundup grounds where the cattle are thrown together in one herd. This is called the roundup. Riders are represented by a buzzard's-eye view of a horse's back; this applies to the other diagrams on the Plate as well. Breaking camp at Lost Camp in the morning, the chuck wagon moves to Hot Springs and camps for noon where the roundup will be made, as indicated by the circle. Splitting up the riders into two bunches, the wagon boss is in charge of one bunch of hands, the assistant foreman of the other. The bosses then proceed to lead the drives which sweep around in a circle. The two bunches of riders go in opposite directions, as indicated by the arrows. The men who lead the drives drop the riders off at intervals of about a mile. The distances separating the riders from each other vary considerably and depend largely on the type of

PLATE 7   *Handling a Herd*

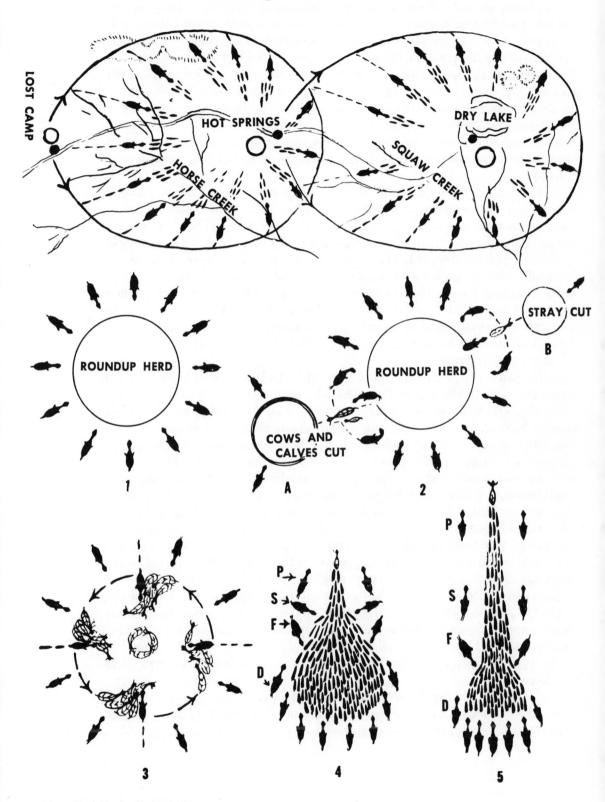

LOST CAMP

HOT SPRINGS

HORSE CREEK

DRY LAKE

SQUAW CREEK

ROUNDUP HERD

1

ROUNDUP HERD

STRAY CUT

B

COWS AND CALVES CUT

A

2

3

P
S
F

D

4

P

S

F

D

5

terrain being worked and the number of cattle in the country. In some regions the riders are two miles apart, and in others less than a mile. When a roundup is to be turned back to the starting point, as is customary in mountain work, the first riders to be dropped off (turned off) generally hold up until the riders on the outside swing can get around. This enables the riders to help each other and keep the cattle from getting away up some canyon or other. The cattle are all shoved (drove) toward the place designated as the roundup ground. When the roundup is thrown together, the riders change horses to work the herd. After dinner fresh horses are caught for the afternoon drive. Then the wagon breaks camp and moves to Dry Lake where the next roundup is made and worked.

Working a roundup or herd: When a drive is made and the roundup is thrown together, as shown on in Figure 1 on Plate 7, the herd is held by two or three riders while the others go to camp and change horses. The men on fresh horses relieve the ones that were left behind who also fetch fresh horses and come back to help work the herd.. These horses that are used to work the herd are generally the best cow horses in a rider's string and are often referred to specifically as cutting horses. They understand the work to be done as well as their riders and need a minimum of direction. The herd is held a while before the cutting-out work is started, in order to give the cows that have become separated from their calves a chance to get together with their offspring and to give them all time to quiet down.

The cattle carrying the brand of the outfit which is running the wagon are generally in the majority and the riders who do the cutting out for that outfit work the herd first. On the average, not more than three riders are allowed to work a herd at the same time, as too many riders cutting out at once will stir the cattle up too much, cows with calves will become separated from them, and the stock might get to milling around. In cutting out the rider should be careful not to work too fast. A slow, steady gait will produce the best results. The cows with unbranded calves that belong to the main outfit are cut out first, into a separate cut that is held together by one or two riders, according to the size of the cut (Figure A). This is called the cow-and-calf cut. When the main outfit has worked the herd, the reps are sent in to look over the stock and to cut out the cattle which belongs to their respective outfits. These cattle are held in the stray cut (Figure B). When the stray men have worked the herd, it is drove off a ways and turned loose. The calves in the cut-out groups are then branded and turned loose with their mothers; the strays are thrown into the stray herd or day herd. Some outfits do not cut out the cows and calves in the manner explained above. Instead, they rope the calves and drag them directly out of the herd to be branded and marked. This method is used for small herds more generally than for large ones.

Checking a milling herd: On Plate 7, Figure 3, is shown how cattle are stopped from milling (going round and round in a solid mass). Milling is often caused by too many riders working a herd at the same time or by the riders working too fast, or by too much excitement of any kind. A stampeded herd will mill for hours after the stampede is checked. Figure 3 shows the riders moving into the herd from different directions; this deflects the cattle from their course and checks those behind the ones in the lead. The cowhands riding slowly among them, cutting straight through the current of movement, will finally simmer 'em down. Another method is to stop working the herd and give it plenty of time and room to spread out. A herd held too close is more likely to start milling than one that is given plenty of room to circulate.

Moving a herd: Figure 4 on Plate 7 shows how a herd is handled by the riders when they are starting it out for a drive. When cattle are well strung out, they will walk better and are more readily handled, therefore the job is much easier on the stock as well as on the riders. In Figure 5 the herd has been strung out by the swing and flank riders. The letters P, S, F, and D designate the various parts of a herd which is being trailed, and the same terms are applied to the riders that take up the four positions alongside the herd: P stands for point; S for swing; F for flank; and D for drags. The two riders on the point are point men, the other pairs swing men, flank men, and drag men, respectively. The point riders are generally experienced cowhands and generally know the country they are traveling through, though not always. They point the herd in the right direction, and it is their job to see that there are no cattle in the way of the herd; they go ahead and drive such obstructing cattle out of the way. Both point men do not leave the herd at the same time, as it is necessary for at least one man to remain with the point to keep the critters on the go. When a point man leaves his position, the swing rider on his side advances and takes over the front position until the point man returns.

The swing men keep the herd from cutting across trails when it is swung to one side sharply and also keep the herd well strung out. The flank men keep the flank and drags (the lagging cattle) narrowed down to only a few head. The narrower the drag end of the herd can be kept, the better the stock will travel and the easier it will be for the drag men to keep the drags moving.

The weakest and the most tender-footed stock are always found among the drags and the strongest and fastest cattle are in the head of the herd.

Handling a herd: A herd moving along in good formation is shown in Figure 6 on Plate 8. In this diagram, the direction a point man would naturally take if he should ride on ahead of the herd—to throw stock out of the way, or for any other purpose—is shown by the arrow. If he rides off at an angle of about 45 degrees from the course traveled by the herd, the cattle will continue to keep moving. If the point man should ride straight ahead, as indicated by the dotted line, the leaders of the herd would stop, or turn off the trail.

In Figure 7 on Plate 8 the point man on the right is bending the leaders to the left. The point man on the left drops back to let them turn.

Figure 8 shows how a point man holds up the leaders when they travel too fast and the drags are falling behind too much. Sometimes the leaders will out-walk the other cattle and it is necessary to hold them up until the others catch up.

PLATE 8   *Handling a Herd (Cont.)*

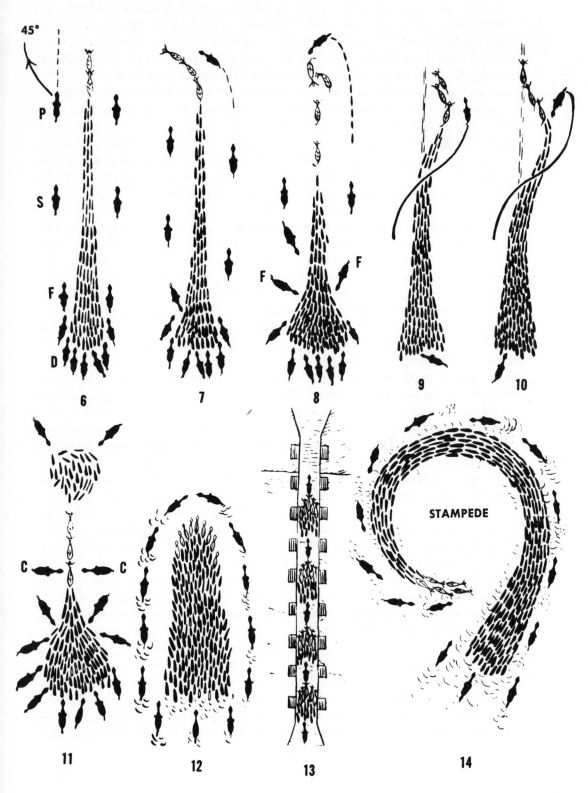

A point man rides ahead and stops the leaders as shown, and the flank men get busy and narrow down the width of the drags and string the critters out so they will travel more freely.

Figure 9 is a diagram showing how two men handle a herd. Here is where a rider's cow sense is clearly shown and the difference between the work of an experienced cowhand and that of an amateur is really apparent. A rider in this situation must be a point, swing, flank and drag hand all at the same time. To keep the herd moving, the cattle must be strung out, and if the leaders should turn off the trail (Figures 9 and 10), the rider who happens to be up near the point can, and generally does cut through the herd at an angle, as indicated by the arrow, thus bending the leaders back toward the trail. In order to straighten the leaders out on the trail when they hit it again, the rider turns back just before the leaders actually hit the trail. The leaders, seeing that the rider is not trying to bend them any more, will hit the trail and follow it, nine times out of ten. The rider who has pointed the herd then rides back alongside the bend in the herd and throws (forces) the rest of the cattle back onto the trail.

Counting cattle: This is shown in Figure 11. Two men do the tallying. The cattle are strung out and pass between the two tally men who are facing each other on their horses and counting the cattle as they pass between them, as indicated at C. Two riders are shown holding up the stock that has been tallied, while the other hands keep stringing the cattle out so they will not be hard to count as they pass the tally men.

A tally string is used by the counters in order to keep accurate check on the stock counted. The end of a saddle rope is often used for the purpose. The tally man holds his rope until a hundred head of cattle have gone by him; then he ties a knot in the rope and counts another hundred head. When the count is completed, the last count is added to the hundreds tallied by the knots in the rope.

Moving wild stock: To move wild stock without spilling them (allowing them to scatter) calls for action and plenty of it. When starting to move a snuffy or spooky herd of cattle, the point and swing men are generally in front of the stock in order to hold 'em up and keep them from running. The riders actually *surround* the herd, as shown in Figure 12. Wild stock that has been trapped, or a bunch of yearlings or calves, when starting out on a drive, will generally break out on a run and stampede if they are not held up until they simmer down. The drags are allowed to travel on their own and are not crowded. The riders keep the gaps between each other pretty well closed up so an animal will not have a chance to break out and make a getaway. Here is where a cowhand should know what is going on *behind* him as well as in front of him. He has got to keep cases on the rider behind him as well as the rider in front of him, and see to it that the space between himself and the others is not too wide, otherwise there will be an opening for some critter to break through. If one should make his getaway, it is best to let it go until a rider back by the drags has a chance to leave his position and circle the escaped critter back to the herd. "Hold what you've got" is the main objective. The riders should not ride too close to the herd but should give it plenty of air, or room. If a rider should quit the herd and take after every critter that breaks out past him this will naturally leave too much space between the riders before and behind him; this simply gives still more cattle a chance to break through. A rider who leaves his post at the wrong moment risks spilling the whole herd. A hand has sure got to use his head in handling snaky stock and keep his place. When the stock has simmered down, it is allowed to string out again and travel.

Corralling a herd: Here you have another situation in which the riders have to take precautions similar to those for handling wild stock (see the Section entitled "Working Wild Stock"). Time has to be given the stock to go through a gate, and if it is crowded too close, some critters will break back between the riders and high-tail it for yonder. Hold the main bunch until it is corralled and then take after those that broke out, circle 'em back and then corral 'em by riding in close formation and shove 'em through the gate of the corral at a rapid pace so they will not have time to turn back to make another getaway. Sometimes it is necessary to rope a critter which has got on the prod and decided that it is not going to be turned back. Such a critter has to be led back on the rope to the corral and turned loose only when it is gotten in.

In the case of a stock break-out handled out in the open, before the stock has been corralled, it is a good idea for all the riders to widen out and give 'em plenty of air to circulate in. Spooky stock will break out quicker if held very close than it will if given plenty of territory. Give 'em plenty of time when starting out on a drive, and when they are used to the sight of a man on a horse, they will generally settle down and travel at a decent gait.

A stampede: How a stampede is checked, is shown in Figure 14. Wild stock —mountain cattle—that have been trapped, or yearlings, are easily jumped or spooked and will stampede, at night especially, with very little reason. Cattle seldom stampede in the daytime because they are able to see what is going on around them. The present-day type of range stock is not easily boogered because it is handled more than stock was in the old days. But, if something unusual happens—such as, for instance, a horse running through the herd kicking at a saddle which has turned under his belly, or a bronc bucking into the herd—even stock today will be pretty apt to make a run.

The way to stop a stampeding herd is to circle 'em and try to throw the leaders back into the drags. For example, if a rider on the right-hand side of the running herd is closer to the leaders than the rider on the left side, the rider on the left side should fall back and let the riders on the right side bend the leaders to the left. If the riders on one side don't fall back and let the other riders on the opposite side bend the leaders, the cattle will be laned and will run straight ahead and will not stop until they are exhausted. The rider in the lead generally uses his slicker, or rope, to turn the leaders, waving it over his head or whipping them over the head with it. Sometimes a rider fires his six-shooter down beside the heads of the leaders and that is often effective in making the cattle turn. The riders behind the point man should fall in close behind him and crowd in along-side the cattle to help circle them. When the leaders have been bent back into the herd, the herd will be thrown into a mill and it will take some time to get 'em simmered down. The riders spread out in order to give 'em plenty of room to widen out and rest.

Cattle that have run a few times get the habit and have to be handled with care to prevent them from making another run. The lighting of a match, a horse shaking himself, the flapping of a slicker, a tumbleweed blown into the herd, or lightning striking close to them will make them leap to their feet and hit out a-running, which is when things begin to *pop*. If cattle have had plenty of grass and water just before they are put on the bed ground, they will be more contented and will lie down and rest. But when cattle are hungry and thirsty, they become restless and will keep getting up and disturbing those that are down—all of which gets them well primed for a run at the slightest provocation. Keeping them contented on the bed ground and giving them plenty of room in which to lie down is the secret of preventing stampedes—always, of course, barring unfortunate accidents.

Crossing bridges: Crossing a pontoon bridge is shown in Figure 13. To prevent cattle from balling up while crossing a bridge, they should be split into small bunches of about twenty head each, with a rider behind each bunch. A rider goes in the lead of the first bunch that is to cross to pilot 'em across. The cattle are forced into a slow trot so they will not have time to stop and turn back and ball up. If the herd is not divided into these small bunches, the critters are apt to stop and turn back when they are somewhere near the middle of the bridge. Then they get to crowding each other until they break down the guard rail; inevitably some of them will then be pushed into the water and lost.

If cattle should refuse to cross a bridge, even behind a pilot, as they have been known to do at times, a good plan is to rope a calf—if there is one in the herd—and lead him across. The calf's bawling and throwing fits as it is being led away will lure the mother into following and this will probably get the balance of the herd to follow too. They will have had their attention diverted from the spooks that have been holding them back. Sometimes it becomes necessary to cut off small bunches with a pilot in the lead and charge them on a run with the riders in close formation, and force them to cross. Or it may be necessary to bait the cattle. This is done by placing a small bunch at the far end of the bridge and holding them there until the others have been lured well along the bridge. Then the bunch used as bait is turned loose. This is often an effective device for getting the herd across.

Swimming cattle: Getting cattle across streams is a pretty big job at times. Once cattle balk at crossing a stream, it is hard to get them into the water again. If the lead steer will take to the water, the others will follow. Generally they will also follow a rider who goes ahead of them to pilot them across. When a rider pilots them, he will be able to bring them out on the other side at the right place. When they will not follow a rider, it is necessary to cut off a small bunch of stock and hold 'em together. Then the riders in close formation charge the bunch into the water before the bunch has time to turn back. As soon as they are started, another bunch is shoved in behind so it will follow the critters already in the water. If cattle are dry or thirsty they are easier to get into the water and across. The riders crossing with the cattle, except for the pilot, swim their horses on the downstream side of the herd to keep it from drifting downstream. The leaders are held up on the opposite side to be used as bait to induce the others to cross; this method is used when it is necessary to force the cattle across in small bunches.

A rider should loosen up the cinches on his saddle horse when swimming him across a wide stream, so the horse will have plenty of room to breathe and have more freedom in swimming. A horse should be given his head at such a time, and if he has to be guided, this is done by splashing water alongside his head. Many a rider has been lost because he pulled too much on the briddle reins; this is apt to cause a horse to go over backwards and drown both himself and the rider. Most horses are good swimmers and, given their head while swimming, are pretty sure to pack a hand across a stream in good shape. If a horse turns over on his side and refuses to swim when he gets into deep water, the rider should get a good hold on the horse's tail and slip off behind him; by kicking and paddling the rider can keep from going under, and splashing water onto the horse's head may make him straighten up and go to swimming. When a rider finds that his horse is a poor swimmer, he should get a tail hold, as described, and give the horse more chance to swim out.

Crossing boggy creeks: Doing this without losing some stock or getting a large number of cattle bogged down is a difficult job. Once the leaders start bogging down, they will naturally turn back and get away from the boggy ground if they can. In such a case it is almost impossible to get the stock started again. It is generally necessary to drive the cattle some distance to find a safe crossing, or to build a temporary bridge across the creek by cutting brush and timber to fill in the creek bed, giving a firm foundation for the stock to cross on. The fill-in material—brush and poles, if there are any at hand—should be tromped down into the mud and then covered over with dirt until you get a fairly solid base. Then a bunch of horses should be driven back and forth over it several times until it is packed down firmly. Then the horses should be taken over ahead of the cattle; the herd will thereupon take courage and follow the horses' lead. This technique for crossing boggy creek terrain will usually give good results and save time and loss.

Holding on bed ground: Cattle prefer to bed down on an elevation because there is more breeze on high ground than low. In case of a storm, high ground will not get as wet and muddy as low terrain will. Also, the higher bed location eliminates danger from floods. The herd is held about two hundred and fifty yards from the camp, or even farther away, so that if anything should go wrong in camp the commotion will not be so likely to booger the cattle. The herd is gradually thrown together by the riders on cocktail (see below) who graze the animals onto the bed ground where they are held loosely so they will have plenty of room to bed down and rest comfortably. By the time the first guard (see below) is ready to take charge of them, they are pretty well simmered down and taking things easy.

Standing, or riding, guard: This is the cowhand's night work. The guard work is split up into four shifts of two hours each. These are designated as the first, second, third and fourth guards. Two riders are assigned to each guard. The first guard goes on herd at 8 P.M. and stands (rides) until 10 o'clock; the second guard goes on then, and stands until 12 o'clock; the third guard works from midnight to 2 A.M.; and the last guard from 2 to 4 o'clock, when it is relieved by the riders who are to take charge of the day herd for the day.

Guards are generally alternated, so there will be no favoritism shown in assigning the men to guard duty. The riders standing first guard the first night out will stand second guard the next night, and the third and fourth guards the following nights. Permanent guard is the job of standing the same guard every night; the riders assigned to this duty have a harder time than some of the others.

Cocktail is the interval between suppertime and first guard. The wagon foreman appoints two or three men each day to go out and relieve the riders on day herd (see below) who then come in for supper and catch up their night horses which they will ride guard on. The men on cocktail gradually work and graze the herd onto the bed ground and hold them there until they are relieved by the first guard. The men who are on last guard are generally the ones who are designated to go on cocktail and they are generally assisted by the wagon boss.

Riding guard: The two men on guard at any time ride in opposite directions, so that they will meet and pass each other twice each time they completely circle the herd. By this method cattle that work out of the herd can be thrown back more effectively and the riders are able to keep cases on each other. The guards ride at a reasonable distance from the stock, forty to fifty feet, so they will not disturb them. Singing or whistling around a herd at night tends to reassure the cattle and makes them feel that all is well and it diverts their attention from annoyances that might cause them to get up and quit the flats. A rider must be cautious about lighting matches, putting on a slicker, jumping his horse off suddenly, or dismounting his horse near the herd. It is best to ride off to a safe distance to do any of these things, or to do any of the many things which might be necessary while on guard. Cattle will spook easily at night and the sudden flash of a match or the flapping of a slicker may booger 'em and cause them to make a run that could prove disastrous. If the herd should make a run, the riders on guard stay with the cattle until the herd is stopped and must hold it until they are relieved by other riders.

When it is time to call a guard to relieve the guard on duty, one of the two riders on herd goes to camp and wakes the men who are to make up the relief. Meanwhile, the other rider holds the herd until the relief comes along.

The day herd: In spring work this is generally the stray herd which consists of stock gathered by the reps of other outfits. They are cut out and thrown over on their home range when it is convenient, or cut out and drove home by the reps when the wagon quits work. On fall work, or beef work, the day herd is stock gathered for shipment, generally with some strays thrown in. The herd follows the wagons and is often in the charge of a day-herd boss. Riders who are put on day herd are alternated each day, in much the same way that the night guards are rotated, so that all will get a good share of the work. The day-herd shift may be for a half day, or for all day, according to the notion of the wagon foreman.

Northern cow work: Work is different in several respects from that in the southwest, largely because of the differences in climate and topography. The spring work in the north, which begins about the first of June, is for the purpose of gathering and branding calves; the fall work, which starts about September 20th, is devoted to gathering beef and other stock for shipment, and of course to branding and marking any calves that need it. The fall program is referred to as beef work and generally lasts until the snow flies.

Southern cow work: The spring work in the southwest is devoted to branding calves and sometimes also to getting yearlings for shipment. The time for starting the work in the different sections of the region varies greatly. Some outfits start about the 20th of May and others start about the first of July. The time for beginning fall work also varies considerably. These variations in starting dates are due to the different methods of handling stock employed by the various outfits. The fall roundup is, as already stated, for gathering calves for shipment and collecting baby beef, and for branding those calves that have been dropped late. The work in the fall may start any time from the 15th of October to the first of December. Because of the variations in the terrain and in the methods used by the outfits, and because of the fluctuations in stock prices on the cattle market, it is impossible to name over-all fixed dates for starting work in either spring or fall seasons in the southwest.

5

ROUNDUP
PERSONNEL

The part each of the hands plays while out on roundup work can be briefly described as follows:

The wagon boss has to be an experienced cowhand who knows how to handle a bunch of men and how to work a range. He knows how to read sign (*i.e.* track—according to one cowpuncher, a good tracker "could track bees in a blizzard").* He savvies what an old cow has to say to her calf, and he also knows how to outguess a cow. He is generally the first man on the job and will get out and do the things he asks his men to do. He is generally agreeable but firm in his demands. A hard-boiled foreman is never liked and can never get real service from his men and seldom holds his job.

Circle riders or *cowhands:* Generally from nine to fifteen hands are employed by the cow outfit running the wagon. They are the men who do the cow work which generally keeps them in the saddle about eighteen hours out of every twenty-four. It is not unusual, in fact, for a rider to cover sixty or eighty miles in a day's work, depending on the type of country he is working in. The number of horses he rides in a day depends on the size of his saddle string and the country being worked. Riding circle—or rounding up, working the herd, holding up the cut, roping and branding, day herding and night guarding, no matter what the weather, these are all parts of his job.

The *rough-string rider* is a bronc rider who is employed to ride the mean

* *Western Words: A Dictionary of the Range, Cow Camp and Trail,* by Ramon F. Adams, p. 124.

horses owned by the outfit. The bad ones are all in one string and are called the rough string.

Reps or *stray men* are cowhands working for some other outfit than the one that is running the wagon. They are there to represent the outfit they are working for and to look after its interests on the range. The rep is expected to do the same work as the other riders, except in the matter of day herding. He cuts out of the roundup the stock belonging to his own outfit and this stock is then cut into the stray bunch, or else is held separately. How the rep handles this stock depends on whether it consists of cows with calves, or of dry stuff that is to be thrown into the day herd or thrown (drove) over to its own home range and turned loose there. If the wagon work is entirely outside of his own outfit's range, all the cattle that he catches are thrown into the stray herd, or day herd, and when the wagon stops work, he cuts out his outfit's stock and together with his saddle string he drives the bunch back to its home range. The rep's board is often paid for by the outfit he is reping for. The number of reps with a wagon often equals, or even outnumbers, the number of riders employed by the outfit running the wagon.

The *wagon cook:* Some of the best wagon cooks are old retired cowhands. Knowing the wants and the ways of a cowhand, they are able to prepare the grub that will satisfy the men. A good wagon cook is particular and industrious; and he is on time with his meals, barring some accident that may prevent him from making connections. He can cook a meal for thirty men in less time than any other type of cook. He makes two moves a day, on the average, of ten to fifteen miles each. He drives the four-horse team that pulls the chuck wagon, helps to tear down and set up his cooking outfit, and has a hot meal ready for a large bunch of hungry riders when they come in off a long, hard drive. A good cook will do more to keep a bunch of cowhands in good humor than anyone or anything else.

The *horse wrangler,* or jingler, herds the saddle horses, or *remuda,* which may consist of a hundred to three hundred head of horses. He rustles wood and water for the cook, helps to set up and tear down the camp outfit, and helps to hook up and unhook the wagon teams. In the northwest he erects and takes down the rope corral and helps to load the wagons. If the cook should happen to need help because of some unavoidable delay, the jingler often peels spuds and chops the wood for the cookfire. When on the move, the wrangler drives the *remuda* behind the chuck wagon or the bed-wagon, and when the camp ground is reached, he turns the herd loose to graze and helps to set up the camp. When camp is made, he gets out and rustles wood and drags it to camp on the end of his saddle rope. If there is no wood in the vicinity of camp, he gets a grain sack and gathers a bunch of cow chips for fuel. A good horse wrangler will let the *remuda* spread out and graze where the grazing is good, see to it that the horses are well watered, and corral them when the riders are about ready to change their mounts. He handles the gate rope of the rope corral while the men are catching horses. Many an old cowhand first broke into the game as a horse wrangler; this is a good place for a green hand to learn the first principles of working stock.

The *night-hawk* has the job of night herding the *remuda*. He takes charge of the saddle-horse bunch when the horse wrangler turns it over to him about sundown and rides guard on the bunch until daybreak. Then he brings the horses in and gets them corralled by the time the cook is ready to yell "Roll out!" The horses are not close herded or bedded down like the day herd, but are allowed to graze in a place where the grazing is the best available and where the night-hawk can keep them in sight at all times. The physical condition of the horses depends to a great extent on the way the *remuda* is handled by the horse wrangler and the night-hawk, as well as by the riders.

The *remuda* consists of the saddle strings (mounts) of the cowhands; each string is made up of from seven to ten head. The number in the string depends on the type of country being worked. The northern cowhand generally has ten head of saddle horses in his string and the southern hand has, on an average, seven head to ride. Northern outfits cover more territory in a day's work than southern ones and this accounts for the difference in the number of horses allowed to each rider. Six circle horses, three cow horses (used for working the herd), and one night horse go to make up the saddle string in the northwest. In the southwest, four circle horses, two cow horses and one night horse constitute the average line-up of the cowhand's saddle mounts. The southern rider rides an average of three horses per day, and the northern hand rides an average of four head, not including the night horse which is a gentle horse used for night-guard riding. The night horse is generally staked out in the northern region, and tied up to a tree or to the hoodlum wagon in the southwest. He is generally saddled all night so he will be ready to ride in case of an emergency. The northern saddle horse gets a rest of three days between saddles (that is, between spells of being ridden), and the southern horse gets about two days rest.

The *horse wrangler's string* averages about six head, two of which are ridden each day. The *night-hawk's string* consists of about four head of real gentle animals that are generally old cow horses no longer able to stand hard riding. Only one horse from this string is ridden each night.

The *rough-string rider's mount* consists of about ten or fourteen head of salty horses; they are generally hard to set on, and it takes a real bronc twister to set above 'em and sap them out. They are horses that need the cold sweat set on them pretty regular to get them down to normal. There are generally several fresh-broke broncs in the string and one gentle horse that serves as the rider's night horse. The rough-string rider is seldom placed on day herd because it is necessary to give the horses a good ride to keep them simmered down—which is the rough-string rider's job.

PLATE 9   *Roundup Camp Equipment*

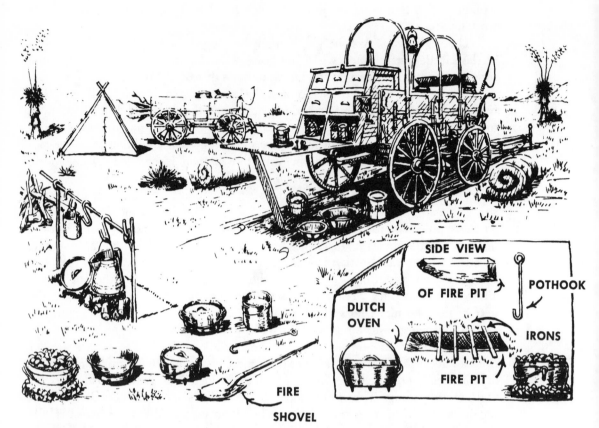

SOUTHERN ROUNDUP EQUIPMENT: CHUCK WAGON & DUTCH OVEN OUTFIT

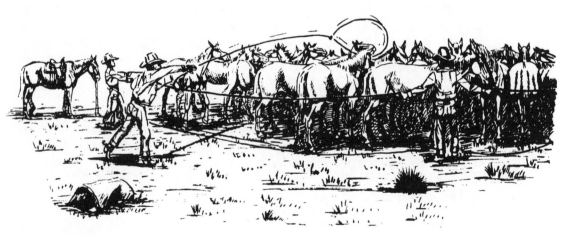

THE REMUDA

6

ROUNDUP
EQUIPMENT

Southern roundup outfit: The equipment used in the southwest is much different from that used in the northwest. The forerunner of the roundup wagon was the Mexican *carreta,* or ox cart, which was used by the Mexican rancheros. The southern outfits are practically the same today as they were in the early trail days. The differences in the type of country and climatic conditions are responsible for the differences in equipment in the north and south.

The chuck wagon, or mess wagon, is an ordinary lumber wagon in which is installed a mess-box, or chuck-box, set in the rear end of the wagon-box, as shown in the illustrations on Plate 9. The lid, or cover, of the box is hinged at the bottom of the box and a folding leg is attached to the outside of the lid, so that when it is let down it will form a table for the cook to work on. Such things as tin plates, knives and forks and cups—which go to make up the cowhand's "reloading" outfit—together with the necessary spices (baking powder, coffee, sugar and other cooking necessities, including pots and pans) are carried in the various compartments and drawers of the chuck-box, as indicated in the drawing. The Dutch ovens and skillets are often carried in a rawhide compartment, or boot, which is attached underneath the running gears of the rear end of the wagon, or in the wagon-box. The chuck, or grub, such as spuds, flour and beans, together with other camp items, including the bedrolls of the riders, are all carried on the wagon. Sometimes an extra wagon called the hoodlum wagon is used to haul wood and water when these will be scarce along the way, as well as extra supplies, etc. But a hoodlum wagon is not used very often.

The cooking equipment consists of a pot rack on the crossbar of which are pothooks (see Plate 9); from these hooks the pots and pails are suspended over an open fire. Dutch ovens serve for cooking all kinds of food—including the baking of bread, beans, or son-of-a-gun. (For the recipe for this concoction, see the Section entitled "Cow Camp Chuck".) Food is cooked in its own juices in a Dutch oven, an old-fashioned method which is now very much in style in modern cooking.

The Dutch oven (see Plate 9) is made of cast iron. The top of its lid, or cover, is flanged around the edge, so that hot coals can be piled on top. The under edge of the lid is offset so that it will set down in the oven about half an inch; this is to prevent it from slipping off. Hot, glowing but no longer blazing coals are placed on top of the oven and underneath it as well. This heat from both above and below causes the contents of the oven to cook evenly and moderately, and when it is handled by a *cocinero* (cook) who savvies his business, there is no other method of cooking that is better, at least in the opinion of the cowhand. No matter what the weather, the cooking is all done in the open and the riders all eat and sleep in the open unless they choose to bring along their own bed tents. Sometimes a wagon fly, or canvas sheet, is stretched above the chuck-box and table; or it may be attached to the side of the wagon, in which case it is held up by a couple of poles at the outside end to make a little shade for the men when they are at the wagon.

Another type of cooking device that is used is the fire pit (see Plate 9), a trench dug in the earth over which four or five pieces of strap iron are placed. The cooking utensils are set on these. One end of the pit slopes up so that hot coals can be shoveled out of it and placed on and under the Dutch ovens. A pothook iron is used to lift off the lids of the Dutch ovens and a long-handled shovel is used to place the coals on them or anywhere else they are needed.

Tepees, or individual bed tents, are often used by cowhands to sleep in; these are their personal property, as the cow outfit does not furnish them for the riders.

To hold the *remuda,* or saddle-horse bunch, an enclosure is formed by the men standing in a circle holding catch ropes, thereby making a rope corral (see the illustration at the bottom of Plate 9). One man, who knows the horses by name and is generally a hand who has been working for the outfit for a long time, ropes the horses. Each rider, of course, tells the roper which horse to catch for him. This method of corralling and roping out saddle horses generally takes most of the roundup crew to handle; a rope corral like that used in the northwest would save much time and trouble in changing horses (see below).

Northern roundup outfit: The chuck wagon is practically the same as the one used in the southwest. The top picture on Plate 10 shows the setup of the mess wagon and cook tent. A wagon fly is stretched from the top of the mess-box to the cook tent. A short tent pole is attached to the back of the chuck-box to hold up the fly, and the other end of the fly is held up by the front pole of the

PLATE 10   *Roundup Camp Equipment (Cont.)*

TYPICAL NORTHERN OUTFIT: CHUCK WAGON & COOK OUTFIT ASSEMBLED

LID BOX

1

2

3

4

5

6

7

LEGS FOLDED

STOVE CART.   HANDLES ON STOVE. STOVE TABLE — AS LID.

SIBLEY.

LEGS BETWEEN
TENT POLES
COOK-TENT TABLE.

STOVES AND EQUIPMENT USED BY THE MAJORITY
OF NORTHERN COW OUTFITS

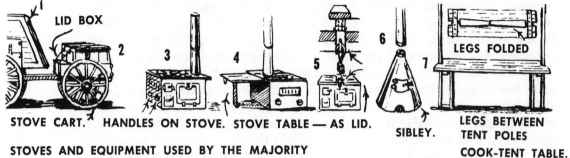

TEPEE

8

9

10

BED TENT & SIBLEY STOVE

ROPE CORRAL SET UP FOR USE

11

12   13   14   15

CATCH ROPE FOR GATE

16   17   18   19

MOUTH OR ENTRANCE
TO ROPE CORRAL

cook tent. There is also a wagon sheet, or cover, which is placed over the hoops on the wagon during a storm. Thus protected, the cook is able to do his work under any kind of weather conditions.

The cook stove is a box-like range especially designed for use on the roundup. (It is also used in the southwest.) It has handles on both sides so that it can be picked up and placed under the mess-box in a stove cart, or trailer, which is attached to the rear end of the wagon when the outfit is on the move. The lids and cross pieces of the top of the stove are removable and are packed in a special compartment located in the front end of the trailer. The stove is then tied down so it cannot make a getaway.

A stove table which was originally devised by a Diamond-A wagon cook known as Noah is shown attached to the side of the stove by hinges. The table is folded over onto the top of the stove to hold the lids (left on in this case) in place while moving camp. A hasp and staple fastened with a snap then holds the table or stove cover in place. This stove table comes in handy for setting down the pots and pails containing grub near the heat where they can be kept warm.

The Sibley (see Plate 10) is a sheet-iron stove which has no bottom; it is much like an inverted funnel. An opening at the bottom provides a draft, and when the draft needs to be cut off, the opening is closed with a pile of dirt scraped off the ground. The Sibley is a good bed-tent heater and is light to carry. The stove and its pipe are carried on the ridge pole of the bed tent and are secured to the side of the bed-wagon when moving camp. An old-time cavalry officer by the name of Sibley was the originator of this type of stove. It was first used by the cavalry during winter campaigns against the Indians.

The cook-tent table is designed to be placed between the center and end poles of the tent. Notches are cut in the ends of the table for the poles to be set in to prevent the table from tipping over. The legs are folded up under the tabletop for convenience in transporting. Grub and the necessary "reloading" tools are placed on the table for the riders to help themselves to when the cook tells 'em to "Come and get it!"

A bed tent large enough to accommodate several beds is furnished by the outfit. During the early spring and late fall work severe cold weather is often encountered and the tents are a necessary protection for the men. Such tents are not needed in the southwest, which accounts for their absence from the standard equipment used in that region. All hands sleep in bed tents in bad weather in the north, but they often sleep out in the open when weather permits.

The bed-wagon is used to haul the bedrolls, tents, branding irons, rope corral, and extra supplies needed for range work. The bedroll of the northern rider is generally twice the size of the "hot roll" of the southern hand, because of the colder climate. This is why there has to be an extra wagon to haul the beds of the northern cowhands. The four-horse team used to pull the bed-wagon is driven by the night-hawk.

The rope corral of the northwest (see Plate 10) consists of two main ropes, one attached to each of the two wheels on one side of the bed-wagon, as shown in Figures 9 and 11. These two ropes are each about one inch in diameter and about fifty feet long. A large honda (loop) is spliced or tied in the end of each rope. These ends are run between two spokes of their respective wheels and the hondas are looped over the hubs, as shown in Figure 17. Two guy ropes are then tied to each of the main ropes, one at the middle and one at the further end, away from the wagon. Then the main ropes are laid out on the ground, and, before the corral is actually raised, they are staked out by use of the guy ropes (see Figure 15). The stakes used are about two feet long and have iron ferrules at the upper end to keep them from splitting when they are hammered into the ground (see Figure 14). The corral is now raised onto crotches in the upper end of poles about three and a half feet long. The corral should be high enough to come well up on the breast of the average-size horse. The mouth or entrance to the corral is closed with a catch rope that is stretched across the opening. The horse wrangler generally uses his saddle rope for this, after the saddle stock, or *remuda*, has been corralled (see Figure 11). When the horses are corralled, a rider can catch his horse at any time without any help.

Figures 12 and 13 show how the corral is done up when it is dismantled. The ropes are tied to the end gate rod on the back end of the bed-wagon. The stakes and crotched poles are all placed in the back end of the wagon so they can be easily gotten at when they are wanted.

7

COW CAMP CHUCK

The following recipes are cow-camp favorites and if properly prepared will prove to be a treat to those who have never sampled them before. They are dishes which only the experienced roundup-wagon cook knows how to build and prepare properly.

S. B. STEW, OR SON-OF-A-GUN

In polite society this concoction is often referred to as Son-of-a-Gun, but that is a very mild version of its real name. Naturally, the polite name makes cowhands and cow-country folk grin when they hear it used by tourists and such. The ingredients, procured from the carcass of a freshly slaughtered beef, are as follows: brains, liver, heart, sweetbreads, kidneys and marrow-gut. Wash them all thoroughly and cut them up into small pieces about an inch square. Put them in a Dutch oven with a piece of suet tallow about the size of a prairie oyster (see below) from a four-months-old calf and enough water to cover. Season with salt and chili powder. Boil until the meat is tender. Mix a small handful of flour with some of the juice or some warm water, add to the stew, stir thoroughly, and let cook about thirty minutes longer. (*N.B.* Marrow-gut is a particularly choice bit of cattle anatomy, the tube connecting the two stomachs of ruminating animals and containing a substance resembling bone marrow. Recipes often specify the quantity to be used by the foot! The best·suet tallow is the fat found around beef kidneys.)

CRISPED MARROW-GUT

Procure the marrow-gut, free from foreign matter, from a freshly slaughtered beef, wash thoroughly, and cut into pieces about two and one-half inches long. Fry in hot, deep fat in a skillet or Dutch oven until nearly crisp. Remove the marrow-gut, salt it, pour off the fat and return the marrow-gut to the skillet to keep warm.

PRAIRIE OR MOUNTAIN OYSTERS

These dry-land oysters are the testicles removed from male calves when they are castrated, or cut. When the calves are branded and marked, the male calves are cut and the oysters are saved and taken to the cook who prepares them in the following manner:

Surplus tissue is removed and the oysters are split open, carefully washed, and then fried in hot, deep fat in a skillet until they are thoroughly cooked; then they are removed from the fat, which is poured off. The oysters are salted and returned to the skillet to keep warm, as in preparing marrow-gut.

CORNED TOMATOES

To a large-size can of tomatoes add a can of corn. Season with salt and pepper, add a chunk of fat and stew until done.

TOMATO RICE

In a skillet brown a cup of rice with just enough fat to cover it when it is well spread out in the pan. When the rice is cooked to a golden-brown color, slice a medium-size onion, add it to the rice. Let this simmer until the onion is about half-cooked, then add a can of tomatoes, season with salt and a little chili, and let cook, covered, until the rice absorbs most all the moisture in the tomatoes. Stir to prevent burning when nearly done.

BLANKET STEAK

There's different ways of fixing steak, but this way is one that "will make a hand let out a couple of holes in his belt when he gets started to wrapping himself around a span of them." The best cooking utensil to use for blanket steak is a Dutch oven. Put the oven on the coals and then cut some fat off the steaks to melt. Prepare the steaks by dropping them in water, salt them, then roll them in flour and put them in the hot oven with the melted fat. Have the lid of the oven hot before it is put on. When the lid is on, pile on some good live coals and let the steak cook until done. Remove the steak when done and add a couple of tablespoons of flour to the juice and stir until smooth. Then add water, salt and pepper. Let stew until thick enough to make a good gravy.

SOURDOUGH BISCUITS

To make the starter, soak half a cake of yeast in half a cup of lukewarm water for about half an hour, or until it is soft. A teaspoonful of sugar added to this increases the action of the yeast. Then build a batter with the yeast and the water it was soaked in, another half cup of lukewarm water, and enough flour to make a thick consistency, or about one and a quarter cups. Stir thoroughly. Place in a stone jar or an enamel pot and put lid on same. Set where the dough will keep warm. If the nights are cold, it is best to wrap the jar in a heavy cloth to keep the dough warm. During the mixing the yeast plant should have developed and the batter should be full of bubbles. Usually the result is better if the mixture has longer than twenty-four hours to stand. If you can let it stand that long, increase the batter the second evening by beating in another half cup of lukewarm water, a teaspoonful of sugar and just enough flour to make a good thick mixture. Let this set overnight and it will be ready for use.

In making biscuits, pour out nearly all of the starter into the mixing pan, add about half a teaspoonful of soda, a pinch of salt and flour enough to make a good thick dough. Knead and work it thoroughly, for the more it is worked the better. Pinch off the dough in pieces about the size of a billiard ball, dip the tops of them in fat and place in a Dutch oven or baking pan.

Always keep a little starter in the jar; add to it some lukewarm water and enough flour to make a thick batter. Stir thoroughly and set aside until wanted. If one does not have yeast to start the dough, a few spuds boiled in water until they fall to pieces can be used. Add flour and a little sugar to the potato water and stir until a thick batter is formed. Then set away in a warm place so it will raise. After that handle as previously explained for good results.

Sourdough flapjacks are made by mixing the starter with a little sugar and lukewarm water, as well as a little soda and a small amount of flour to make a good batter.

A COWHAND'S COFFEE RECIPE

To two gallons of boiling water add two pounds of coffee. Boil two hours, then throw a horseshoe into the pot and if it sinks, the coffee is not yet done. "Trouble with most coffee-makers, they're too generous with the water," says Frank King.

S. B. IN A SACK

To two-thirds of a quart of flour add two cups of suet which has been chopped fine and one teaspoonful of salt. Add a large handful of raisins and sufficient water to make a heavy dough. Mix and roll in another third of a quart of flour. Place in a small sugar sack and boil in a pot of hot water for one hour.

S. B. SAUCE

Beat 1 egg, add one cup of sugar, a hunk of butter about the size of an egg, three tablespoonsful of hot water and the juice of a lemon, or some lemon extract, or a wine glass of brandy. Cook in a double boiler until thick. Pour on S.B. pudding (S.B. in a Sack) and watch 'em take to it.

SUCAMAGROWL

This is not so hard to take as its name might imply and it is a good substitute for pudding or pie. The ingredients are:

3 cups of water
2 cups of sugar
2 pinches of cinnamon
    or nutmeg

1 cup of vinegar
2 tablespoons of flour

First, put the water and vinegar together and bring to a boil. Mix the sugar and flour together and stir this mixture into the boiling liquid until it is thoroughly dissolved. Let cook for fifteen minutes and then add the spice. Have a dough ready, like a biscuit dough prepared with baking powder. Break it off by the tablespoonful and drop the pieces in the simmering liquid. When the dumplings are done serve them right off on tin plates while they're still hot.

PLATE 11 *The Cowhand's Bed*

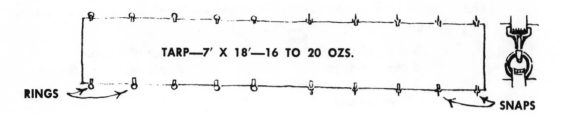

RINGS   TARP—7' X 18'—16 TO 20 OZS.   **SNAPS**

BED COMPLETE

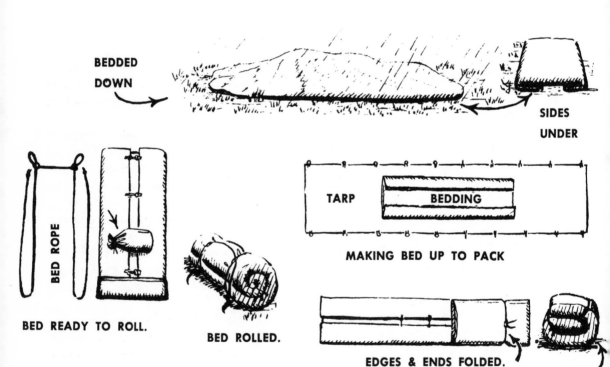

BEDDED DOWN

SIDES UNDER

BED ROPE

BED READY TO ROLL.

BED ROLLED.

TARP   **BEDDING**

MAKING BED UP TO PACK

EDGES & ENDS FOLDED.

ROLLED.

8

THE

COWHAND'S BED

A cowhand's bed is designed for roundup work and is often called a "roundup bed." It is constructed to give the service and comfort demanded by hands working the range and it must keep a person warm and dry in any kind of weather.

A good "tarp" is a tarpaulin or canvas sheet of heavy-weight, waterproof ducking used as a covering for the bedding. A tarp is shown at the top of Plate 11. It is about seven feet wide by eighteen feet long, with snaps and rings attached to the edges so the sides can be fastened together when the tarp is doubled. The average size of a tarp is seven by sixteen feet, but one seven by eighteen feet is better, as it will be long enough to extend well over the sleeper's head when doubled over and will protect his clothing, etc., in case of a storm.

The tarps are made in various weights, in sixteen-, eighteen-, twenty-, and twenty-two-ounce ducking, but the eighteen-ounce type is the one most generally used. It is a good water excluder, is not too heavy to manage and will stand a lot of rough handling.

The bedding proper consists of "soogans" (quilts) and blankets. Generally, three or four soogans are doubled and used as a mattress. A pair of double cotton blankets is placed on top of the mattress to sleep between, and two or three single woolen blankets are used for covering. The amount of bedding necessary for comfort depends a good deal on the climate of the locality in which the bed is to be used. The roundup bed used in the northern states consists, naturally, of much more bedding than that used in the southwest.

"Bed Complete" at the top of Plate 11 shows how a bed looks when it is made up. The doubled tarp forms a protection for the bottom of the bed as well as the top, and the sides are fastened together with the snaps and rings to keep the wind from blowing the top off.

For a pillow the cowhand often uses his war-bag, or war-sack, in which are kept certain pieces of clothing and such things as toilet articles, writing materials, tobacco, etc. Extra clothing such as shirts and pants is often placed between the folded soogans used for a mattress and is smoothed out to keep it free of wrinkles.

The top half of the tarp should be two and a half to three feet longer than the bottom half so that it will extend well over the cowhand's head when he is bedded down and will protect his clothing, etc. "Bedded Down" on Plate 11 shows how the bed should be arranged to protect a person from a storm. At the right, the arrow indicates how the sides of the bed are folded under to keep the wind and water out, forming a sort of sleeping sack. The elevation in the center of the bed formed by the body of the sleeper causes the water to run off much as it does off the top of a tent.

A bed rope, shown in the left-hand lower corner of Plate 11, is usually a piece of worn catch rope about twenty-five feet long in which a couple of loops are tied near the center, about twenty-two inches apart, and is used to tie around the bed when it is rolled up. The loose ends of the rope are placed around the bed, run through the loops and then drawn up tight and tied, as shown in the drawings "Bed Ready to Roll" and "Bed Rolled."

"Making Bed Up to Pack" shows how the bedding is folded and placed in the center of the tarp and how the edges are folded over on top and fastened together. The ends of the tarp are folded over as shown in "Edges and Ends Folded." The arrow indicates how a rope is tied around the folded ends to hold the bed in place while it is being rolled.

"Bed Ready to Roll" illustrates how the edges of the bed are folded over on top and then fastened together to hold them in place while the bed is being rolled, and shows how the war-sacks used as pillows are placed on top near the center. The head of the tarp is folded over to start the roll. The outfit should be tightly rolled so it will not be large or bulky and it should not occupy any more space than is absolutely necessary when it is placed on the bed-wagon.

9

PACKS
AND
PACKING

The style of packsaddle and rigging shown in Figure 1 on Plate 12 is the type most generally used by professional packers. It is completely rigged with breast strap (C), breeching (E) and double cinch (G). This is the only satisfactory style of rigging for a pack outfit. The tree (B) is the sawbuck type and is the humane pack tree shown in Figure 12. The side bars (sides of the tree) are lined with sheepskin to prevent the saddle blanket from crawling or slipping out from under the outfit. A lash rope (A) and lash cinch, a necessary part of the equipment, are also shown on the side of the tree in Figure 1.*

Figure 3 on Plate 12 illustrates the Springerville type of pack outfit used a great deal in Arizona and New Mexico but little known in other states. The tree has extended crossbars (see arrows) which are designed to prevent the packs from resting on the rigging; this eliminates rigging sores on the pack animal's back. Figure 7 shows a single-rig burro-pack outfit widely used for burro packing. Figure 8 shows the Decker pack outfit which is used mostly by forest rangers. It is not designed for heavy packing like the outfits described above.

Figure 2 is a drawing of a pannier, or pack bag, made of canvas or leather and attached to the pack tree by two leather loops over the crossbars. Small articles to be packed, such as cooking equipment, etc., are placed in the bags, while the larger articles are placed on top of the outfit and covered over with a piece of canvas called a pack cover. The whole outfit is lashed down with a lash

* See Sections entitled "Saddles," "Trees and Riggings," and "Cinches" for descriptions of various terms and pieces of equipment not fully defined in this Section.

PLATE 12   *Pack Outfits*

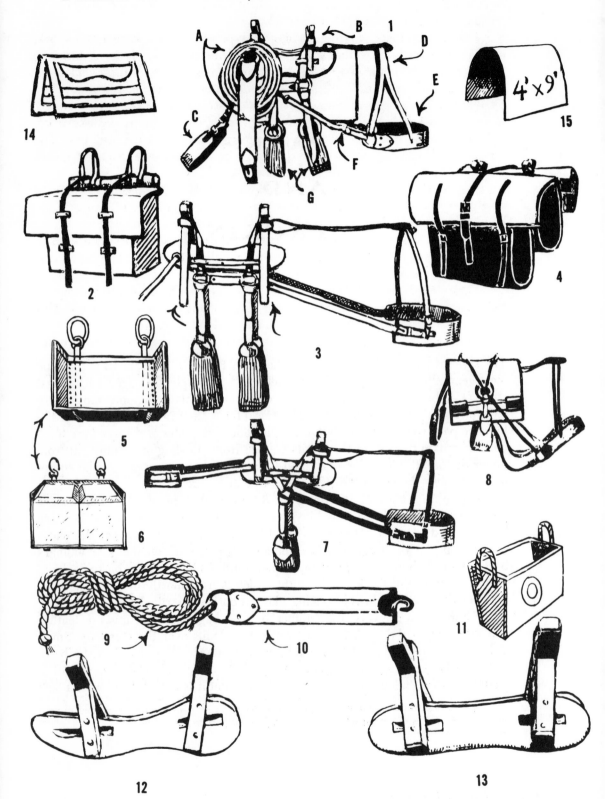

A B 1

C D E F G

14

15 4'x9'

2

3

4

5

6

7

8

9

10

11

12

13

rope which is put on with different kinds of hitches shown in the diagrams of packing hitches on Plates 13, 14 and 15.

Figure 4 on Plate 12 shows a different type of pack bag known as a kyack, or kyax. It is made of leather with a canvas cover, as shown in the illustration, but it can also be made of wood which is sometimes covered with rawhide.

Figure 5 shows the Willis metal salt kyack, designed by the foreman of the Double Circle outfit in Arizona to carry salt. Two blocks of salt will fit closely in each such kyack and are prevented from slipping out by the kyack's being tipped so the outside edge will be up when it is attached to the pack tree. The blocks of salt can be easily removed because of the open side. Figure 6 shows how the two blocks of salt are placed in the kyack.

Figure 11 is a homemade wooden kyack, often covered with rawhide to strengthen it and hold it together. It is heavier than other types of kyacks but it is substantial and when covered with rawhide will last indefinitely.

Figure 9 shows a lash rope and Figure 10 a lash cinch. These are used to lash the packs onto the pack animal. The rope is about thirty feet long and a half inch in diameter; it is usually made of hemp or cotton.

Figure 12 shows the Visalia humane pack tree which has side bars designed like those on a stock saddle, conforming to the shape of the horse's back. This is a desirable improvement over the ordinary style of pack tree.

In Figure 13 you have the burro-pack tree, a type used in the pack outfit shown in Figure 7 (see above). The side bars are not shaped like those in the horse or mule pack rig because the burro's back is not shaped like that of a horse or mule.

Figure 14 shows a style of packsaddle pad designed to protect the back of the pack animal. A heavy or thick pad is necessary for packing work because the dead weight is hard on the animal's back. If precaution is not taken in arranging the padding, a sore back will be the result.

Figure 15 shows a pack cover. A piece of heavy canvas about four feet wide and nine feet long is used to cover the pack outfit to protect it from the elements and to hold things securely in place.

The packing hitches shown on Plate 13 are for packing beds on a horse or mule. They are hitches which the cowhand uses to pack his roundup bed. The first hitch, shown in Figures 1 to 4, is the one man hitch, so called because it is easy for one man to put it on. Figure 1 shows how the rope is placed on top of the bed. Figure 2 shows how the two loose ends of the rope are run down and in under the horse's body, then through the two loops which hang down on the off side* of the horse. The ends are then brought back in under the horse, as indicated by the dotted lines, and run in under the rope across the center of the pack, as diagrammed in Figure 3. By pulling on the ends of the rope, front and back, as indicated at A in Figure 3, the slack can be taken out, causing the cross piece

* The off side of the horse is his right side. The near side of a horse is his left side, the side from which a rider mounts a saddle horse.

to bind or hold the ends of the rope. The more the rope is tightened, the more the cross piece will pull down on the loose ends and prevent them from slipping. When the rope is tight enough, the two ends are tied together on top of the pack, as indicated in Figure 4.

How the W hitch is formed and completed is shown in Figures 5 to 7. The two ends of rope are run through the two loops hanging down on the off side of the horse, in the same manner as in the one man hitch in Figure 2. They are brought back in under the horse as shown in Figure 6. The ends are run through the center loop of the W, in the manner indicated in Figure 7 which shows one end of the rope carried in *under* the loop and the other carried *down through* the loop from the top. The purpose is to cross the ends so they can be tied effectively. The slack is pulled out, as in the one man hitch, but the center loop will not hold the ends of the rope as in that hitch. It is necessary to hold onto one end of the rope to keep the center loop of the W from slipping if one person is operating the hitch. Two men are required, generally, to tighten the hitch, one at each end of the rope. When the hitch is tight enough, the ends are tied together.

Figure 8 illustrates how the S hitch is formed on the top of the pack and Figure 9 indicates how the two ends are run down and in under the horse and then passed through the two loops. The two ends are brought back in under the horse and tied across the top of the pack, as shown in Figure 10. Two men are required to handle this hitch because the ends of the rope are brought back in under either side of the horse, where the packers respectively stand. The ends of the rope are tied in a square knot.

The stirrup hitch, illustrated in Figures 11, 12, and 13 on Plate 13, requires two men to handle it. A man works on each side of the horse and when the two "stirrups," or loops, are formed on each side of the horse, as shown in Figure 11, the stirrups are placed over the edges of the bed, as indicated in Figure 12. Each packer holds onto a free end of the rope and, placing a foot in the stirrup, draws the loops down on the bed and pushes them in under the horse to the opposite packer who runs the end of the rope through the loop received from the opposite side. This is indicated at A in the detail to the left in Figure 12. The ends of the rope are pulled to take the slack out of the hitch and then they are tied together on top of the pack, as seen at A in Figure 13.

Figure 14 shows a top view of a pack outfit, before it is loaded, when it is placed on a horse, and Figure 15 shows a side view of the same outfit.

Figure 16 illustrates the *tapaojos* (from the Spanish meaning "eye cover" or "blinders") which are used to place over the eyes of a pack animal so it will stand still while being loaded. They are made of leather with strings attached to tie around the animal's neck just back of the jaws.

The half-diamond hitch is seen in its various stages in Figures 1 through 10 on Plate 14. Note that the last pull on a pack rope is always towards the back so the pack will not tend to be pulled forward. Usually two men work together in

PLATE 13 *Bed Hitches*

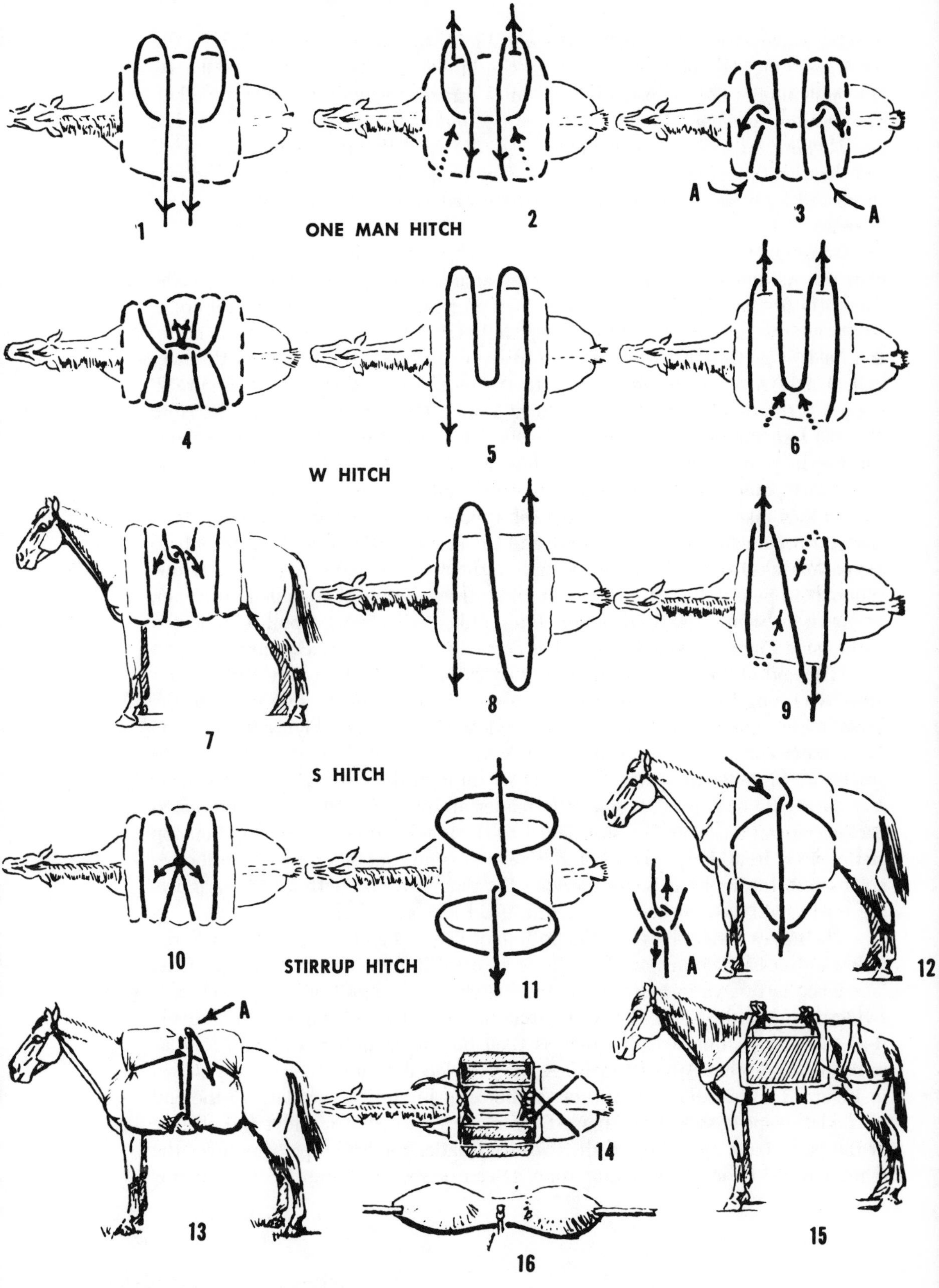

ONE MAN HITCH

W HITCH

S HITCH

STIRRUP HITCH

packing, so that one man can be on each side of the pack animal to handle the lash rope. One man can put on any of the hitches shown herein, if necessary, but most hitches are more easily and quickly made if two men work together.

In order to show how the slack is pulled out of the rope, arrows inserted in the diagrams indicate the point in the rope at which the pull should be applied and the direction of the pull. The points from which the rope is to be pulled are numbered in proper order, as in Figure 6 on Plate 14 and in Figures E and 4 on Plate 15.

To return to the half-diamond hitch which is shown in its various stages on Plate 14: Assume that a packer is working alone on the left, or near, side of the horse. He first arranges the lash rope on top of the pack as shown in Figure 1. He throws the lash cinch over the pack, catches it as it swings in under the horse, and holds it and the bight of the lash rope in one hand; then he pulls the loop indicated at A over the bight and into the cinch hook, as shown in Figure 2. Figures 3 through 8 show how the slings around the pack bags are made. Note that the lash rope must pass between the cinch and the pack bags. The slings not only help to hold the pack firmly, but they also hold the bags out slightly so they won't pound so hard against the horse's sides.

How to take the slack out of the lash rope is shown in Figures 6 and 7. The first pull is indicated at 1 in Figure 6, and the arrow on the rope indicates where the packer takes ahold of the rope to pull in the direction indicated by the arrow. When the rope is pulled, it is drawn in under the pack and then pulled out again, as shown in Figure 6 at 2, in the direction indicated. The next pull is indicated in the same Figure at 3, and the slack is carried in under the pack and pulled out at 4. The end of the rope is then drawn down in the direction indicated in Figure 7. The sling loops are shown loose around the packs in the side views of the horse in Figures 5 and 8 in order to give a clear view of them. Figure 9 shows the slack drawn out of the rope just before tying the end of the rope into the lash-cinch ring in under the pack. How this tie through the cinch ring looks can be seen in Figure 8. Figure 10 gives the reader an over-all view of the completed packing operation. Note the so-called half-diamond formed in the rope on top of the pack, from which the hitch derives its name. The hitch just described is not hard to throw; by closely observing the diagrams and with a little practice, the reader will have no trouble doing a good job of packing.

The squaw hitch, shown at the bottom of Plate 14 and continued over in the following set of diagrams on Plate 15, is an easy hitch to throw. The end of the lash cinch is thrown over the pack and caught in the hand of the packer as it swings in under the horse. When the rope has been hooked into the cinch hook, it is doubled to form a loop which is then pushed in under the main line, as indicated by Figure A on Plate 14. A sling is placed around the pack as shown in Figure B and in the side view of the horse in Figure C. On Plate 15 the end of the lash rope is shown in Figure D being carried down in under the off side of the pack, back up on top of the pack and under the first rope, then over the main line and under its own sling rope, as can be seen in Figure E. The hitch is now ready to be tightened up. The technique used in taking the slack out of the rope is practically the same as the one employed in the half-diamond hitch. The hitch in this case, however, must be pulled tighter than is done in the half-diamond, because the sling rope is on the outside of the main line. The sling rope should be drawn up close in under the pack bags so they will pull against the bottom. Figure F shows how the end of the lash rope is run around in *under* the sling ropes, but *over* the main line, and then half-hitched around the rope leading to the cinch, as shown in G. This completes the squaw hitch. The circle shown on top of the pack closes up when the knot is tightened.

The diamond hitch is the most widely known hitch of those described herein and is not difficult to throw if the reader will follow the diagrams closely. Again we will assume for the sake of clarity in describing the work that the hitch is put on by a lone packer. Standing on the off side, the packer throws the end of the lash cinch over the pack, catches the end of the cinch in his right hand, and loops the lash rope around the hook, as indicated at A in Figure 1 on Plate 15. A loop is formed in the center of the pack by pushing the rope in under the main line as shown in Figure 2. The sling loop hanging down on the near side is placed around the kyack and then drawn up through the center loop, to form the sling loop for the off side of the pack, as shown in Figure 3 and indicated by the arrow. The sling is then placed around and under the off kyack, as shown in Figure 4. The slack is pulled out as shown by the numbered indicators in the diagram. The first pull is back and down, as shown at 1 in Figure 4. This pull is followed by pulls 2, 3, 4 and 5. The last pull is toward the back, as it should be in packing. Note that the slings are on the outside of the main line, as they also are in the squaw hitch. Figure 6 shows the diamond shape formed by the hitch on top of the pack when the slack is drawn out after the last pull is applied toward the back. Figure 7 illustrates how the end of the lash rope is tied into the ring of the lash cinch to complete the diamond hitch.

The sling hitch shown in Figures 8 and 9 is used in packing sacks of grain and other bulky things which can be handled with that type of hitch. A lash rope about fifteen feet long is double half-hitched over the front of the crossbars, as shown in Figure 8, and each half of the rope is looped over the back crossbars to form a sling loop, with the end of the rope in under the sling loop, so that it can be brought up under the sack to be tied with a couple of half-hitches as shown in Figure 9. With this hitch grain and other things can be packed and do not have to be put in kyacks.

The professional packer is particular about the arranging of his packing equipment so that it will set right on the pack animal. The padding placed under the packsaddle tree is smoothed out so that it cannot hurt the animal's back. The padding should extend about seven or eight inches beyond the ends of the tree and should also extend well down on the sides of the pack animal to prevent the packs or kyacks from rubbing against its sides and causing pack sores. It must be remembered that galls and saddle sores are much easier made than cured. In cinching the packsaddle on the pack animal, it is best to tie the latigos

PLATE 14   *Packing Hitches*

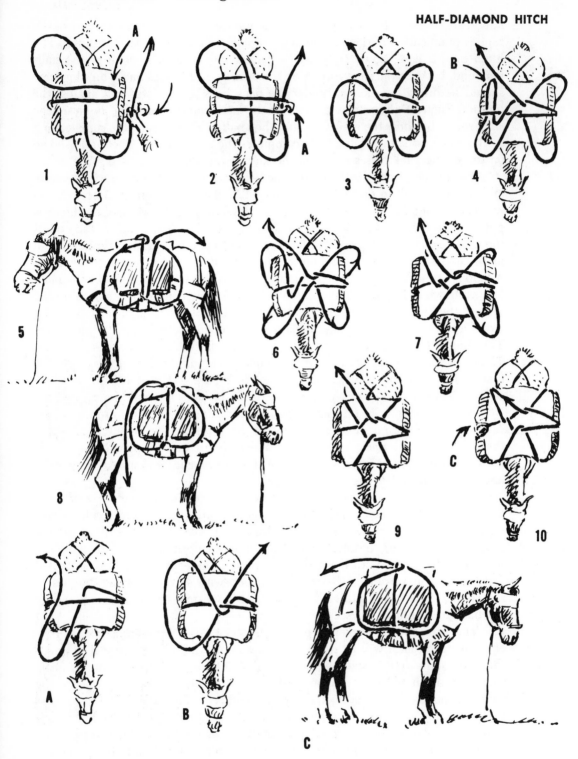

HALF-DIAMOND HITCH

SQUAW HITCH

PLATE 15 *Packing Hitches (Cont.)*

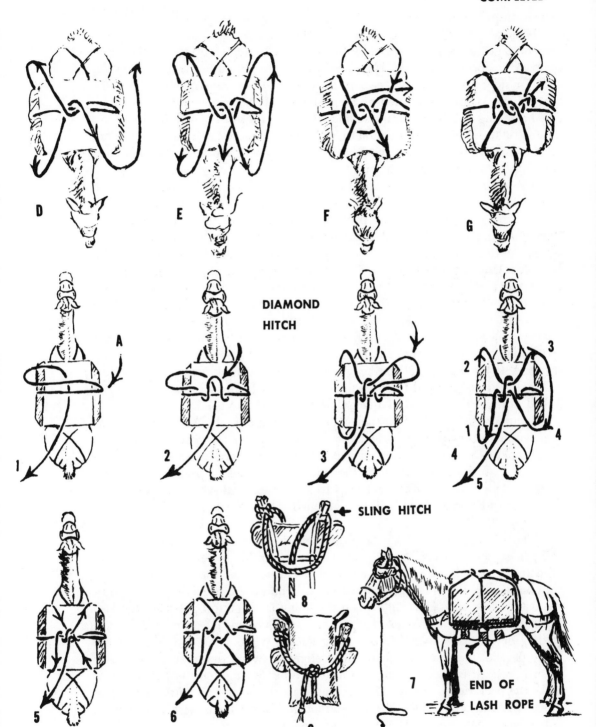

SQUAW HITCH COMPLETED

D E F G

DIAMOND HITCH

A

1 2 3 4 5

SLING HITCH

8

9

7 **END OF LASH ROPE**

5 6

(cinch straps) in the cinch ring instead of in the rigging rings of the saddle. This will eliminate knots bunching up in under the packs and also make it more convenient to get at the latigos should it be necessary to tighten up the cinches after the pack has been completed. If buckle tongues are placed in the cinch rings on the near side, it will not be necessary to tie the latigos; consequently the possibility of any knot being formed by the fastening of the latigo will be eliminated. The breeching and breast straps should be drawn up so they will fit snugly but not too tight. If they are drawn too tightly, this will cause the breast strap to cut off the animal's wind, and if too loosely, the pack will slip when the animal is going up or down a mountain.

Extra rope for lash ropes and for pannier or kyack sling ropes should be carried in case of an emergency, as well as extra padding for the packsaddles.

In arranging the load to be packed, the packer aims to divide the articles into equal parts as far as possible, taking into consideration both their bulk and weight, so that the load will be as nearly balanced in size and weight as can be managed. Unbalanced packs will cause much shifting and slipping and this may ruin the back of the pack animal. In packing cooking utensils and small articles, place them close together so that they will not rattle or get jammed up. When the kyacks or panniers have been packed, the extra equipment, such as warbags containing the cowboys' personal belongings, coats, hobbles, sacks and other articles are placed on top of the kyacks and across the packsaddle to round up the load. If the load is not too heavy, a cowboy bed is thrown over the pack. (This should be arranged for packing as shown on Plate 11.) Then the pack is lashed down with any one of the packing hitches mentioned.

Long articles, such as tent poles, guns, spades, etc., should be arranged so they will not gouge the pack animal or equipment or be in a position which will cause them to hang up or catch on a tree or limb or otherwise cause trouble.

It is a good idea to lift up on the sides of the kyack or pack when placing the sling loop under it. This will help to give slack, and when the pack is let down again the whole hitch will be tightened. The tighter the hitch, the better the pack will ride.

The average weight of a pack placed on a horse is about 175 pounds, about 225 pounds for a mule, and 200 pounds for a burro. Much depends on the kind of material packed, the type of country to be covered, and the distance the pack is to be carried. When on the trail with a pack outfit, the packer generally stops the outfit every once in a while when the going is rough to tighten up the lash ropes and take out any slack that might have developed because the load is settling or the pack animal is becoming gaunt. While some pack animals are being packed, they have the habit of swelling up when the hitch is tightened; in such cases it is necessary to stop after a time and tighten the lash ropes to make the pack ride properly. The pack animals should not be permitted to trot downhill. Always pick the best trails and let the pack animals set the pace when going over rough ground. Halt frequently to let them rest while making a hard climb.

10

HOW A BRANDING
CREW WORKS

The ropers who catch the calves generally lead or drag 'em out, depending on the size of the calves. The little calves are usually roped around the neck and led out to the rastlers who flank them (see below), throw them down and hold them as shown on Plate 16. The rope is taken off the calf after it has been thrown and the roper goes back for another calf. The big calves are generally heeled (roped by the heels); this throws them and they are drug out, thus saving the rastlers the work of flankin 'em. A good roper can keep two sets of rastlers busy picking the calves off his line. When working in a corral, he can keep three sets of flankers going without busting an artery.

In order for a roper to tell what brand belongs on a calf, he first makes sure that it is follerin' its mammy. When he is satisfied that it is follerin' the *right* cow, he ropes the calf and heads for the fire. The brand mark that was on the calf's mother is called by the roper when the rastlers receive the calf. The brand is called first and the marks are called second. For instance, the roper calls out, "N.A.N.; crop the right, an' swallow-fork the left." The rastlers repeat the call given by the roper so the iron men and the markers (see below) will know what is to go on the calf.

The flankers, or rastlers, are split up into working teams, or sets, of two men each. When a calf is led out, one hand flanks it—that is, reaches over the calf's back, grabs two handfuls of skin, one at the flank and one near the foreleg, leans back, and flips the calf over on its side (see Plate 45). Once the calf is down,

PLATE 16 *How a Branding Crew Works*

Katherine Field .53

the rastler catches its top foreleg and holds it down while his pardner catches the top hind leg, pulls it out backward and holds it stretched out, at the same time bracing his foot against the other hind leg, as shown on Plate 16. The calf is helpless in this position; it is branded, marked, vaccinated and castrated (if it happens to be a bull calf), one thing right after the next, while it is being held by the rastlers. Each set of rastlers works in turn when a calf is brought out by the ropers, unless something happens to throw things out of line. In any event, they take 'em as they come and like it!

The iron men are kept busy branding and looking after the fire so the irons will be kept hot. There are some pointers which a hand operating an iron must keep in mind: If a brand is not burned deep enough, it will not peel, and if the iron is too hot, especially when a complicated stamp iron is used, it is pretty sure to blotch the brand. This often happens when there are sharp turns or points in the brand, like those in Diamond A which is often called Scab A because so many of these brands do run together from too hot an iron being used. Another thing, if too much pressure is applied with a real hot iron, the iron is apt to burn a hole through the hide. Very little pressure is necessary to put on a good brand with a hot iron. Also, the hand operating the iron must be careful not to let the iron slip; this will naturally result in a blotched brand. The men delegated to handle the irons are generally hands who savvy their business and know how to put a brand on right when it is called.

The markers are men who know how to handle a sharp knife when it comes to whittling on a calf's ear. When marking the top ear of a calf, the marker generally puts his foot on the critter's nose to help hold its head still. The rastler holding the foreleg turns the nose of the calf up when the marker wants to get at the bottom ear to mark it. When the ears have been marked, the marker castrates the animal if it is a bull calf. While castrating a calf, the marker generally places his foot on the lower hind leg of the calf in order to hold it still while he is operating.

Modern methods of castrating with special instruments which eliminate the necessity for removing the lower half of the bag (scrotum) and for removing the testicles are now being used by some outfits. The new method severs the cord of the testicles without cutting the hide. This new method has proved successful when used by those who really know how to handle it. However, some stock owners have condemned the new method when they have tried it out because the operators have been careless or not sufficiently expert. If the operator does not make sure that the cord is in the proper position at the time he applies power to the castration instrument, the operation will be a failure. Moreover, you cannot find out whether or not the operation has been successful for several months because it takes that long for the testicles to dry up. For these reasons, some cowmen have given up the new method in favor of the old, reliable sharp knife. However, the new castration technique eliminates the danger of screwworms attacking the part affected by the operation. Also, the new method requires much less time than the old.

Some male calves are usually left for bulls. The new method of operating leaves no visible outward evidence on the castrated critter; so in order that a cowhand won't get the calves mixed up, the outfits using the new method use a special earmark to distinguish the "reserved" calves from the others.

The gun man is the hand who handles the vaccinating syringe and shoots the dope to the calves to immunize them from blackleg. Practically every cow outfit vaccinates to eliminate the danger of this incurable disease which caused much loss to cowmen before vaccinating was generally adopted.

Tallying calves while branding and marking them is done by saving pieces of ear which have been removed by the marker. The pieces of ear removed from the bull and heifer calves are placed in separate piles. When the bunch is all branded and marked, it is only necessary to count the pieces in each of the two piles to determine the number and sex of the calves branded. By keeping such records each season, the outfit can generally tell how many steer or heifer calves of a certain age they will have to sell.

Dehorning calves which run on the open range while they are being branded and marked was practiced by some outfits because they had been led to believe that the market demanded hornless stock and that they would profit much by dehorning. Generally, those who have dehorned their stock have been unable to realize the additional profit that they had anticipated and have discontinued the practice. They found that dehorning cost more than the profits realized because of the extra work entailed in doctoring the calves for screwworms which had attacked the wound where the horn had been removed. The loss in flesh by those that had been set back by handlin' also cut into profits. The cowmen as a whole do not admire a muley, because it reminds 'em of places where man and beast are confined in small enclosures. Such things are not of the cow country where horns have been on cattle ever since the beginning. Horns are the only weapon of defense a range cow has to do battle with and without them she is practically defenseless against any enemy which might attack her or her offspring. Then, too, a horned critter is easier to handle when rope work is to be done, such as pulling out of a bog, roping, and leading out of rough country; a critter roped around the horns is easier handled than one roped around the neck. There are many other instances that could be cited where horns are more beneficial *on* a range cow than *off*, many more, in fact, than most people have any idea of, and it is the opinion of the majority of cowhands that it will be many snows before the range country is converted into small feed lots and dairy farms where hornless cattle belong.

11

BRANDS
AND
MARKS

The branding and marking of range cattle and horses is necessary to establish ownership of the stock. It is said that Cortes was the first to introduce branding on the North American continent when he burnt the Three Christian Crosses (see top, left, of Plate 18) on the few head of Andalusian cattle he brought over from Spain when he landed at Vera Cruz and proceeded to conquer Mexico. Since that time many million head of range stock have had their hair scorched and their ears whittled.

Brands were run on stock with a running iron. A branding ring was carried tied to a saddle string for range branding work because it was much lighter and more compact than a regular branding iron. Any type of brand could be run with a ring. A folding running iron designed to be carried in a scabbard attached to the back skirts of a saddle is shown in the drawings of branding irons on Plate 17.

Laws were enacted in some range states prohibiting the carrying of a running iron by a range rider, but he was permitted to pack a stamp iron bearing the brand of the outfit he was working for. However, because of the extra weight and unhandiness of such an iron, the practice of carrying an iron was abandoned. The reason the carrying of a running iron was prohibited was, of course, to eliminate the practice of running a brand on stock that was the property of someone other than the wielder of the iron. Some crafty individuals who wished to build up a herd in the least possible time used to indulge in the practice of branding cattle that didn't belong to them.

PLATE 17   *Branding Irons*

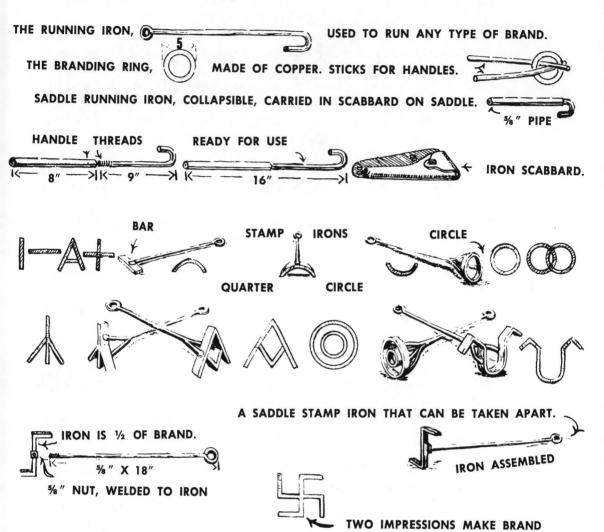

THE RUNNING IRON, USED TO RUN ANY TYPE OF BRAND.

THE BRANDING RING, MADE OF COPPER. STICKS FOR HANDLES.

SADDLE RUNNING IRON, COLLAPSIBLE, CARRIED IN SCABBARD ON SADDLE.

⅝" PIPE

HANDLE   THREADS   READY FOR USE

8"   9"   16"

IRON SCABBARD.

BAR   STAMP   IRONS   CIRCLE

QUARTER   CIRCLE

A SADDLE STAMP IRON THAT CAN BE TAKEN APART.

IRON IS ½ OF BRAND.

⅝" X 18"

IRON ASSEMBLED

⅝" NUT, WELDED TO IRON

TWO IMPRESSIONS MAKE BRAND

A stamp iron is generally the completed brand made in one piece, so the brand can be stamped on the animal in one operation. A collapsible stamp iron designed to be carried on a saddle is shown at the bottom of Plate 17. The iron consists of one half of the brand (in this case a swastika) which requires two operations to put it on the animal. By turning the iron around one quarter turn, the second half is stamped on. This iron was designed by Grover McSherry. Stamp irons of intricate brands which have sharp corners or turns are apt to blotch a brand if the iron is too hot, because then the flesh between the brand markings is scorched.

Brands are generally made up of certain characters or marks which are designated by names or terms peculiar to the cowhand's vocabulary. The component parts of brands are shown on Plate 18, and their names are given so the uninitiated can learn how to read a brand.

Brands are made up of letters of the alphabet, numerals, and designs of familiar objects such as animals, birds, and articles of commerce, all done in outline. Legitimate brands are recorded in order to protect their owners. Stock branded with an unrecorded brand is subject to seizure and confiscation and any person caught running an unrecorded brand on an animal is subject to prosecution. Cattle-growers' associations have framed protective measures for cowmen and these have been enacted into range laws.

In order to designate the location of a brand on an animal without giving a picture of the animal itself, certain letters of the alphabet are used and so arranged that it will be easy for a cowhand to understand how the brand is put on. Brands listed in state brand books are designated in this manner in order to save space in listing the great number of brands that are recorded. In the following paragraphs examples of how the brands are indicated and located are given:

Brand –H– is listed as follows: "–H–, L.S.R.H.C." The first letter indicates the side the brand is on, in this case L for the left side. (R, of course, is used for the right side.) The last letter indicates the kind of stock the brand is on. C in this case stands for cattle. (H stands for horses and M for mules.) The letters in between the first and last indicate the location of the brand on the animal. The different parts of an animal are designated by the letters J, N, S, R, H, and TH: J for jaw; N for neck; S for shoulder; R for ribs; H for hip; and TH for thigh. These indicator letters of the –H– brand, "S.R.H.," mean that the brand is on the shoulder, ribs and hip, which would place the first bar of the –H– on the shoulder, the H on the ribs, and the other bar on the hip.

The brand 77777 is listed as "77777, R.J.N.S.R.H.C." The indicators show that the brand is on the right side, that it is for cattle, and that there is a 7 on the jaw, neck, shoulder, ribs and hip. If there is only one letter between the first and last letters, this means that the brand is located in only one spot, but if there is more than one such letter, this signifies that the brand is spread out in different locations (see Plate 19). Brands are read from left to right and from top to bottom.

Most brands can be called (read) quite easily, but there are brands that even the most experienced cowhand cannot call. These are the Mexican brands which the owners themselves cannot call by their proper names, if any. Those are the odd designs at the top of Plate 18. The first two Mexican brands can be called and are famous in Mexico's range history. The first brand is the Three Christian Crosses which Cortes burned on the ancestors of the old-time longhorns. The second is the famous Terrazas brand, called T R S Connected.

The component parts of our American brands and some complete brands are shown and called on Plate 18. The reader will be able to understand why a brand is called as it is by noting the names of its component parts. If the brands and their parts shown on this Plate are carefully studied, the reader will be able to call a brand nearly as well as an experienced cowhand.

PLATE 18   *Brands*

MEXICAN BRANDS

COMPONENT PARTS OF BRANDS AND HOW TO READ 'EM.

BAR (NOT "LAZY BAR")	DRAG Y (DRAG ATTACHED)	N SLASH N
SLASH	SWINGING DIAMONDS	P CROSS CONNECTED
QUARTER CIRCLE	ROCKING K	DIAMOND A
	FLYING CIRCLE	TRACK L CONNECTED
HALF CIRCLE	FLYING X (WINGS ATTACHED)	
CIRCLE		QUARTER CIRCLE H
RAFTER	BARB BARB F	CIRCLE C
	SPEAR	DOUBLE CIRCLE
OPEN A	ROUND-TOP T	P BENCH CONNECTED
BENCH		
HALF BLOCK, OR HALF BOX	CROW FOOT, OR TRACK	INDIAN SIGN
	ROUND-TOP A	HOOKED H CONNECTED
BLOCK, OR BOX	STAPLE STAPLE L	POTHOOK
TRIANGLE	MASHED O, OR LINK	
DIAMOND	TURKEY TRACK	ANCHOR
LAZY S (LYING DOWN)		POT RACK
REVERSED F	LONG X LONG S	HORSESHOE
	RAIL (EXTRA-LONG BAR)	
TUMBLING K (FALLING)	RAIL N	SQUARE TOP HAT
CRAZY K	RAFTER J	PITCHFORK
Y DOWN	FORKED S (FORKS ATTACHED)	QUIN SABE (DON'T KNOW)
CROSS	HALF BOX H	HASH KNIFE
H N CONNECTED	BAR Y	HATCHET
T UP AND T DOWN	WALKING F (LEGS ATTACHED)	BULL HEAD
RUNNING W (SCRIPT)		FIDDLEBACK
WALKING A	BOX T	TERRAPIN

Marks made with a knife are shown on a steer in the drawing on Plate 19, with the marks indicated by arrows. The terms used to designate them are also given:

The wattle (tadpole) shown on the side of the jaw and on the shoulder is made by cutting a small strip of hide about three inches long so it will hang down and form a sort of jinglebob. The wound will heal over quickly.

The dewlap is shown under the jaw and below the neck.

The jug handle is also shown, below the brisket; it is made by slitting the loose hide also known as the dewlap.

These marks are not used extensively, especially not in the southwest because of the possibility of screwworms attacking the exposed spots. Nevertheless, such marks are an effective method for identifying stock at any season of the year and serve to block the activities of brand workers (forgers), because if the marks are removed the scar is always plainly seen.

Earmarks are employed to protect a brand and to assist in identifying the

PLATE 19   *Marks Made with a Knife*

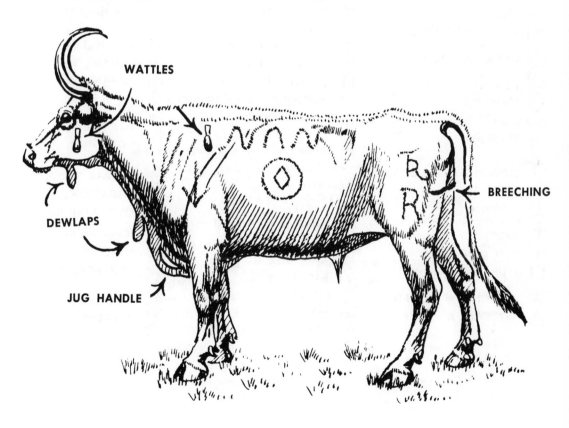

stock branded. Earmarks are easily read and can be used to identify stock in the winter when the hair on an animal is long and conceals the brand to a certain extent. Then, too, when working a herd in cases where cattle are held closely or are milling around, and dust is thick so that brand reading is difficult, the earmarks are generally visible since the critter usually holds his head high. An earmark is harder to work over than a brand, and because of the nature of the mark it often foils the brand worker. There are very few brands which are not run in conjunction with an earmark. Brands that do not employ earmarks are for the most part those of breeders of high-grade stock who do not mark the ears because this detracts from the appearance of the critter's head.

Reading earmarks requires plenty of practice and a heap of experience. Even then there are plenty of real cowhands who can't call them all correctly. The earmarks shown on Plates 20 and 21 are selected from marks which have been used in conjunction with thousands of different brands and are representative of the structure and makeup of earmarks in general use. The cowhand who can call correctly all the marks shown in these diagrams, "without cuttin' plenty of sign on 'em, is a hand that has never been fooled," says Red Hawkins.

In calling an earmark, the right ear is called first and the left ear is called second. The diagrams of earmarks represent the position the ears would be in if the critter were standing looking at the reader; that is, the ear on the left side of the diagram would be the right ear of the animal. Always remember that the animal is supposed to be facing you. The earmarks on Plates 20 and 21 are correctly called, in sequence, on the list that follows them, in order to give the reader an idea of how a roper would call the marks when dragging a calf up to the fire to be branded and marked. After the list follows a glossary of terms to be applied to the marks illustrated and to the names they are called by, which will explain how the marks are made. By referring to the diagrams, to the list of names of earmarks, and to the glossary of terms, a clear idea can be had of how the marks are built.

LIST OF EARMARKS

Note: "Right" is used for "right ear" and "left" for "left ear" in calling earmarks.

1. *Slick-ear.* Term used to designate an unmarked animal or a maverick.
2. *Crop* the right, and *Swallow-fork* the left.
3. *Under-bit* the right, and *Over-bit* the left.
4. *V-under-bit* the right, and *V-over-bit* the left.
5. *Under-half-crop* the right, and *Over-half-crop* the left.
6. *7-under-bit* the right, and *7-over-bit* the left.
7. *Reversed-7-under-bit* the right, and *Reversed-7-over-bit* the left.
8. *Under-slope* the right, and *Over-slope* the left.
9. *Sharp,* or *Point,* the right, and *Grub* the left.
10. *Under-split* the right, and *Over-split* the left.

11. *Under-hack* the right, and *Over-hack* the left.

12. *Under-round* the right, and *Over-round* the left.

13. *Round-swallow-fork* the right, and *Round-crop* the left.

14. *Under-slope-crop* the right, and *Over-slope-crop* the left.

15. *Tip* and *Split* the right, and *Over-slash* the left.

16. *Double-swallow-fork* the right, and *Double-V-under-bit* the left.

17. *Under-straight* the right, and *Over-straight* the left.

18. *Over-* and *Under-straight* the right, and *Over-* and *Under-straight* the left.

19. *Split* the right, and *Full-split* the left.

20. *Key-swallow-fork* the right, and *Key-under-bit* the left.

21. *Key-split* the right, and *Key-under-split* the left.

22. *Comet-under-split* the right, and *Comet-over-split* the left.

23. *Curl-under-split* the right, and *Curl-over-split* the left.

24. *L-split* the right, and *Under-half-slope crop* the left.

25. *Tip* and *Double-split* the right, and *Under-slash* the left.

26. *Curved-under-slash* the right, and *Curved-over-slash* the left.

27. *Rimmed-under-slope* the right, and *Rimmed-over-slope* the left.

28. *Curved-* or *Bent-under-split* the right, and *Curved-* or *Bent-over-split* the left.

29. *Swallow-fork* and *Split* the right, and *Y-split* the left.

30. *Under-slope* and *Split* the right, and *Over-slope* and *Split* the left.

31. *Quarter-over-* and *Quarter-under-crop* the right, and *Over-slope-split* the left.

32. *Curved-over-slash* and *Under-half-crop* the right, and *Double-split* the left.

33. *Tip* and *Over-slash* the right, and *Tip* and *Over-* and *Under-slash-hack* the left.

34. *Drop-split* the right, and *Over-half-swallow-fork* the left.

35. *Under-slope-half-crop* the right, and *Over-slope-half-crop* the left.

36. *Tip* and *Under-half-crop* the right, and *Slash-split* the left.

37. *Half-V-under-bit* the right, and *Curved-* or *Bent-under-split* the left.

38. *L-under-split* the right, and *L-over-split* the left.

39. *Lightning-crop* the right, and *Reversed-lightning-crop* the left.

40. *Under-step* the right, and *Over-step* the left.

41. *Fantail-split* the right, and *Tip* and *Split* the left.

42. *Tip* and *Under-half-swallow-fork* the right, and *Over-slope* and *Under-half-crop* the left.

43. *Over-slope* and *Crop* the right, and *Half-V-over-* and *Under-bit* the left.

44. *Quarter-over-* and *Under-tip* the right, and *7-over-bit* and *7-under-bit* the left.

45. *Over-slope* and *Under-slash-hack* the right, and *Under-slope* and *Over-slash-hack* the left.

46. *V-over-bit* and *V-under-bit* the right, and *Over-straight* and *Under-round* the left.

47. *Key-under-half-crop* the right, and *Key-over-half-crop* the left.

48. *Key-under-slope* the right, and *Key-over-slope* the left.

49. *Over-round* and *Under-round* the

PLATE 20 *Earmarks*

SLICK-EAR

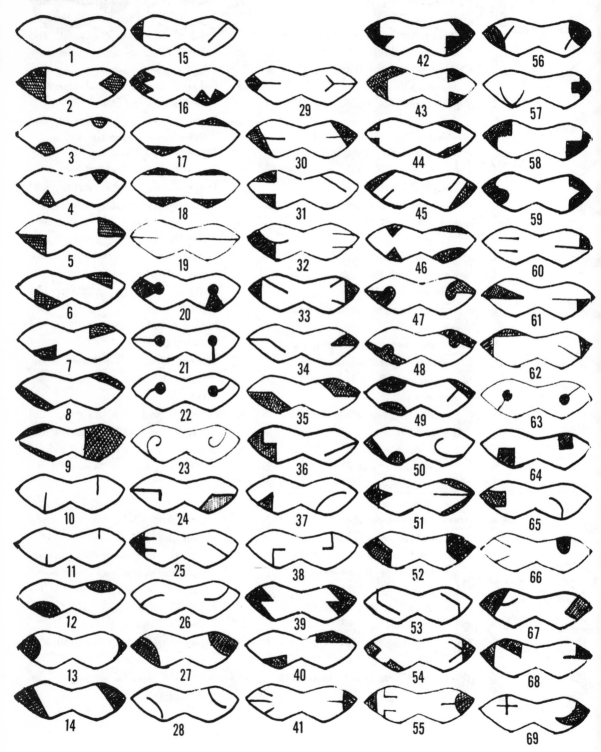

PLATE 21 *Earmarks (Cont.)*

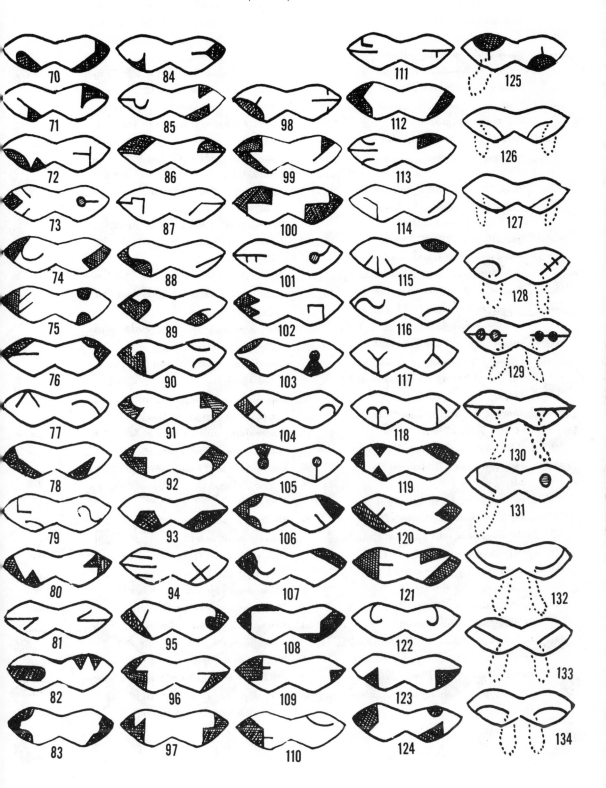

right, and *Over-slope* and *Over-slash-hack* the left.

50. *Under-slope* and *Under-bit* the right, and *J-under-split* the left.

51. *Tip* and *Swallow-fork* the right, and *Point* and *Split* the left.

52. *Half-under-slope-crop* the right, and *Half-over-slope-crop* the left.

53. *Drag-over-split* the right, and *Drag-under-split* the left.

54. *Swallow-fork* and *V-under-bit* the right, and *Tip* and *V-split* the left.

55. *Tip* and *Over-* and *Under-L-hack* the right, and *Round-swallow-fork* and *Split* the left.

56. *Rimmed-under-slope* and *Under-slope hack* the right, and *Rimmed-over-slope* and *Over-slope-hack* the left.

57. *Under-jigger* the right, and *Tip* and *Square-swallow-fork* the left.

58. *Over-half-crop* and *Tip* the right, and *Tip* and *Under-half-crop* the left.

59. *S-crop* the right, and *Point-crop* the left.

60. *Double-slit* the right, and *Over-half-tip* and *Split* the left.

61. *Full-over-half-swallow-fork* the right, and *Split* and *Under-half-tip* the left.

62. *Over-straight* and *Tip* the right, and *Tip* and *Under-slash* the left.

63. *Under-sloped-key-split* the right, and *Over-sloped-key-split* the left.

64. *Square-under-bit* the right, and *Square-over-bit* the left.

65. *Square-swallow-fork* the right, and *Curved-under-split* the left.

66. *Over-slash-hack* and *Under-slash-hack* the right, and *Full-over-bit* the left.

67. *Over-slope-crop* and *Under-slope-hack* the right, and *Under-slope-swallow-fork* the left.

68. *Reversed-7-over-bit* and *Tip* the right, and *Over-half-tip* and *Split* the left.

69. *Cross-over-split* the right, and *Squedow* the left.

70. *Dutch-under-bit* the right, and *Tip* and *Under-slope* the left.

71. *Under-slope-split-under-bit* the right, and *Flicker-over-half-crop* the left.

72. *Under-rim* and *V-under-bit* the right, and *Under-split-split* the left.

73. *Swallow-fork* and *Over-* and *Under-slash-hack* the right, and *Key-slit* the left.

74. *Over-slope* and *Rocker-split* the right, and *Under-slope-swallow-fork* the left.

75. *Tip* and *Double-under-slope-split* the right, and *Over-bit* and *Under-bit* the left.

76. *Over-slope* and *Split* the right, and *Point-over-slope* the left.

77. *Over-jigger* the right, and *Full-jingle-bob* the left.

78. *Tip* and *Under-slope* the right, and *Chihuahua-under-bit* the left.

79. *L-over-split* and *Under-flicker* the right, and *S-under-split* the left.

80. *Under-slope* and *V-under-bit* the right, and *Tip* and *Over-half-swallow-fork* the left.

81. *Drop-barb-split* the right, and *Raised-barb-split* the left.

82. *Dutch-split* the right and *Double-V-over-bit* the left.

83. *Chihuahua-crop* the right, and *Button-under-slope-crop* the left.

84. *Kin-savvy-under-bit* the right, and *Swallow-fork* and *Split* the left.

85. *Under-half-key-split* the right, and *VV-over-bit* and *7-under-bit* the left.

86. *Over-slope-half-crop* the right, and *Dutch-over-half-crop* the left.

87. *Ching-gow-split* the right, and *Drop-split* the left.

88. *S-under-slope* the right, and *Under-slope-split* the left.

89. *Kin-savvy-swallow-fork* the right, and *Curved-under-slope-split-under-bit* the left.

90. *Tip-hook-crop* the right, and *Over-flicker* and *Half-jinglebob* the left.

91. *Pelow-swallow-fork* the right, and *Tip* and *Over-half-crop* the left.

92. *Round-top-under-half-crop* the right, and *Reversed-pelow-swallow-fork* the left.

93. *Bench-under-bit* the right, and *Under-slope-half-crop* the left.

94. *Finger-split* the right, and *X-under-bit-split* the left.

95. *Under-slope* and *Under-slash-hack* the right, and *S-crop* the left.

96. *Over-slope* and *Under-half-crop* the right, and *Pelow-crop* the left.

97. *Ching-whala-crop* the right, and *Tip* and *Under-half-crop* the left.

98. *Under-rim* and *Hack* the right, and *Over-* and *Under-hack* and *Split* the left.

99. *Over-half-crop* and *Under-slope* the right, and *V-over-bit-slash* the left.

100. *Three-quarter-over-crop* and *Tip* the right, and *Tip* and *Three-quarter-under-crop* the left.

101. *Double-hack-split* the right, and *Comet-over-split* the left.

102. *Double-swallow-fork* the right, and *Tipped-L-under-split* the left.

103. *Dutch-point* the right, and *Key-under-bit* the left.

104. *X-split-swallow-fork* the right, and *Tip-flicker* the left.

105. *Key-over-bit* the right, and *Key-under-split* the left.

106. *Chihuahua-crop* the right, and *Over-slope-crop* and *Under-slash-hack* the left.

107. *Chingadero-jinglebob* the right, and *Over-slope* the left.

108. *Over-straight* and *Tip* the right, and *Half-under-slope-crop* and *Under-straight* the left.

109. *Three-quarter-over-crop* and *Hack* the right, and *Under-half-tip* the left.

110. *Half-under-slope-crop* and *Hack* the right, and *Over-flicker* the left.

111. *L-over-hack* and *Split* the right, and *Hack-split* the left.

112. *Over-slope* and *Drop-under-slope* the right, and *Under-slope* the left.

113. *Flicker-tail-split* the right, and *Reversed-7-over-bit* the left.

114. *Sloped-under-split* the right, and *Drag-over-split* the left.

115. *Fanned-under-split* the right, and *Over-round* the left.

116. *S-split* the right, and *Jinglebob* the left.

117. *Y-under-split* the right, and *Y-over-split* the left.

118. *Pelow-under-split* the right, and *Barb-under-split* the left.

119. *Tip* and *V-over-* and *Under-bit* the right, and *Over-slope* the left.

120. *Under-slope-hack* the right, and *Swallow-fork* the left.

121. *Crop* and *Split* the right, and *Reversed-7-over-bit* and *Under-slope-crop* the left.

122. *Curl-over-split* the right, and *Curl-over-split* the left.

123. *V-under-half-crop* the right, and *Under-half-crop* the left.

124. *Half-over-slope-crop* the right, and *Over-bit* and *7-under-bit* the left.

125. *Over-round* and *Hack* the right, and *Under-round* and *Hack* the left.

126. *Flickerbob* the right, and *Flickerbob* the left.

127. *Under-slope-flickerbob* the right, and *Under-slope-flickerbob* the left.

128. *Full-curved-jinglebob* the right, and *Ching-gow-jinglebob* the left.

129. *Sonora-jinglebob (Holy-split)* the right, and *Sonora-jinglebob* the left.

130. *Chihuahua-jinglebob* the right, and *Chihuahua-jinglebob* the left.

131. *Drag-over-split* the right, and *Punch* the left.

132. *Rocker-split-jinglebob* the right and left.

133. *Over-slash-jinglebob* the right and left.

134. *Jinglebob* the right and left.

Note: Where the mark is the same on both ears, the marks can be called as in the last three numbers (132, 133, 134). There are many more types of earmarks not shown herein because of lack of space, but if the reader will memorize those shown, he will be better posted on the subject than the average cowhand is.

GLOSSARY OF TERMS USED IN CALLING EARMARKS

Crop—The outside half of the ear is removed. (To cut off the end of the ear.)

Tip—To cut off the tip end of an ear, one half as much as is removed by a crop.

Split—The ear is split halfway, lengthwise or sidewise, from the center to the outside edge of the ear.

Full-split—A split that extends three-quarters of the length or width of an ear, or even further.

Hack—A short split about half the length of a split or slash (see below).

Slash—This is a diagonal split, running at an angle, much like the brand of the same name.

Rocker-split—A long, curved under-split, starting at the top end of the ear.

Drag-split—The inner end of a split, running at an angle from that of the outer end.

Slope—A diagonal split, or cut, on the outside edge, running at an angle.

J-split—Cuts made with the bottom generally curved to the left.

Key-split—Represents the form of cotter keys of different shapes.

Comet-split—Similar to a key split, except the tail end is curved.

Slits—These generally are cuts made on the inside of the ear and have no outlet.

Points—The ends of the ears are sharpened into points by cutting two similar marks converging at the outer end of the ear. *Sharp* is another term for this mark.

Hooks—These are cuts that are curved at one end like a fish hook.

Barbs—These are sharp, V-shaped angles on the ends of splits and slashes, etc.

Drop—The sudden downward angle of a cut or mark.

Curve—The gradual bending of the line cut.

Rounds—Parts of a perfect circle.

Bits—Small sections removed from the ear which represent a simple mark or design, such as a V, U, quarter circle, square, etc.

Swallow fork—A section removed from the end of the ear, forming two divergent points that fork out. Similar to bits, only larger.

Rim—The curving of a straight edge; a long, shallow, curved edge.

Fanned split—Pieces of ear which have been formed, by splitting, so that the outside ends will be wider than the ends which remain attached to the ear.

Flickers—Small narrow strips formed on the outer edge of the ear by cutting the ear parallel with the outer edge for a distance of about two inches.

Jinglebob—Pendant sections of skin which hang from the bottom of the ear. They are formed by different types of splits. (See dotted lines in diagrams Nos. 128 through 134 for some examples.) The best-known jinglebob is that of John Chisum who was involved in the famous Lincoln County cattlemen's war. (See earmark No. 111, Plate 21.)

Gotch ear—Term used for an ear which has been deeply undercut near the base, which causes the ear to hang below its normal level. This is an earmark that is seldom used.

Grubbed—A grubbed ear is cut off close to its base. This mark is now prohibited by law because it is possible to use it to eliminate earlier earmarks. Grubbing was effectively used by rustlers and brand workers to get rid of legitimate earmarks.

Odd or intricate forms of earmarks which were difficult to call or were apparently nameless often had names hung on 'em by some inventive cowhand who was unable to identify them. Names were coined on the spur of the moment while a hand was trying to figure out how a mark was made and what the form represented. Some chance phrase might suggest a name that was spontaneously adopted by the particular bunch of cowhands present at the impromptu christening. Spanish terms or names were naturals for very intricate designs because of the odd forms generally used across the border for both brands and earmarks. Some examples of these odd terms for earmarks are: *Quien Sabe, Chihuahua, Chingadero, Pelow, Jigger, Jinglebob, Dutch Split, Flicker, Gotch, Quedow,* etc.

The terms used for a brand or mark in the southwest country may be entirely different from those used in the northern sections, but in general the same terms apply throughout the cow country.

In making the marks, the marker—the hand operating the sharp knife—generally starts a split from the inside of the ear and works out. An under-slope (see "slope" in Glossary), for instance, is made by starting the cut in the center and splitting out both ways. There are a number of such techniques which eliminate the danger of cutting too far or of whittling up the marker's hands.

12

HOW BRANDS
AND MARKS
ARE WORKED

How brands and marks are "worked" by rustlers (cow thieves) is an interesting subject and has been an absorbing topic to cowhands and cowmen ever since the range stock industry first broke out down in old Mexico. Many an ingenious method for working a brand or mark has been devised and many a promising herd of cattle has been built up by crooked range practices. Many a long-rope and hot-iron artist has been leaded or necked to a tree or has suddenly changed his current range for one that seemed healthier—and all because he had been sort of careless with a rope and iron.

In order to combat the methods employed by the cattle rustler, the cattlemen's stock associations have drawn up drastic stock and range regulations, and these regulations the associations have had enacted into range laws. They have proved effective in eliminating many of the brand-burning tricks pulled by certain unscrupulous cow gentry. Before the stock associations framed regulations to check brand burners, a person could design a brand and put it on his stock without recording same. This proved to be a great factor in encouraging the brand artist. However, for a while after the law made compulsory the recording of all brands, a person going into the cow business could still design a brand for his own personal use and usually have it recorded.

After the enactment of the laws, the rustler adopted a new tactic. He selected the brand of some good-sized cow outfit in the territory where he proposed to operate. Then he would devise or design an intricate brand of his own into which he could incorporate the brand of the outfit whose stock he wished to work over. This was easy enough to do. The outfit's brand would be used as a base or foundation for the rustler's proposed new brand. The slick brand worker would generally manage to make up a design which would change the character of the worked brand, used as a base, so completely that it was often difficult to recognize the original brand within the structure of the rustler's new brand.

To illustrate how brand working was done, the most famous case recorded in the history of the art is described herewith, to wit, the working of the XIT brand of Texas into the Star-Cross brand. This is always cited as the ultimate in hide forgery and is famous all the way from Alaska to the Argentine as a piece of superb craftsmanship. But a majority of the people who talk about this bit of trick handiwork cannot themselves work the XIT into the Star-Cross, nor do they know exactly how it was done. The T in the XIT is the stumbling block because the top of the T was horizontal and this would seem to have made it impossible to incorporate it into the pattern of the star of the Star-Cross.

PLATE 22

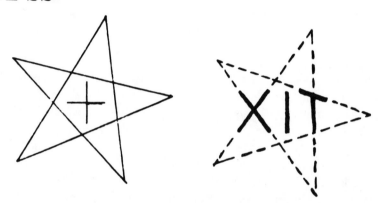

STAR CROSS, MADE FROM X I T

But the brand workers found a way out. They noticed that the XIT brand was on the left side of the animal, reaching from shoulder to flank; that furthermore this placed the T well back towards the flank. Now, they also noticed that when the hind leg of the calf was pulled straight out behind the critter (see Plate 16), preparatory to running the brand, the hide was stretched somewhat out of position. And so, after the T had been burnt into the hide, by an unsuspecting (or perhaps not so unsuspecting) iron man, when the calf was released the hide slipped back to normal again and caused the top of the T to be on an angle, with its left-hand end tipped a bit up. This resulted in a sort of tumbling T which could be incorporated by the brand worker into the star of the Star-Cross. Plate 22 shows graphically how the trick was worked.

Not all of the XIT brands could be tampered with in the manner described, because in many cases the T's were put on in their proper position with the upper part horizontal. However, there were lots of "tumble T's" which could be worked on. And they were worked, plenty.

Earmarks were often in the way of the rustler, as they could not often be altered effectively into the marks which were being used in conjunction with the phoney brand. And because of that, many a cowman remained unmolested by the brand forger. But, in order to overcome the handicap of the unworkable earmark, the ear was removed altogether by grubbing (cutting the ear off close to its base). To eliminate this practice, a law was proposed prohibiting the removal of more than one half of a cow's ear, or to sharp or point more than one ear. Not more than one ear may be cropped on a critter since the cropping might destroy earlier earmarks.

For some time now it has been practically impossible for a person to record a brand which he himself has created and submitted to the brand recorder. A substitute brand is given in place of the brand wanted and it is a case of take it or leave it alone. Also, not more than one brand is allowed to any one individual. Cowmen used to run several different brands, which generally made it very convenient for them to do a little manipulatin' that was not in the books. But that practice was also strangled by rigid regulations sponsored by the stock associations.

"Markers" were often used as bait to catch an over-industrious brand worker. A calf with some peculiar markings or coloring by which it could be easily identified by its owner would be turned loose where the *hombre* to be caught couldn't help seeing it. Sometimes a calf that was given a secret identifying mark not easily detected would be used as the bait. The owner of the calf kept cases on the whereabouts of the rustler or rustlers. If a marker, or baited calf, should be found in the possession of the suspected brand worker and should happen to have the rustler's brand on it, and he claimed it after it had been claimed by its original owner, then things would start "circulatin'." It would then become a matter of a quick getaway by the *hombre,* or shoot the works!

Character brands are so called because they are used to test the character of certain individuals who are suspicioned of brand artistry. The brand is so designed that it can be easily worked over into the brand of the person suspicioned; and it is a brand which is not known in the locality in which it is found. All this, of course, constitutes a special inducement to an enterprising rustler to try out his artistic ability with a hot iron.

Sleepering calves is another favorite pastime of the brand worker and is much practiced in some regions, especially where there is plenty of open range. The rustler has to be something of a psychologist; he has to know how the average rider acts and thinks. Now, the first thing the average rider notes when looking for unbranded stock is the animal's ears. If they are unmarked, he assumes that it is a slick-ear and not as yet branded. But if the ears are marked, he takes it for granted that the critter has been branded as well and doesn't give it any further thought, unless he happens to be a very *cautious* rider. So the rustler catches an unmarked calf belonging to some outfit, not his own, of course, marks its ears with the same mark as those on the mother's ears, and then turns the animal loose. If and when this particular calf reaches weaning size and has not been branded yet, having been overlooked because of its earmarks, the rustler separates it from its mother, drives it some distance away from where it was picked up, and then either places it in a corral with other stock, or shoves it over into a remote territory. After the calf has been weaned in this fashion, its earmarks are altered and it is branded with some other brand than that of its original owner. There are many variations to this type of rustling, details of which, for lack of space cannot be given here.

Sometimes, instead of leaving the calf, which is to be rustled later on, unbranded, it is hair-branded with the brand of its mother. In hair branding, the hair is burned down close to the hide, but not close enough to burn the hide. At a later period the hair brand can be wiped out by a brand that burns into the hide. The owner of such a hair-branded calf and his riders will note that the calf has been both marked and, apparently, branded, and may easily overlook the fact that the brand has burnt away only the hair. After that, the calf is handled by the rustler in much the same way as described above.

Detecting a worked brand is difficult, but if the superimposed brand is examined before it has peeled off and healed, the ridge of the old brand can be traced out by feeling along the new brand. Of course, the under side of the hide will always show up the old brand plainly, but the critter would have to be killed and skinned in order to identify the old brand underneath. Where absolute proof is necessary, the hide will have to be used as evidence.

The burner, when running on a brand, is careful not to burn deeply the old brand which he is incorporating into his new one, because the ridge of the old brand can form a healing scar only once. So he touches it very lightly with his iron when operating on it so as not to arouse suspicion that the brand has been tampered with—a suspicion that would arise if an unhealed, old ridge were noticed. A wet sack is sometimes placed over the old scars, and then a hot iron is run over the sack. This has the effect of scalding the old ridge and making it peel off with the scabs of the new brand the burner wants. But this is a rather difficult process and is therefore seldom resorted to.

Burning with a hot iron is not the only way to run on a forged brand. Some operators have had success with acids which will make a fresh brand look like an old one in a very short time. But, generally speaking, such processes have certain characteristic results by which a close observer can spot the work of a rustler. However, there did come on the market a branding compound which altogether eliminates the need to use a hot iron. It has been tested by stockmen. The cold iron is dipped into the compound and is then stamped on the hide of the animal just as would be done with a hot iron. The chemical will eat away the hair and cause the brand to peel like a burned brand and will leave a scar which is as permanent as one put on with a hot iron.

Picking a brand was another technique employed by the brand artist as a temporary measure while sleepering a calf, or used to work over an old brand. This process was similar to that of hair branding, except that the hair was picked off with a knife or pulled out with a pair of pliers. When the animal is drove out of the country, the picked brand can then be burned over and made into the brand wanted.

Picking a brand is also used for legitimate purposes of identification. If a brand has been blotched or is difficult to read because of a long or heavy coat of hair partly concealing it, the critter can be roped and thrown down and the hair picked off around the brand so it can be identified. As was explained in the Section "How a Branding Crew Works," sometimes a brand is blotched because of too hot an iron having been used, or because the iron slipped when the critter was being branded. It is difficult to keep an iron from slipping on the hide of an animal when it is struggling during the branding process, and this is usually the reason why a brand is blotched.

13

WORKING

WILD STOCK

The term wild stock applies to cattle running on the many mountain ranges of the west, including old Mexico. Because of the ruggedness of the country in which they range and because they get accustomed to living among and like wild animals, without ever coming in contact with human beings, such cattle become as untamed and wild as their surroundings.

The work of gathering wild stock is very different from ordinary roundup work carried on in country where a chuck wagon can go along with the gang. Pack outfits are used to transport the equipment necessary for rounding up wild cattle. In working mountain ranges, traps must be set and worked in the roughest areas to catch the stock, though drives (circles) are made wherever possible in the rest of the country to get the critters collected.

The construction of the traps and the various ways in which they are used are shown in the illustrations on Plates 23 and 24. These drawings will give a hand an idea of how a trap is made and operated. The methods for handling wild stock are also shown and explained below in a way that we think will prove of value to a rider who has never yet made connections with this line of work.

The drawing on Plate 23 shows how a cattle trap is constructed. A corral about fifty or sixty feet in diameter is built with an inlet set of trap entrances called triggers on one side and an outlet set (exits) on another. The inlet set of triggers is located at the bottom of the diagram where the trail leads to the trap. Not all traps have outlets, but the most successful ones do. A holding pasture, strongly constructed (see upper part of the drawing), is often used to hold the stock after the critters have been caught. The pasture may enclose forty to one hundred acres of land, according to the size needed, and is generally around a watering place that serves as an inducement to the cattle to enter the trap. The enclosing fence should be from five to six feet high, with posts set about twelve feet apart to which are strung six strands of barbed wire. Four staves, more or less, should be driven into the ground between the posts to make the fence strong enough to hold the brush snakes once they are caught.

A pole gate-wing, running from the gate that leads into the holding pasture, is connected to the wire fence. The pole gate-wing is a great help when the cattle are being corralled. There is also a pole wing running out from the left-hand corner of the corral, to which the wire fence is connected. These pole wings are reinforcement to prevent the cattle from breaking out when they are being corralled. The gate leading into the holding pasture can be closed so that stock can be held in the corral. At the top of the holding pasture are seen two sets of inlet triggers, indicated by the arrows. They are on other trails leading into the trap.

Traps are generally located where the holding pasture connected with the corral can be set up to enclose a watering place, if one is available. Salt is placed in the corral. The triggers are left open so the stock can go in and out if no outlet triggers are used. No attempt is made to catch the cattle until they have got used to going into the trap, so that when the triggers are finally set the critters will think nothing of it. When there is water inside the holding-pasture fence, it is not necessary to work the traps every day, except in the spring when small calves are lying out. Where no water can be fenced, the trap consists of a corral only and salt is the only inducement to the cattle to walk into the trap.

Cattle-trap entrances, as shown on Plate 24, are of several types and the ones that are described here are those most generally used. Figure A shows a single-trigger trap, so called because it has only one trigger. (A trigger, as will be seen from the drawings on Plate 24, consists of a horizontal portculis that is drawn shut after the animal has been lured into the trap.) The center Figure B shows a double-trigger trap. The double triggers are shown open, in Figure C, for stock to walk in and out of the trap when the latter is not being used. The construction of a trigger is shown in Figure D. It is built much like a corral gate, but with the ends of the cross-poles sharpened. The double triggers are shown being shut in Figure E.

The single trigger is located in the corner of a corral and when it is set, a space of about six inches is left open between the corral fence and the sharpened ends of the trigger so that the cowhand can squeeze through. When the trigger is not set, but is thrown back, the stock can go in and out at will, as shown in Figure A.

Triggers are hung very much like a corral gate and the ends of the triggers are suspended by wires attached to the crosspiece of the trigger arch, as indi-

PLATE 23 *Cattle Trap*

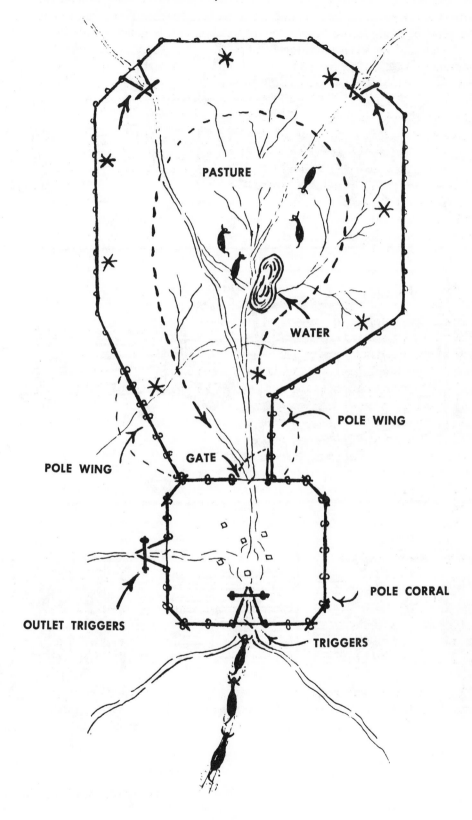

PASTURE

WATER

POLE WING

POLE WING

GATE

POLE CORRAL

OUTLET TRIGGERS

TRIGGERS

PLATE 24 *Cattle-Trap Triggers*

A

B

C

D

TRIGGER

E

A

cated by the arrows in Figure C. When the triggers are about to be set, the suspension wires are moved over towards the center of the cross-pole, as shown in Figure E. To keep the triggers together, a connecting wire is attached to the two suspension wires, as shown by the arrow at A in Figure E. On the single trigger, a connecting wire is attached to the single suspension wire and to the side of the trigger arch on the opposite side to hold the trigger in place when it is set.

An opening about six inches wide is left between the sharpened ends of the double triggers, when they are set, for the cowhand to squeeze through.

The starting stick is a stick about fourteen inches long which is placed between the ends of the two triggers to hold them apart. This is done to coax the first critter through the entrance. The starting stick should be placed near the top of the triggers so the critter will go under it. When the leader, or first animal, goes through the set triggers, the starting stick will fall to the ground and the triggers will swing together behind him. The cattle immediately behind the leader will naturally try to follow and will crowd their way through the entrance. Several blocks of salt are placed near the ends of the triggers to induce the cattle to enter the corral. Five or six feet is close enough to get them started.

The use of outlet triggers in a trap (indicated on the left side of Plate 23 by the arrow at the side of the pole corral) is a great help in trapping wild stock. The diagram on Plate 25 of how the triggers should be arranged shows, at B, how the two triggers are brought together to close the entrance, just as though they were gates. When thus brought together and tied, they will close the outlet. By using an outlet set of triggers as well as an inlet, the critters, if they are still to be allowed to circulate, will be forced to go out through an opening other than the one they came in by. This will prevent them from learning to "work" the triggers (see below) and also will get them used to going through the triggers the right way when these are set. ("Set" in this connection means that the triggers are in such a position that a cow can squeeze through—the wire allows enough play for this; but if the cow tries to go through them the other way, the wire will hold the triggers closed enough so that the cow will get stuck on the points.) Outlet triggers can be set all the time, even when no attempt is being made to catch the stock.

When stock is to be caught, the outlet triggers are folded together as shown at B on Plate 25 to close that entrance. *Closing* the outlet in this way will prevent the stock from going out, whereas if the triggers were merely wired loosely together, as used to be done, the cattle would be continually trying to get out through the outlet. If all the triggers were arranged so that entrance to them could be closed by *folding* them together, this would eliminate the objection to having outlet triggers in a corral that is being used to work stock in.

A wise old brush snake learns to throw a set of entrance triggers with his horns so he will be able to get his head in between the triggers, push them apart, and then proceed to work his way out. When an outlet set of triggers is provided,

PLATE 25   *Combination Inlet & Outlet Trap Triggers*

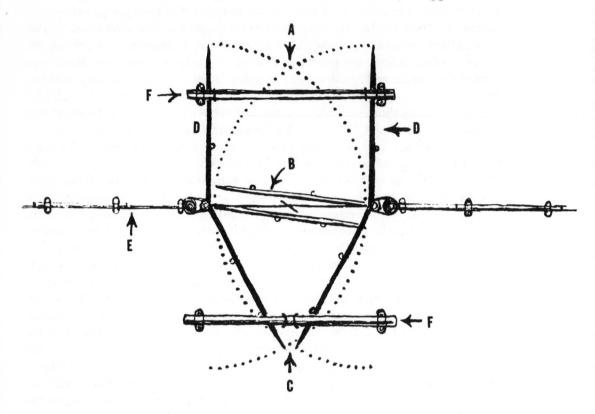

he will not get into the habit of trying to get out the way he came *in,* because he is used to going out a different way. When the entrance to the outlet is securely fastened, he will be blocked because his mind will be fixed on the outlet instead of the inlet.

The triggers can be designed so they can be used as a gate to close the entrance to the corral and can then also be reversed to be used as outlets as well as inlets (see Plate 25). Such combination triggers have proved useful in different ways when working stock in the corral and when taking 'em out. The triggers can be folded out of the way against the outside of the corral fence, leaving the corral clear for action except for the trigger arch which is located just inside the entrance. The combination trigger set was designed by the author with the idea in mind of overcoming the inconvenience of having a set of triggers inside the corral while stock is being worked. Such triggers formerly were always in the way; these designed by the author have the added advantage of working both as outlets and inlets, as needed.

The dotted lines on Plate 25 indicate the course on which the triggers swing in, the same as that traversed by an ordinary corral gate that can be swung both ways. The two D's are the trap triggers. A in the diagram shows the triggers opened up, like other triggers that are not in use; B indicates how the triggers are brought together in the center to close the entrance˙after they have been opened either inward or outward. The upright braces on the triggers, as shown, are so placed that they will not be in between the triggers when they are folded together to close the entrance. C shows the same triggers swung the other way and set for an outlet. E is the corral fence. The two F's represent the trigger arches. All that is necessary to convert a trigger set into this combination set is to erect a trigger arch on *both* sides of the corral fence.

The triggers can also be operated as gate-wings when stock is being corralled or being turned on the outside in a certain direction. If one trigger is swung toward the outside and the other left as a wing on the inside of the corral, this will help materially in heading the stock in the right direction when they are let out *or* being corralled.

In the spring of the year it is necessary to work the traps every day because the young calves do not follow their mothers but lie out when she goes to water. Cows with calves that are lying out have got to be turned loose, if they are trapped, so they can go back to their calves. The calves that happen to be caught in the trap are branded and turned out with their mothers and the rest of the stock is placed in the holding pasture until the outfit is ready to take the animals out.

If there is no holding pasture connected with the corral, the cattle that have been caught in the corral and are now wanted by the outfit are taken out and driven to a holding pasture located in lower country.

There are various methods of handling stock that has been trapped; those described below are the ones most generally employed:

A holdup, that is, a gentle bunch of cattle, is thrown into the holding pasture to mix with the wild stock and the riders are quietly stationed around the inside of the fence. The riders' respective positions are indicated by the stars on Plate 23. They are stationed in this way so they can bend the cattle back when they make a run for the fence. A rider now slowly rides around the cattle to get them used to a rider and to get them well mixed with the gentle stock. He gradually drives the whole bunch around the enclosure until the snuffy stock has simmered down and seems to be willing to stay in the herd. Several hours are generally required to tame 'em down enough so it will be safe to take them outside. The other riders gradually close in on the stock, completely surrounding the bunch, but keeping far enough away to give them plenty of air so the critters will not try to break out of the herd. With a rider in the lead as a pilot, the cattle are led from the holding pasture into the corral and held a while to get them a little more used to contact with human beings, and then they are taken outside. To do this, all the riders but one get outside the gate and spread out in a wide circle so the cattle will be completely surrounded when they come out of the gate. Give 'em plenty of air and let them take their time and never crowd them. If all the hands are in the right place at the right time, which is all the time, there is not much danger of spilling the works.

Handling without a holdup (without a bunch of gentle cattle) is done in practically the same way as with a holdup; the only difference is that it takes more time to simmer the animals down so they can be handled. The riders keep shoving the stock around from one rider to the other to keep the critters circulating until they are tired enough to settle down and walk decently. If there are a few renegades in the bunch determined to make their getaway, it is a good idea to rope them when they are corralled and tie their heads down to one fore foot, or to sideline 'em (*i.e.*, tie one front foot to the tail—see p. 98), which will take the sap out of them before they can go very far. Never crowd the cattle but be sure to give them plenty of room, let them take their time while traveling, and you'll be more certain to put 'em where you want 'em.

Working traps without a holding pasture calls for rope work because there is no chance to get the stock simmered down as can be done in the holding pasture. But, generally, there is a holdup of gentle stock on the outside of the trap into which the wild stock can be run when turned out of the trap. The snaky critters are roped—by the head and heels—and stretched out on the ground and then sidelined. Or the head is tied down to the forefoot, so the animal can't hightail it when the bunch hits the open. Otherwise, the handling of the stock on the outside is the same as previously explained. In handling wild stock after it is taken out of the traps, the riders generally pack a hungry loop (carry their ropes ready for a throw) in case an ox should decide to break out by 'em regardless of how well the bunch is being handled. When these critters make up their minds to take to the brush, nothing can stop 'em except a rope or a bullet. If a hand is good at forefooting or tailing an ox (see Plates 43, 44, and 51), he can turn him over and head him back towards the herd. When timber or brush is thick, it is best to spread a loop around the ox's horns, then bed him down and tie his head down to his foreleg, or sideline him, to make him stay with the herd. But too many hands roping at the same time may cause the whole herd to be spilled.

Throwing the steer by crossing him over the rope is done more often than outright busting (a violent type of throwing described on p. 169) and it is not so hard on the ox. It is generally referred to as pulling down or dragging down, which it really is. After a catch has been made with the rope over the animal's horns and the critter has been stopped, the idea is to pitch the slack in the rope so it will fall in front of the steer. He will most probably step over the rope with his front feet, and when he does so, the rider hauls the slack up taut around the critter's forelegs. The critter's head will now be pulled, by the rope around his horns and forelegs, down toward his forelegs. Then, if the cowhand rides round him in a circle, the steer will lose his balance and topple over on his side. If the horse savvies his business, he will keep the rope taut and so keep the critter down while it is being hog-tied (see Plate 46). Some outfits object to a rider busting or fair-grounding (another violent method of throwing an animal) a critter and insist that the cattle be pulled down. As already stated, pulling down is much easier on the stock, and that is what tallies in the owner's checkbook.

When making drives in open country in which salty stock are caught, a holdup of gentle stock is used to run the wilder critters into. The object is the same as in handling trapped stock (see above). A couple of riders are designated to pick up a bunch of docile animals and hold 'em where the roundup is to be thrown together. Mixed with the docile animals, the snaky stock will be easier to hold. The herd is not always worked where the roundup is made but is sometimes driven to where there is a good opening in order to have plenty of room to work the herd in. The driving helps to get the stock simmered down so it will be easier to hold.

Tying them down to make them stay in the cut used to be necessary when handling a herd with a bunch of salty old renegades in it that had to be cut out and held up. If one renegade was cut out, he would naturally try to make a getaway and would have to be roped and tied to keep him in.

The cattle gathered each day on the drives as well as those that are trapped are generally driven to a good-sized holding pasture and turned loose. No night guard or day herding is necessary, as the stock gathered each day is thrown into the enclosed holding pastures located at various convenient points. When the work is over, the stock intended for shipment is cut out, driven together and headed for the shipping pens. The herd is guarded at night when necessary, but whenever possible it is thrown into these pastures to eliminate the work of standing guard and to give the cattle a chance to graze.

To catch wild stock without traps in the toughest country, the cowhands have to rope the critters, tie them up to trees, and then lead them out of the country the next day. Handling wild stock in this way is the roughest kind of cow work; it takes a man with plenty of guts to be a good hand in the pinnacles. Two riders generally work together in order to help each other out in case of an accident.

The riders carry head ropes with which to tie the cattle to trees, as shown on Plate 26. The ropes are from ten to twelve feet long and are doubled up so they will not hang up on (get tangled in) the brush. The ropes are tied to the backs of the riders' saddles. Some outfits use hard-twist rope for this purpose because of its light weight and because it is much stronger than ordinary hemp rope. Others use hemp rope five-eighths or one-half inch thick. Each rider carries about four head ropes, which is generally sufficient for a day's work. Two catch ropes are carried by some hands, though this is unusual. But with two catch ropes a rider can save time by tying the first critter up to a tree with the catch rope that is on the animal and taking off with the second rope after another ox that has been jumped at the same time. The rider returns later and ties the first steer to the tree with a head rope and removes the catch rope.

Riders carry hogging strings cinch-tied to a rigging ring on the saddle and to the chap belt. These ropes are used to tie down or hobble the critters caught. A piece of hard-twist rope about seven feet long, with one strand removed, is approximately the right length after a honda and knot have been tied in it. For rodeo work the free end of the rope is thinned out and wrapped (whipped around) with twine. The idea is to eliminate the possibility of a knot hanging up the rope (keeping it from running smoothly) while a tie is being made. (A piece of rope six feet long is ample for a pigging string to be used to tie a calf with.)

Armed with catch ropes tied down to the saddlehorns, hogging strings and head ropes, with a six-shooter bedded down in the right-hand chap pocket, and mounted on able rim-rockers* with good double-rig outfits screwed down on 'em, two brush hands start out and work the country where the wild stock is ranging. By reading sign they can tell whether cattle are in the locality. If fresh sign is found, the riders usually halt, let their horses rest awhile, and cinch up so they will be primed to make a run. Now, with ropes in hand and loops half-cocked, they are ready for action. When a bunch of brush snakes is jumped, the riders build to 'em, each trying to catch the first ox he can make connection with. When a critter is caught, the rider crosses the animal over the rope (see above) and drags it down. Quitting his horse, he now proceeds to hog-tie the steer. If the latter should try to get up on his feet before it is tied, it can be held down by one foreleg or by a hind leg until a rope can be gotten on its feet. The rider, when he grabs a hind leg will usually hold it up, and by doing this, keep the critter down until the top foreleg can finally be grabbed, and, still keeping the animal down, get him tied. The idea is to keep the animal off balance till it decides to quit struggling. When it quiets down, then it can be tied (see below). A good horse will hold the animal down by keeping the catch rope taut while the rider is doing the tying, as shown at the bottom of Plate 46.

After the steer has been tied, the rider proceeds to hobble the animal with one of the hogging strings. The hind legs are tied together, as shown in the drawings L and M on Plate 26. The hind legs should be pulled close together so the critter cannot walk when he is on his feet. A good method is to tie a square knot in the rope after it is passed around the first leg, then carry the two ends of the rope around the other leg and tie them in a hard square knot. Be sure that there is no slack left in the rope, or the critter may get its feet out. This method is exactly the same as that used in tying a steer to a tree, as shown in diagram B on the same Plate.

Wild stock will often die if tied down and left that way for several hours exposed to the hot sun. Some riders who have roped and tied down an ox, and left him tied while they go after another critter that got away, often have found the first critter dead when they returned to tie him up to a tree. Therefore the main reason for hobbling a critter behind after it is caught is to let the animal

* Good cow horses agile enough to climb steep hills, scramble over rocks and come down sharp pitches.

PLATE 26 *Working Wild Stock*

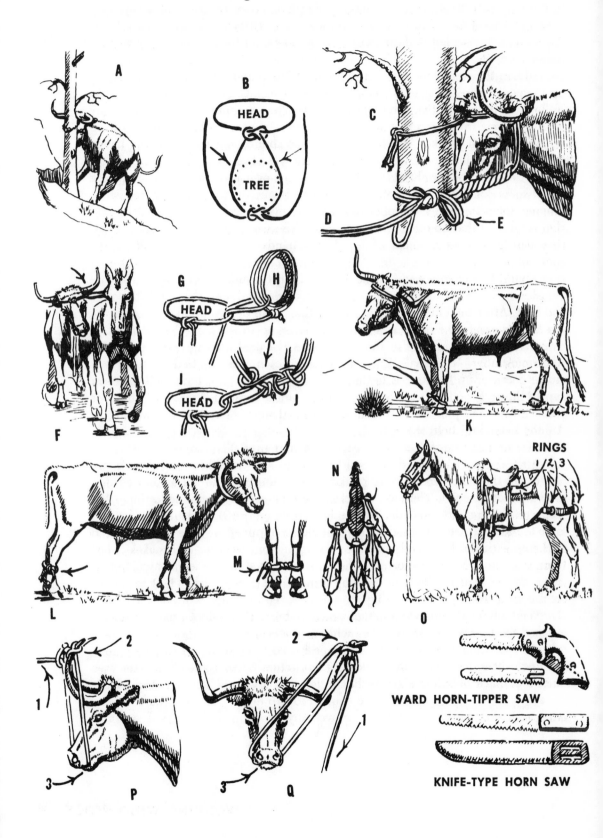

A

B
HEAD
TREE

C
D
E

F
G
HEAD
H
I
HEAD
J

K

L
M
N
O

RINGS
1 2 3

P
1 2 3

Q
1 2 3

WARD HORN-TIPPER SAW

KNIFE-TYPE HORN SAW

get up on its feet. A horse can stand being tied down longer than a cow can. The heat has a lot to do with the problem; if a critter has been run a lot and then is caught and left tied down for several hours, it's the hot sun that generally cashes him in.

When the steer is hobbled, first the catch rope and then the hogging string are removed and the steer is left to its own devices while the rider proceeds to follow up the cattle that have gotten away. The escaping cattle are generally found not far from the place where they were last seen, as they often bush up in the first good patch of brush they can make connections with. Trailing has to be relied on to locate old renegades, for they will often lie down in thick brush and let a rider come right close to them without ever making a move. But once they know that they are spotted, the brush begins to pop as rider and stock charge down through the timber like a young cyclone in action. (Let it be said here and now that no other class of riders in the world surpasses or even equals the daring and recklessness of top brush hands working wild stock in the pinnacles.)

Tying a steer to a tree is done by snubbing the animal up close to the tree trunk. The rider circles the tree to get a wrap around it, and then pulls the steer up to it. After the animal is up close, another wrap or two is taken around the tree. Now, while the horse is holding the steer up to the tree, the rider gets a rope around the hind legs of the critter—this is called heeling—and pulls them out from under the animal. When the steer is down, it is hog-tied. Another way to get a critter up to a tree is to throw the catch rope over a limb, pull the steer up to the tree, and then proceed to handle him as explained above. (The rope used to heel and pull the critter down is a head rope.) The next operation is to tie the animal to the tree.

Tying to a tree, as shown in Figures A and B of Plate 26, is an easy job— sometimes. The rope is looped around the horns and tied in front with a square knot, and then the two ends are passed around the tree and are again tied in a square knot (see B). The loose ends of the rope are then wrapped around the rope on the tree, as indicated by the arrows in Figure B, and then tied again into the loop around the head by half-hitches. Wrapping the rope that is around the tree with the loose ends prevents the rope from wearing and makes it last longer. If the rope is too short, or the tree is too big around, the ends will not be long enough to reach back to the loop around the head. A tree eight to twelve inches in diameter is large enough to tie to. A ten-foot rope will not leave ends long enough for the rope-wrapping operation, but a twelve-foot rope will do the trick if the tree is not over twelve inches in diameter.

In tying an animal to a tree, the rope is tied loosely around the horns so it will not cut in and the animal's head is not actually tied right against the tree trunk—a space of about eight inches is left in between. The rope around the tree, as shown in Figure B, is loose enough to slip up and down and around the tree to give the animal a chance to move. Any knots on the tree trunk or limbs in the way of the rope should be trimmed off so the rope will have free play. After the critter has been properly tied, the other ropes are removed and the animal is let up.

Another way to tie an ox to a tree is to tie one end of the rope loosely around the horns with a bowline knot, then pass the other end around the tree and bring it back to the rope around the head and tie it into the horn loop by half-hitching it around the rope. But be sure to leave plenty of slack in the rope around the tree so that it can slip up and down and around properly.

When the last critter has been caught and hobbled, the riders generally help each other tie them all up for the night. The animals will be found close to the place where they were left because, of course, they aren't able to travel. The first ox the riders come back to is roped and hazed up to the first tree they find suitable for the purpose; then the animal is snubbed up to the tree. While the hazer heels it and pulls it down, the other rider quits his horse, gets on the steer and holds it down while the hazer ties its feet. After the animal is tied down, the tips of its horns are sawed off (see below). The animal is then tied up to the tree. When all the cattle have been tied up, the two riders return to camp and stay there until the next morning, when the cattle will be led in.

When cattle are left tied up overnight, their heads become sore from pulling back on the rope. When they are led in in the morning, they will not pull back as much as if they had not been tree-tied and they are more easily handled. Sometimes, if there is no one else to do the job, the riders who caught the cattle go back the next day and lead them in. Many outfits, however, have special hands to catch the cattle and others to lead them in to camp.

Leading them in in good shape is the main idea and there are several ways of doing it, all of which have proven successful and are described as follows:

Necking to mules is claimed by some cowmen to be the most practical method because of a lower percentage of loss from injuries. Figure F on Plate 26 shows how a steer is necked up to a mule. A five-eighths-of-an-inch soft Manila rope, twenty-two feet long, is used for the necking operation. One end of the rope is tied around the mule's neck and then wrapped around five times in order to make a wide collar (see Figures H and G). These drawings also show the head rope with which the steer was tied to the tree. One should be careful to avoid having the rope collar too loose around the mule's neck, as it might then come off over the mule's head. If the collar is made too tight, however, it will cut into the creature's neck. It is actually best to have the collar six or seven strands wide, though five strands use less rope. When the rope is ready around the mule's neck, he is led up beside the steer and the free end of the Manila rope is run through the loop of the rope around the steer's head (see Figure G); then the Manila rope is passed back through the collar and back through the steer's head rope again. The steer's head is pulled up to within six inches of the mule's collar. If the steer is not up close enough, he has too much play and he can hook the mule with his horns. When the two animals are close enough together, the end of the rope should be run through the collar and head ropes several times more to make it secure and to keep the head rope from cutting the neck rope out. Figures I and J show how the end of the necking rope is half-hitched around both sides of the knot in the rope collar; double half-hitches should be drawn up tight on each side of the knot to make it safe. The head rope is now untied from around the tree and the ends should be tied up into the collar or in the rope around the horns.

A good lead mule will lead a critter to camp by himself. It is best to ride ahead of him to keep him from going too fast; an ox is likely to get to sulling if he is forced to walk fast. If the critter does sull, the mule is apt to hurt him by kicking at him to get him to move up, and that don't pay. In leading a bunch of cattle out with mules, the whole bunch should be driven around together until all the cattle have been gathered, and then they should be headed for camp. One rider should be in the lead and the other behind the stock to keep the animals going at a slow walk. If worked this way, there will be very little difficulty bringing them along and they will not get jammed up. Some outfits turn the mule and steer loose by themselves and no attention is paid to them. Eventually the mule will show up at camp with the ox. When a mule is necked to a critter, he is naturally anxious to get loose and he knows that the sooner he makes camp the quicker he will get rid of his charge.

Working cattle too fast when leading them in will get them to sulling and then trouble begins. Give them plenty of time and humor them when starting out by letting them go in the direction they want to go until they get to walking decently; then, gradually circle them around into the direction of camp.

Necking to burros is done in much the same way as necking to mules, but it is not so easy on the critter, owing to the fact that a burro will fight a critter more than a mule will and if he is turned loose with an animal to do as he pleases, he is apt to injure it. But when a bunch of burros are necked up to cattle and handled by a couple of riders in the same way as in necking to mules, the stock can be led out in good shape.

Necking cattle together requires more work than necking to mules or burros and the stock is harder to drive when handled this way, therefore this method is seldom used. Cattle caught in a trap are sometimes necked and tailed together so they cannot get away when being driven. The animals are roped and tied down close to each other and then a rope is tied around their horns, leaving enough space between their heads so they can travel but still be kept close together. The ends of their tails are also tied together with a hogging string to keep them headed in the same direction and to keep them from hanging up in the brush. Cattle necked together in this fashion travel better in a herd than in isolated pairs. Also, to make any progress, they have to be given plenty of time.

Lead steers, or *cabestros*, are used in some parts of Mexico. Some have a hole large enough to pass a rope through made in one horn. A rope is fastened to the lead steer's horn and then tied around the horns of the critter to be led out. The lead steer is turned loose and leads his critter to camp just as a lead mule does—but better, if anything.

Leading out on a horse is actually the method most used in leading cattle out of rough country. A short, hard-twist lead rope about eight feet long is used. One end of the rope is tied around the critter's horns with a bowline knot while the critter is still tied to the tree. Then the rider gets on his horse and snubs the animal's head up close to the saddle fork by running the rope through the fork of the saddle from the front. Then he dallies (wraps) the rope around the saddle-horn and ties it in a dally-and-tie. The rider then gets off his horse, unties the head rope from around the tree and ties the ends up around the critter's horns so the rope will be out of the way; or he takes the head rope off entirely. When an ox fights too much, he is heeled and pulled down, his feet are tied, and *then* the lead rope is put on him and the head rope is removed. He is snubbed up to the saddle as close as possible while he is down, the rope is dally-tied, and then the rider unties the critter's feet and gets back on his horse. When the critter gets up, he is snubbed up closer to the saddle so he will not have much slack to charge around in. By working the ox around easy and giving him plenty of time, he can be gotten to walking along with the horse and then can be led into camp without much trouble. Avoid as much as possible leading the critter over steep, narrow trails and keep out of close places if you want to save time and a lot of unprintable language.

Leading out with a catch rope, holding the rope in the hands, can also be done. Just place the loop of the rope over the critter's horns, snub him up close to the saddle and tie the rope. Then untie the head rope from around the tree and get back on the horse. Now give the critter about fifteen feet of slack in the rope to play on and gradually work him around from one side to the other by pulling on the rope lightly. Be careful not to get him on the prod. By partly driving and partly leading him, you will get him to walking and following the horse. Never try to force him by dragging him, because he will sull and more time will be required to get him going. If the critter tries to get away, he can be stopped by taking dallys around the saddlehorn. You will have to take plenty of time if leading on the catch rope is to be successful.

Driving on the end of a catch rope is done in much the same way as leading on the catch rope, only in this case the critter is hazed, or driven, along and has to be pulled out of the brush. All of this will most likely get him on the prod and give the rider more trouble than if the critter were being led.

A critter can be led out as soon as it is caught if it is blindfolded. While the animal is tied down, a rider's brush jacket, or jumper, is placed over the critter's head. The sleeves are tied around the horns so that the body part of the jumper will hang down over the animal's head. The catch rope is left around the horns and used to lead the critter with. When the animal is untied and let up onto his feet, he won't be able to see where he is going and the idea is to get him to follow the horse by sound, thinking that he is following another ox. The rope is held in the hands to give the critter slack to play on and is dallied around the saddle-horn when necessary to stop the animal when he goes wrong. It will take some time to get the animal started. The rider gets him going by working around him, riding up alongside of him, riding off ahead of him, but never trying to force him by pulling on the rope too strongly. Eventually, with plenty of humoring, the critter will get to following the horse and when he does, take it easy so he can feel his way along.

A come-along is a halter especially designed to compel an animal's obedi-ence (see p. 138). Cattle can be led with the come-along when first caught if the rider will only take the time required to get the critter started, in the same way that is necessary in halter-breaking horses. The come-along is applied in the same manner as is later described for horses and will work here too if no attempt is made to drag or force the critter. Hold the rope in the hands and dally when necessary; otherwise handle the ox as in leading on a catch rope. Cattle that have been tied up to a tree can also be led out on the end of a catch rope by using the come-along.

Leading six head of cattle at one time may seem impractical, but it has been done. The rigging used for the purpose, and especially designed so the cattle can be tied to it and led behind a horse, is shown in Figure O on Plate 26. It was originated by the CCC outfit in Arizona to save time when a large number of cattle had to be led and taken out of the country as quickly as possible. A strong breeching, like that often seen on a harness or packsaddle, is used (see E in Figure 1 on Plate 12). It is attached to the saddle as shown in Figure O on Plate 26. Then, rings—one on each side, and one in the center at the back—are securely fastened to the breeching. The rings are indicated by arrows on the drawing. The two back rigging rings on the saddle and these three rings on the breeching—five in all—are used to tie the head ropes of five of the cattle in. The sixth steer, which is the last one picked up, is snubbed up to the saddle fork and led as was described for leading on a horse above. To handle so many animals at one time in this way requires a gentle horse that will not go out of his head when a horn happens to hit him in the flank. A squaw's saddle horse might fill the bill.

The rider doing the leading out starts in by leading the first steer picked up and snubbing him to the saddlehorn. When the second critter is reached, the first one is tied to the back rigging ring of the saddle on the near side of the horse. The rings numbered 1, 2, and 3 (Figure O) represent the order in which the first three head of cattle are tied to the outfit as they are picked up; the other cattle are tied in consecutive order as *they* are picked up. A lead rope is tied onto the second steer and he is led, as was the first, until the third steer is reached. The second steer is then tied to the front breeching ring on the near side, next to the first steer. The third steer is then tied up to the rear breeching ring (3 in the diagram). The other cattle are tied to the remaining rings in the order stated, until all six head are picked up. Cattle should be tied up short enough to keep their horns from hitting the horse, but with enough slack to give them room to walk freely. Figure N shows how four head of cattle are led in this way. Three are tied to the breeching and one is snubbed to the saddlehorn.

Two riders should work together, one to lead and the other to haze and help turn the cattle loose from the trees, etc. One rider can do all the work, but two working together is best for all concerned. In leading the cattle, close or narrow places must be avoided, such as narrow trails or thick timber, for the cattle must have room to walk freely. Time, and plenty of it, will be needed to make headway in bringing them out.

Tipping and dehorning wild stock call for methods that differ from those used on the average run of cattle. The horns of wild stock that is caught and led out are tipped by sawing off six to ten inches of the sharp ends. This is done to prevent the horns from doing damage to the horses the cattle are led out with. The sharp edge around the tipped horn is rounded off by using a rock to hammer the edges down, or the edge is trimmed off with a knife. The sharp edge of a freshly sawed horn can do a lot of damage when it makes connections with an animal or a human. The tipped horns are a mark which easily identifies an animal that has been led out. Generally a critter is tied down before it is snubbed up to a tree to be tied up, so it is while it is down that the horns are tipped; then it will not be necessary to tie him down again to do this work later.

Dehorning with a rope has been done in cases of emergency when no saw was handy to do the job with. When an ox is a confirmed bunch-quitter and will fight everything that gets in his way, it is a good idea to make a muley of him by jerking his horns off altogether. He is roped, bedded down and hog-tied to make him stay bedded while he is being worked on. In Figures P and Q on Plate 26, the rope is shown attached to the horn by a double half-hitch, right back of the honda (indicated by the arrows at the numbers 2). The loop is placed in the critter's mouth (see at the numbers 3). The half-hitches on the horn should be drawn tight so they will not slip down. The top horn should be jerked off first. The critter is then turned over and the other horn is removed.

First the skin at the base of the horn is cut all the way around so that when the horn is jerked off the hide will not hang to it. The main line of the rope runs straight out in front of the animal (see at the numbers 1 of Figures P and Q). Then the rider ties the rope hard and fast to his saddlehorn, and, riding straight ahead of the steer, he has to hit the end of the rope on a run so the horn will snap off instantly. The rope will slide out of the steer's mouth when the horn comes off. The arrangement indicated in these drawings is the best one to use. Be sure to cut around the base of the horns first, though.

Horn-tipping saws are shown down in the right-hand corner of Plate 26. There are two popular styles. The Ward horn-tipper is designed to be carried in a chap pocket, folded up, or to be carried in a holster like a six-shooter; its saw blade is removable and easily replaced, and its handle fits the hand like a Colt

.45. The knife-type saw is carried in a scabbard like a hunting knife. Both saws are light and easy to carry. When wild stock in the pinnacles is being worked and led out, the riders generally pack a saw to tip the ends of the horns.

Tying a steer's head down, as shown in Figure K on Plate 26, is a technique often used when stock is being trapped. The snuffy steer is roped and tied down, a hogging rope is looped around the horns and the end is tied around a foreleg, just above the hoof, with a bowline knot so the rope will not tighten on the leg. In tying the head down, the head should be pulled to just below the level of the back and the foreleg should be straight down from the animal's body in its normal position. Tying an animal's head down will prevent it from running and will help to discourage it from trying to make a getaway while being driven with other stock. The critter will eventually have to be roped and stretched out in order to remove the rope that ties his head and foot.

Sidelining is another technique that is used in handling wild stock caught in traps. A horse is shown sidelined on Plate 33 in Figure J. The animal is roped and tied down, and then sidelined. A hogging string is generally used for this operation. One end of the rope is tied around the front leg just above the hoof in the same way as in tying a head down to a foreleg (above). The rope is again tied with a bowline knot so it will not tighten around the leg. The other end of the rope is then tied to the critter's tail, as indicated in Figure I on Plate 33. Make sure that the rope is tied short enough to prevent the animal from stepping forward. You can do this by having the foreleg extend straight down from the body as if it were in a normal standing position while making the tie. The critter will then not be able to travel fast and will be unable to break out of the herd.

Releasing the ox from the tree is shown in Figure C of Plate 26; it is carried out after the rider has got on his horse. (Sometimes an animal turned loose in this way is run into a holdup of gentle cattle that is first brought up close.) A catch rope is used; the rope is doubled and then passed around the steer's neck in such a manner as to leave the double end five or six feet longer than the looped end. This long end is later used to untie the rope (see at D). The ropes are twisted, not tied, together between the critter's neck and the tree; then they are looped around the tree and tied in a single bowknot, or slip knot, as indicated at E, so the rope can be untied when the long double end at D is pulled. After the critter has been necked to the tree, as shown, a rider can untie the head rope, take it off the steer, then get back on his horse and, by dallying the catch rope around the saddlehorn, untie the knot by pulling on it. It will untwist from around the critter's neck and turn him wild loose. The rider will be on his horse and will be able to get out of the way if the steer charges. The same technique can be employed with a single strand of rope, but doubled it is stronger and will not break if an ox should set back on it. This technique can also be used when an animal has been necked to another, to release them from each other.

Kneeing cattle was an operation sometimes practised in the early days to prevent snaky stock from traveling too fast. The idea was to hold in the herd.

A tendon in the front of the knee was cut, which prevented the critter from running. Kneeing had the same effect on a critter as sidelining, that is, it prevented the foreleg from advancing. Other methods, however, are more practical, just as effective as kneeing, and do not injure the stock handled.

Eyeballing was also practised before more modern methods were adopted, but has gone the way of the longhorn. Brush snakes (cattle that stayed in the brush during the day and grazed out at night) were the type of stock that was eyeballed when it was caught, to prevent the critters from going back into brushy spots. The animal was caught and tied down and then its upper eyelids were cut off, after which it was turned loose. Then the first bunch of brush the critter ran into proved to be surprisingly hard on the eyes. Not being able to close its eyes to protect them when it shoved its head into a thicket soon made it change its mind about camping in such unfriendly territory. The open country then offered more attraction and the result was that an outlaw became civilized.

Eye-openers also were once used on cattle that were especially fond of thick brush. Used as a temporary expedient, eye-openers proved nearly as effective as eyeballing. The critter was roped and tied down, and small sticks about the size of a match were used to prop its eyelids open. Sometimes a small stick was cracked in the middle and inserted in the eye in the shape of an inverted V to hold the eyelids apart. This was easier on the eye since it straddled the eyeball. At the same time it exposed the eyeball more to every little branch and twig that reached out to poke the critter in the face. Cattle that submitted to this treatment also soon found that the open places were more hospitable and that his fellows in the herd were really quite congenial. When the critter was finally introduced to its new range, the eye-openers that had so convincingly demonstrated to him that wild ideas should be forgotten were removed.

Blinding by sewing the eyelids together was a method often used in the days of the longhorns to cure the critters of any wild notions they may have had. After a time the threads rotted out and the much-tamed wild ones were able to see again.

Tying a jaw to a foot was an operation similar to tying a head down described above. The difference was that the rope was tied around the critter's lower jaw instead of around its horns. This early method was harder on the animal than using his horns as is done today.

Time has changed the methods of handling range stock to such an extent that nearly all the old-time practices have been discarded and in their place improved methods, more humane in every way, have been substituted.

A good catch dog is highly valued in extremely rough country where it is very difficult to catch wild stock. In such terrain the catch dog plays an important role. No special breed of dog is used for the purpose. A good catch dog will trail up a critter and hold him up (at bay) until the rider can get to the spot. The rider has no trouble locating the dog who makes plenty of noise. If the ox should break out and run before the rider arrives, the dog will catch the animal by the ear or by the nose and hold on until the critter stops or breaks the dog loose. After the first run the ox learns to stay in one place and defend itself. As long as it will stay in one place, the dog will not harm it. A vicious dog is not good for catching cattle because he is apt to tear a critter up when he gets ahold of it. A dog that will catch by an ear is preferable to one that catches by the nose. By using a catch dog to hold an ox up, the rider is able to get to the critter and rope it; once caught, the animal is tied up to a tree and handled in the same manner as other wild stock.

It should be noted that the brush hand's equipment is different from that of the open-country cowhand because of the nature of the country and of the work described above. It is necessary for a rider to protect himself from the wear and tear of the timber or brush and the rocks which he encounters in his everyday work. He is generally rigged out with a brush jacket or jumper, heavy chaps, leather cuffs (sometimes), gloves and a small hat. A large hat is easily knocked off and is generally in the way of every limb that the rider has to duck under; he has no time to keep cases on a hat when he jumps brush snakes. Short taps on the stirrups (see Section on "Tapaderos"), breast straps and sometimes a breeching on the saddle are used in extremely rough country. The equipment carried is generally arranged so it will not get hung up on a limb or other obstruction while the hand is riding.

14

MUSTANGING

There are many factors to be taken into consideration if any measure of success is to be attained in the business of catching wild horses, or mustangs, as they are generally called. A great deal of work and a lot of hard riding, combined with a lot of good luck, are necessary to achieve profitable results in such work. In wild horse country watering places are few and far between and it is necessary to locate such places in order to plan out the work of catching the horses.

When the horses that are to be run are located, the next thing is to locate where they are watering so that a favorable spot can be selected for the construction of a trap. The trap consists of corrals so arranged that it will be difficult for a horse to escape once he is inside the enclosure. The trap must be located in a place where it will be well concealed, as, for instance, in a canyon, where the horses will not be aware of the trap until they are practically in it. The trap, naturally, is more easily concealed in a deep draw or canyon than out in the open. The deeper the canyon the better, for it will serve as a sort of chute that helps prevent the wise ones of the bunch from breaking out and making their getaway. A trap located in a sharp bend of a canyon is better than one in a canyon that has no bend, because then the horses can be forced into the trap before they catch on to where it is. A trap that has been used with good results by mustangers is shown on Plate 27.

The trap shown is an elaborate arrangement designed for country where it is difficult to find a depression deep enough to prevent the horses from getting away when they are being forced into the trap. The more natural the enclosure appears, the less suspicious the mustangs will be. This is a point which must be taken into consideration. The mustang is much wiser than he is given credit for. The more the horses have been run, the wiser they become, so they will be on the quedow (alert) for anything that doesn't look natural. Once they sense something is wrong, they are pretty sure to make a break, and once they start back, nothing but lead or a well-placed loop will stop 'em from high-tailing it back for the high spots. The trap shown on Plate 27 has a round catch corral constructed of poles or pickets set into the ground close together and fastened together with wires twisted around each post (see the drawing of a section of picket fence at the top of the Plate). A pole corral is best, but where it is difficult to secure timber, heavy woven wire is used instead, reinforced at the top, center and bottom to break the strain the fence will be subjected to when a horse hits it head on. The catch corral is generally from forty to fifty feet in diameter and from eight to nine feet high, and sometimes higher. Horses have been known to go over some pretty tall corrals when they took a notion.

Pole wings are shown on Plate 27 extending out away from the gate of the catch corral, forming the point of the heart-shaped forcing corral; they are necessary when the mustangs are being run into the catch corral. The material used in the construction of the forcing corral is heavy woven wire, doubled, to form a fence eight to nine feet high. Heavy posts, twelve to fourteen feet long, are set three to five feet into the ground and are placed about six feet apart; the woven wire is fastened to and supported by these posts. The wire is on the inside of the posts, which makes for strength and eliminates chances of injury to the stock. The woven wire is attached to the ends of the pole wings running out from the catch corral, as indicated in the drawing.

A second set of wings, running out from the entrance to the force corral, is constructed of the same woven wire as the corral. These wings are extended out some forty to fifty feet from the entrance and are spread out to a considerable width so the horses can be run between them without crowding. They should be about forty-five yards apart at the outer extremities to give ample room to push 'em into the trap.

Booger wings, which consist of a single strand of smooth wire, are attached to the ends of the woven-wire wings and run still further out, for a distance of five or six hundred yards, to form a very wide V. The wire is placed up about five feet from the ground and is fastened to posts and trees wherever possible. Rags consisting of old clothes and sacks torn into wide strips about three feet long are fastened to the wire and placed about six feet apart. The rags will swing and flap in the wind and will help booger the mustangs away from the fence when they head toward it. The posts of the force corral are camouflaged by placing limbs cut from trees on them to make them look like trees. The more the enclosure can be made to look like the natural surroundings the horse is used to, the better. All trace of sign showing where work has been done in the vicinity of the trap should be removed or concealed and as many precautions taken in

PLATE 27

Wild Horse Trap

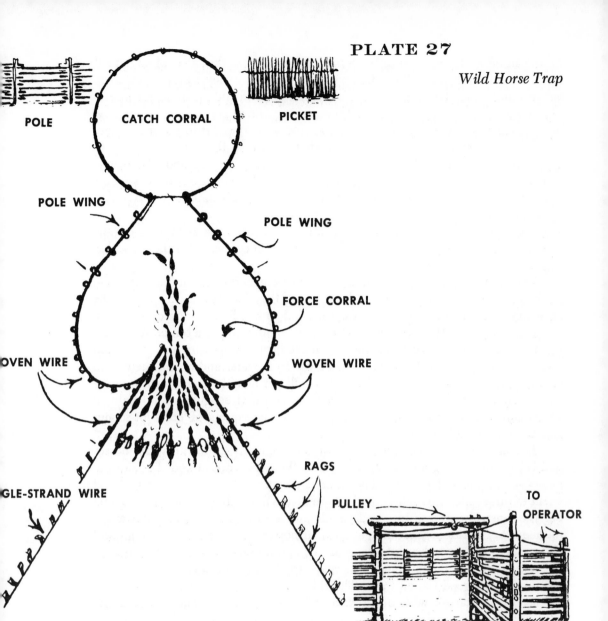

POLE CATCH CORRAL PICKET

POLE WING

POLE WING

FORCE CORRAL

OVEN WIRE WOVEN WIRE

RAGS

GLE-STRAND WIRE PULLEY TO OPERATOR

TRAPPING GATE

placing and arranging the trap as would be used in making a set for a coyote. A wise old mustang can read sign, at times, as well as a wolf, and if that fact is not taken into account, the consequences may turn out to be costly.

Where horses are run in rough country, it is best to place booger wires across the trails and draws forking off the main trail that leads to the trap. This will keep the horses from turning off the trail in an attempt to make a getaway.

Traps can be well concealed in timbered territory and in that kind of country it is not necessary to place them in very deep canyons. They can be located in between hills near the head of a creek or draw—often good locations for a trap. The less a human circulates around the scenery where the mustangs run, the better. Precaution must be taken when constructing a trap not to put it too close to where the horses range; any activity taking place near them will cause 'em to get suspicious and quit the country for a new range. The trap should be some distance from the main trail leading to the water hole, which is a trail the mustangs travel every day. If the trap is set up too close to this trail, they will probably notice what is going on before the trap is ready to use, which will never do. The traps have to be some three or four miles away from the locality where the horses circulate if they are to be kept from coming in contact with the work that is going on.

The saddle horses used by the mustangers are generally grain fed to put 'em in condition to stand up under the hard riding they have to do in running the mustangs. From five to seven riders are needed to handle a bunch of real mustangs. It often takes three or four days of hard running to get a bunch of broomies simmered down to where a rider can make connections with 'em. The main idea in mustanging is to keep the horses away from water and to run them until they are pretty well played out. Then they will not be able to do much running when they are headed for the trap. Water holes are often guarded at night to keep the horses from drinking. This helps to take the sap out of 'em a lot sooner and saves time and labor.

In starting a run, the riders are stationed around the territory the horses will be run in—that is, around both the area the horses are in and the land between the trap and the horses. The riders are stationed at intervals of two and a half to three miles, on high ground where they will be able to see what is going on. The mustangs are run in a wide circle and are relayed from one mustanger to the next. The riders generally get off their horses and lie down on the ground if there are no trees or brush to conceal them on horseback. The idea is to keep out of sight so that the mustangs will come up close to the rider and give him a chance to get a good run on them. The rider bends 'em back in the direction of the nearest mustanger who, in his turn, will give 'em a run. The mustangs are kept on the jump all day and generally cover from seventy-five to a hundred miles in that time. At the end of the day the mustangers go to camp. They are out early the next morning, mounted on fresh horses, to start the mustangs to running again. The mustangers generally take up new positions each day to keep the mustangs from knowing where the riders are.

When the horses are ready to be corralled, two riders are located at the trap to help lane the mustangs into the mouth of the force corral. The riders are stationed about seventy-five yards back from the ends of the force-corral wings and are cached so the mustangs won't see anything suspicious until the riders dash out alongside them. In corralling mustangs, good timing must be used so the horses will not have a chance to plan a getaway. As the mustangs are run into the booger wings, the riders charge 'em and walk on their hocks until the critters are in the trap. Ropes and hats are put into action and this, combined with a few panther squalls (cowboy yells), helps divert the mustangs' attention from the trap they are headed for. No room or time is given the horses to stop or turn around and no opening is left for them to break through if everybody is at the right place at the right time.

Once the horses are corralled in the catch corral, they are left there for a day or so to get them used to a fence. This makes it easier to hold them in a horse trap (pasture) later on—which is what they will be put in when they are taken to the ranch. Before taking the horses out of the corral, they are forefooted (roped by the forefeet) and thrown in order to sideline them, as shown in the illustrations for the Section entitled "Bronc Busting." The side line is put on to prevent the horse from traveling too fast, so he can be kept in the herd. He cannot step ahead with the foot tied, but he can draw it up into the position shown in Figure J on Plate 33. When all the horses are sidelined, they are turned out into the force corral to circulate around for a while. Some gentle horses are generally thrown in with 'em to help lead the bunch to camp. After the horses are drove into the corral at the ranch, the side lines are often left on them for a few days till they become used to the fence and are a bit more docile. Then they are caught and the side lines are taken off. When the mustangs are turned loose, they are not allowed to drink all they want the first time they make connections with water. A little at a time is best, as they are apt to overdo the thing if left to themselves. Safety first is a good maxim to be guided by.

The gate-closing arrangement shown under the wild horse trap on Plate 27 is a trapping gate designed to close the ordinary corral gate when stock has entered the corral. Stock that is hard to corral will watch its chance when no human is around to slip or sneak in for a drink or for salt, but if someone attempts to close the gate while the critters are in the corral, they usually high-tail it before the gate can be shut. The drawing shows how one end of a rope is attached to the top of a two-by-four piece of lumber that is nailed or wired to the end of the gate. The two-by-four holds the rope up high enough for stock to pass under it when entering the corral. Two pulleys are used, as indicated by the arrows in the diagram. One pulley is wired to the gatepost and the other is attached to the crossbeam above the entrance. The rope is run through the pulleys and out to one side. The operator who pulls the rope to close the gate is supposed to be concealed some distance away where he can still watch the stock that enters the corral. When the stock he wants is in the corral, he pulls the rope and closes the gate. Before the horses know what is happening, they are trapped. A long piece of wire can be used to lengthen the rope if it is not long enough to reach out to where the operator intends to conceal himself. A self-locking latch on the gate will hold it closed; if there is no such catch on the gate, it will be necessary for the operator to keep the rope tied taut until he can get to the gate and fasten it.

15

BRONC BUSTING

The terms bronc busting, bronc snapping, bronc twisting, peeling broncs, bronc stomping, and bronc breaking all mean the same thing, but the actual work in this field is done in many different ways. The term "bronc" is from the Spanish *bronco,* meaning "wild," but the word was used by the Americans to designate a wild horse and is still used with that meaning.

Bronc buster, bronc peeler, bronc snapper, bronc stomper, bronc twister, and bronc breaker are all terms used to designate a man who makes a business of breaking range horses to the saddle. There are many different methods used in breaking horses for saddle-horse purposes. The majority of riders who break broncs do so in a rough-and-tumble way, depending on main-strength, no matter how clumsily applied, to get results, whereas the job really requires much time and patience as well as kindness to the animal.

These heavy-handed methods are reminiscent of the early days when the main object was to stick onto a horse and let time and hard riding do the rest. The general technique was to rope the horse around the neck, and, while one or two men eared the horse down (held him by the ears), the rider saddled the animal and stepped above him. Then, when he was ready, the rider told 'em to turn 'im loose, whereupon the battle between horse and rider took place, with another rider on a properly broken horse standing by to haze the bronc out of bad places. When the bronc was exhausted, he was turned loose and another bronc was handled in the same way. Such were the methods usually practised in the old days and still practised to a certain extent by some bronc fighters.

The majority of broncs broke are intended for range or cow work. Broncs broke by incompetent riders seldom become good cow horses unless they happen to be turned over to a cowhand who knows how to handle a fresh-broke horse. Some bronc breakers seem to think that all that is necessary is to set the cold sweat on a bronc even though it may wreck the animal's constitution. "Bronc fighter" is a term that should be used only to designate those bronc riders who do a horse more harm than good. No doubt but what the term was originally coined for this type of rider; it certainly fits 'em and it will be used herein only in this sense.

The methods for handlin' broncs described in the following pages are based on the principle that the horse deserves humane treatment and that there should be due regard for the safety of the rider. The old rough methods of breaking a horse to the saddle are not discussed and only the most practical and up-to-date methods are described. These methods have stood the test of time and have been developed through many years of bronc-busting experience. They require that every effort be made to prevent possible injury to the horse and to keep him in good condition. If the horse is properly handled, he will be in as good condition (flesh) as when he was first caught. The only marks which should be visible and which will indicate that the horse has been broke are the changed appearance of his tail; this will have been pulled, or trimmed, to shorten it. The bronc fighter's handiwork, on the other hand, will be quite evident because of the numerous tracks (skinned places) on the bronc's anatomy. "Bear sign" and "panther tracks" linked with the scary expression and wild actions of a green-broke horse are clearly indicative of his past contact with a bronc fighter.

What is a "broke" horse? This is a question often discussed by riders. Since the term applies to the breaking of a green bronc for saddle-horse purposes, from the bronc breaker's standpoint as well as the owner's it means a bronc that has been taught to stand while being handled; that is, to stand still while being saddled and while a rider mounts and dismounts. Also, the horse should turn freely from one side to the other when being reined. He also should be well halter-broke (taught to lead) and not afraid of a rope or a slicker being used on or around him. And, last but not least, a horse that has been properly broke can be controlled and will not pitch or buck when being rode.

Time, patience, kindness, and system are the main factors for breaking horses successfully for whatever purpose. It must be borne in mind that the average horse is a highly intelligent animal, and it is necessary that the person attempting to teach the horse how to do things be endowed with at least as much (if not *more*) sense as the horse is supposed to have. If the methods described below are intelligently applied, there is no doubt but what success will eventually crown the rider's efforts.

Safety first is a maxim the rider should always keep in mind. The positions of the bronc buster, shown in the illustrations (Plates 30 through 34), are to be carefully noted; they are intended to show the need for the rider being in the right place at the right time. The horse will then react favorably and much work and time will be saved in breaking him.

Broncs are generally handled in a round corral built of poles or posts set close together; such corrals are referred to as pole corrals and picket corrals, respectively. The pole corral is used mostly in the northwest and the picket corral generally in the southwest. The type of corral used is determined to a great extent by the character of the timber grown in the territory. The round corral is designed expressly for catching and handling horses. It places a roper within easy throwing distance of the horse and prevents the bronc from getting a straightaway run from the roper when being forefooted. Also, a horse can be kept moving easier in a round corral, which makes it more convenient for the roper to make a catch. Moreover, when a bronc is being ridden in the corral the first few times with a saddle, the round shape makes it easier for the rider to turn the bronc and keep him going. There are a number of other reasons for the round corral, but space will not permit enumerating them all here.

The first thing on the program when breaking a bronc is to catch him. There are two methods generally used in roping a bronc. One consists in catching the horse by the neck and choking him down; the other is to rope the horse by the forefeet (forefooting him), and then to throw him down, which is generally referred to as busting (see Plate 40). The forefooting-and-busting method is regarded by a majority of bronc breakers as more productive of good results than roping a bronc by the neck and choking him down. It is maintained that a bronc roped by the head (neck) is more likely to be injured than when he is forefooted.

A brief analysis is perhaps necessary to explain just why the method of roping around the neck is less desirable than forefooting. In the first place, a bronc roped around the neck and snubbed to a post is generally choked down before he is gotten under control. This often results in pulling the horse's head down. In nine cases out of ten a horse is ruined for saddle-horse purposes once his head has been pulled down. And when a horse falls when he is roped around the neck, he is more apt to injure himself than if he is forefooted and busted. A bronc will be more inclined to fight back when he is roped around the neck because he is convinced his life is at stake; this panic is not conducive to good results. Also, it takes more time to handle (saddle and mount) a bronc the first few times when he has been roped by the neck rather than forefooted. When a bronc is forefooted, he can be thrown and hog-tied (feet tied together) all within the space of a few minutes; he is then in a position where he can easily be hackamored (haltered) and have his hind foot tied up if necessary. Tying a bronc down (see Plates 28 and 29) helps to convince him that a man can and will handle him without much trouble and that the man is not trying to kill him, which is the impression he gets when he is roped around the neck and choked down. The bronc forefooted and tied down is also in a subdued frame of mind, and this is essential for good results in handlin'.

It is not always necessary to throw (bust) a bronc after he has been forefooted in order to handle him. A horse can be forefooted and left standing and then his forelegs are tied together. This is the easiest method of handling a bronc when a bronc buster is working alone; he can handle a bronc this way without too much trouble even though he does not bust the horse. The idea is to hold the horse's feet once he has been forefooted. After the horse has been stopped, the roper gradually works up close and manages to throw the end of the catch rope around the bronc's forelegs, forming a half-hitch (clove hitch) above the loop which is then drawn up tight, thus tying the feet together. A soft rope (hemp or cotton) can then be used to tie the forelegs together more securely, as shown in Figure 17 on Plates 30.

Two methods used in forefooting a horse are shown and described in the Section entitled "Ropes and Roping"; the slip catch is shown on Plate 40 and the sneak catch on Plate 44. In the majority of cases a bronc buster does have someone to help him when he catches a bronc the first time, because if the horse does have to be thrown, it is difficult for one man to do this by himself. When a horse is busted, it is necessary for the roper to get up close to the horse to keep the bronc's feet pulled out from under him when he tries to get up. The horse's forefeet should be pulled straight out from his body so that he will not be able to get them in and under when he struggles to get back on his feet. When the horse is down, the roper's helper gets on the bronc's head and pulls the nose up and back, as shown in Figures 1, 15 and 16 of Plates 28 and 29. This is done to prevent the horse from getting up while the roper ties his feet together. Figure 1 on Plate 28, shows how the roper holds the horse's feet pulled out straight from the body with a short hold on the rope.

The drawings on Plates 28 and 29 show all the various steps in tying a horse down, giving buzzard's-eye views of a horse lying on the ground; this was necessary to show correctly how the rope is handled to make the ties. Being all set to make the tie (Figure 1), the roper half-hitches the forelegs (Figure 2) in order to hold the legs securely together. When the half-hitch has been drawn tight enough, the rope is doubled to form a loop, as shown, and then passed between the forelegs and slipped over the lower hind foot (Figure 3). It is then drawn up close to the forefeet and held there while the rope is again doubled to form another loop which is passed down, under and around the hind leg (Figure 4 at B) and then passed between the forelegs and drawn up tight. The loop end and the free end of the rope (Figure 4 at A) are tied together with a square knot as shown by the arrows in Figure 5. If the tie is made right, the horse will be unable to kick loose. The bottom hind foot is tied in this way so that the top hind foot can be tied up separately.

Figures 6, 7, and 8 on Plate 28 show how to tie up a hind foot so that the rope will not burn the foot or ankle. This is a tie from which a horse cannot kick loose and it is also easy to remove later. A soft hemp or cotton rope, about thirty feet long and about three-quarters of an inch in diameter, is generally used for a foot rope. One end of the rope is tied around the horse's neck to make a collar;

PLATE 28 *Tying Horse Down*

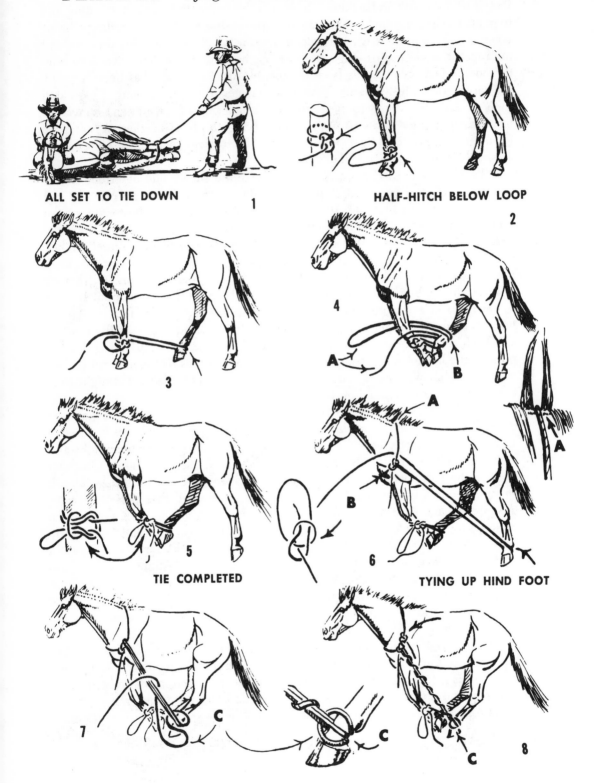

ALL SET TO TIE DOWN 1

HALF-HITCH BELOW LOOP 2

3

4

A
B

TIE COMPLETED 5

A

A

B

6

TYING UP HIND FOOT

7 C

C

C

8

PLATE 29 *Tying Horse Down (Cont.)*

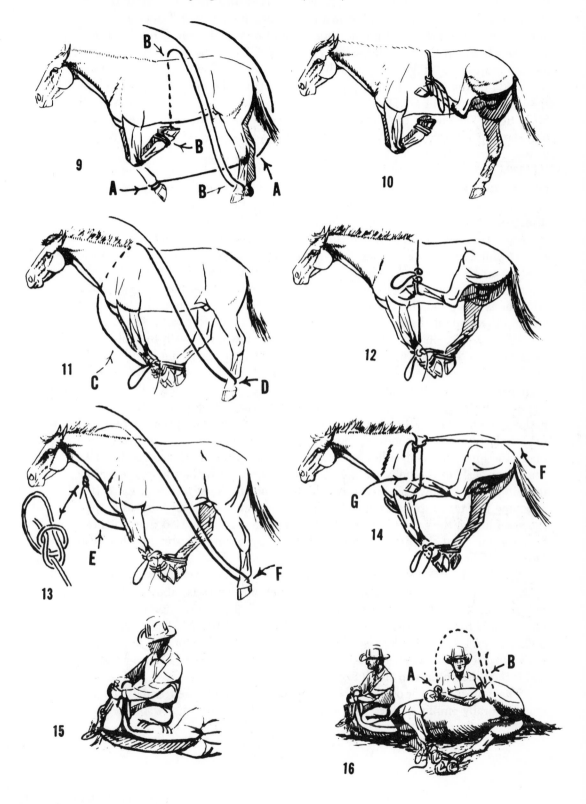

this is tied with a neck-rope knot (bowline), as shown in Figure 6 at B. The collar should be large to set well down on the shoulder so it will not cut off the horse's wind. The other end of the rope is run down and around the hind foot and then back up through the collar (Figure 6). The rope is again run down and around the leg (Figure 7), and then a loop is formed which is run down on the inside of the main line (the line extending from the collar to the foot) as shown in Figure 7 at C. The loop is then slipped over the foot and drawn up fairly tight. The end of the rope is then wrapped around the main line (Figure 8). The end of the rope is half-hitched around the collar, as indicated by the arrow.

When the foot rope is tied, the collar is fastened to the top of the horse's neck by two wisps (tufts) of mane, indicated by the two A's in Figure 6. The two bunches of mane are crossed and wrapped around the collar rope in opposite directions. The mane thus wrapped around the rope on top of the neck prevents the collar from slipping down over the horse's head when he lowers it.

The hind foot should be tied so that it can rest on the ground when the horse is let up on his feet (see Figure 18 on Plate 30). If the foot does not rest on the ground as indicated in this drawing, it will be difficult for the horse to stand still while he is being handled. When removing the foot rope, unwrap the main line and flip the loop off the hind foot without bending down to take it off.

While we are on the subject of tying a horse down, it is well to explain the three different methods used in tying a horse down for castrating, as illustrated on Plate 29. These methods are as follows: The three-feet, single-rope method is shown in the two top Figures. The horse is forefooted and tied with one and the same rope. The forelegs are half-hitched below the loop to hold them together, as was done in tying a horse down (see above description of forefooting). In Figure 9, the A's indicate how the rope is carried from the forefeet, down under the hind legs, and pulled in under the horse's body so the forefeet can be drawn up close to the belly (Figure 9 at B). The rope is then looped over the top hind foot as shown, and is drawn high up on the horse's side (Figure 10). The rope is then wrapped around the foot a few times and half-hitched around the main line of the rope (Figure 10). When a horse is being tied down, it must be borne in mind that he is being held down by a helper sitting on his head (Figures 15 and 16).

The four-feet, single-rope method is the second one used in tying down a horse for castration. It is similar to the first method described above. The three feet are tied as shown in Figure 5 of Plate 28. The end of the rope is carried in under the horse's neck as shown in Figure 11 at C on Plate 29. The rope is then pulled in under the shoulder so that it will be in position for the finished tie shown in Figure 12. The rope is looped around the hind foot (Figure 11 at D) and is then drawn up and tied (Figure 12).

The four-feet, two-ropes method is the third method used and is the one most generally employed for tying a horse down for castrating. A soft hemp or cotton rope about twenty feet long and five-eighths to three-quarters of an inch in diameter is the size of rope commonly considered best for tying up a hind foot. One end of the foot rope is passed around the lower foreleg and tied so as to form a large loop, just as was done in tying the collar around the horse's neck (Figure 6 on Plate 28). Figure 13 at E on Plate 29 shows how the loop is formed around the leg and tied with a neck-rope knot (bowline), as indicated by the double arrow. The loop is drawn in under the horse's neck and then the rope is run down and looped over the top hind foot (Figure 13 at F). The end of the rope is then run through the top of the loop which should be long enough to reach up over the horse's back (Figure 14). The hind foot (Figure 14 at G) is pulled up into place and the rope is wrapped around the foot and tied around the main line in the same manner as in the first two methods described above. This method of tying a hind foot up is carried out on the same principle as that shown in Figure 6; the only difference is that the loop is tied around the horse's foreleg instead of around the neck. The foot can be tied in exactly the same way as in Figure 8 after it is drawn up in place, but it is not necessary to wrap the rope around the main line.

The swing or string method of holding a hind foot is shown in Figure 16 on Plate 29. This is the surest way to hold a horse in correct position to give the operator a chance to work freely and unhampered by the horse's struggles. The end of the foot rope, used as shown in Figure 14, is formed into a large loop (see the dotted line). When the foot is tied up, the man passes the rope around behind him and then passes the end of the rope around the horse's hind leg. Then, holding the sides of the loop thus formed (Figure 16 at A and B), he sets down on the ground with the loop around him, and with his feet braced against the horse's back, he holds the hind leg up out of the way of the operator. A horse handled in this manner is powerless.

How to hold a horse's head is shown in Figures 15 and 16 on Plate 29. When a horse is thrown, a man gets on the horse's head and pulls the nose up and the head back; he will be well out of the way of the horse's hind feet when the horse kicks to free himself. Then the roper can tie the horse's feet without any trouble. The head should not be turned back too far, as this may twist the horse's neck too much and cause him to struggle to relieve the pressure.

Figures 17 and 18 on Plate 30 show two different methods of placing a green bronc under control in order to handle him for his first saddling. The hackamore (a type of halter; see the Section entitled "Hackamores") and the foot ropes were put on the horse while he was tied down. The arrow in Figure 17 shows how the horse's forelegs are tied. With the hackalea (a type of hackamore) rope and the foot rope held in the hands of the man, the horse can't get away or harm the twister. The animal soon learns that it is best to stand and wait for what is going to happen. The forefeet should be drawn close together so the horse cannot step. The feet are shown wide apart in the insert (under the horse) in Figure 17; this was necessary to illustrate how the rope was half-hitched

PLATE 30 *Bronc Busting*

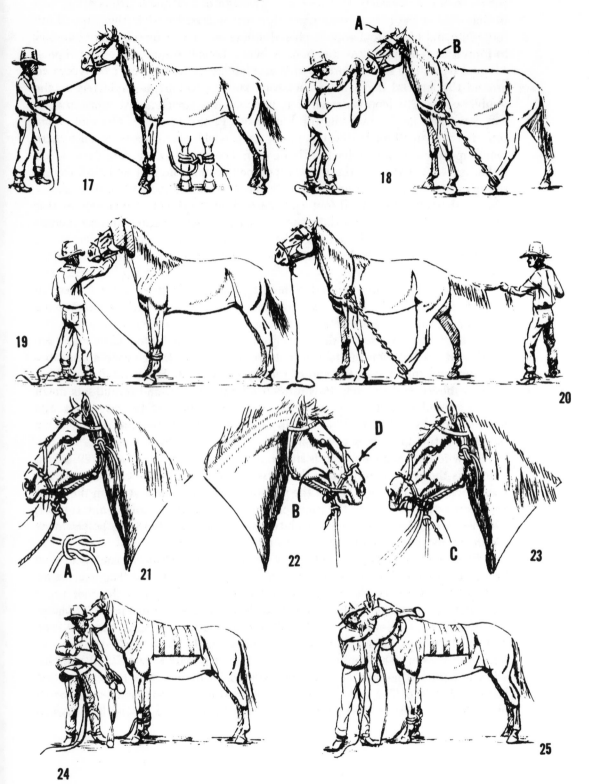

between the horse's legs. In principle the half-hitch is much the same as hobbling, but the man keeps control of the feet by holding on to the rope. A soft rope (hemp or cotton) about twelve feet long and about five-eighths of an inch in diameter is used for this purpose. A honda is built in one end of the rope so that a loop can be formed in it similar to a catch-rope loop. This method of tying the horse's forefeet is one used by the author in preference to tying up a hind foot. By pulling the horse's head from one side to the other a few times to make him conscious of the foot rope, he is soon convinced that he is really tied. The thought that he is apt to be busted if he moves, which he does not want to have happen *again*, will cause him to stand while the twister works him over.

The reason for *not* tying the hind foot is to eliminate the possibility of burning or skinning up the foot with the rope. (When the foot rope is put on when the animal is down, however, there is no trouble about burning.) Another reason for not tying the hind foot is that the horse can stand in a natural position with only the forefeet tied. Moreover, the rope is placed more easily on the forefeet than on the hind feet. It is not necessary to go the trouble of tying the hind foot in the majority of cases where a green bronc is being handled. (Still another method is to hobble front and back legs and—using a blind over the animal's eyes while at work—tying the lead rope to the back hobble and turning the horse loose to battle it out.)

Figure 18 on Plate 30 shows how the hind foot is tied so it will be well advanced but at the same time be in a position to rest on the ground. Tying up a hind foot is the old reliable method of putting a bronc or a mean horse under control. In exceptional cases the author has used this method of handlin' a mean horse; it does no harm in the beginning, as it helps a horse to get used to a rope around his feet and also softens him up considerably. Whether or not to tie up a hind foot depends on the temperament of the horse and on the time that can be taken in handling him.

Figure 18 at A shows the old-style blind which was often used by bronc fighters in the early days. The leather blind was attached to the hackamore in such a way that it could be slipped down over the horse's eyes while he was being saddled and was often left over the eyes while the rider mounted and then was raised by the rider afterwards. The blind is seldom used now and has gone the way of the bucking roll. B in Figure 18 indicates where the neck rope is held in place by the mane that is wrapped around it as was described above (see Figure 6 at A on Plate 28).

Sacking is a technique generally adopted to get a horse used to things touching him and is necessary in gentling him. It is really the first lesson a bronc learns when he is being broke. A grain sack is usually used for the purpose or, if one is not handy, a piece of saddle blanket or other similar material will answer the purpose. This method is often referred to as "slicker breaking," but it is not really slicker breaking though it is a very similar procedure. The rider is shown starting the process of sacking the bronc in Figure 18 on Plate 30. The sack is held up in front of the bronc to let him smell it so he will know that it is not something that will harm him. The sack is then lightly rubbed over the horse's head in a leisurely manner. Pains should be taken to rub it over his eyes in particular, because this will tend to make the horse relax—a condition the rider always strives to attain. Talking to the horse in a friendly manner while rubbing the sack or the hand over a horse's eyes is important in breaking the tension the horse is naturally under when he makes his first contact with a human being. Time and slow deliberate motions applied with patience and the determination to treat the horse right are vitally important in making friends with a bronc. If the reader will keep these essentials in mind when working with a horse, he will be well on the trail to success. The twister must first convince the horse that this man is a decent sort of animal and one that the horse will do well to throw in with. It is necessary to gain the horse's confidence before any headway can be made in obtaining satisfactory results. These things are stressed in order to impress their importance upon the rider so that he will be sure not to overlook them in his work. Once the rider has gained the horse's confidence, the bronc will respond readily to attempts to teach him how to do the things wanted of him.

Figure 19 on Plate 30 shows how the sack has been swung in under the bronc's neck and then up and over his ears. This was done so easily that the horse never batted an eye. Why? Because the horse knows that there is nothing to be scared of in the man's actions or in the sack he is playing with. The sack is left on for a few seconds at a time and then is slowly drawn away. Never whip the sack around the horse where it will fall in such a way as to cause him to flinch, for this will make him think that he is about to be hurt and that would never do. When the horse has been well sacked around the head and neck, the sack is gradually swung so it will wrap around the horse's forelegs and underneath his body and over his back and hips and hind legs. Every part of the horse's anatomy is touched reassuringly. Both sides of the horse are worked over in the same way so that he will get used to being handled on both sides. One bad mistake a great many bronc busters seem to make is that they do not take the pains to work on both sides of a bronc, which naturally results in a one-sided horse. If a horse is not worked on both sides, then later, when it becomes necessary for a hand to do some work on the off side,* trouble begins and it is usually a case of man and horse having a regular battle. When it is necessary for the man to work alongside of the horse in sacking, he should hold the horse by the feador, or theodore, rope (a safety device, or throatlatch, used on the hackamore; see Section on hackamores) under the horse's jaw, as indicated by the position assumed by the rider in Figure 26 on Plate 31. If the horse should jump or whirl, the man will be pulled forward and out of the way of the hind feet if the horse should attempt to kick at him. Always have a good hold on the horse

---

* As was mentioned before in the Section entitled "Packs and Packing," the off side of a horse is his right side. The near, or left, side is the side from which he is mounted and from which he is usually handled.

under all circumstances, then the chances of getting into a jack pot will be greatly diminished. Never be in a hurry when working with a bronc, especially during the first five saddles (the first five times a green bronc is ridden); there is no need to be in a hurry, time must always be taken in such work, and if you are in a hurry to go someplace, ride a gentle horse.

Figure 20 on Plate 30 illustrates what can be done with a horse when he has a hind foot tied up. The rider is shown pulling, or trimming, the horse's tail and the horse apparently is convinced that this is perfectly all right, though he may not really like it. The position may seem rather dangerous, and it would be if the hind foot were not tied up. It is quite safe for the rider to get on the horse bareback and "waller" all over the animal and then slide off over the horse's tail if he chooses to do so. The horse can move, but his efforts are checked to a certain extent and this makes it quite useless for him to object to being handled. As has already been pointed out, the method of tying up a horse's hind foot is a satisfactory procedure in handling a mean horse, for the more he tries to battle, the more he is working against himself, as he soon finds out. Some horses will not stand for kind treatment; like some humans, they are born that way and in that case it is necessary to use a convincer to bring them to their senses. This does not mean that the rider should abuse the horse in any way, but it is often necessary to make a horse do a thing against his will. After he has done it, he should be praised in such a manner as to make him think (yes, a horse does *think*) that it had to be done.

Trimming a horse's tail is often done when the bronc is being tied down (if the hind foot is not to be tied up) to avoid having to do the job after the horse has gotten back on his feet. A knife is often used to trim out the surplus hair; this is easier on the animal than pulling the hair out by quick jerks. The tail should be trimmed so that the end will reach to the bottom of the hocks. A horse looks better with a neat, trimmed tail which, moreover, is not likely to get tangled up in a rider's spurs. Also, it is easy to tell a broke horse from one that has not been handled by the shorter tail. Trimming off the short mane on the top of the horse's withers which comes under the saddle blanket also marks the handled bronc. Then it is not necessary for a rider to get up close to a bunch of range horses in order to tell whether or not there are any broke horses in the bunch; he can easily pick out the broke horses by their shorter tails and trimmed manes.

While a bronc is being broke, he is ridden with a hackamore or with a hackalea, a special type of hackamore. The hackalea and how it is used is shown in Figures 21, 22 and 23 on Plate 30. The construction of the hackalea is explained on pp. 144-146. A mouth rope or biting rope is used in conjunction with the general outfit; a piece of sash cord is used for the purpose. The rope is about sixteen inches long and is run over the part of the noseband that is under the horse's jaw, around through the horse's mouth, and is then tied on the side of the mouth, as indicated by the arrow in Figure 21. The rope is tied in a square knot (Figure 21 at A). The noseband is pulled down low and close to the horse's chin and is held in place by the mouth rope, so that when the reins are pulled on, the mouth rope will be pulled on too. This will give the rider more purchase on the horse's head. The rider is cautioned against tying the mouth rope so tight that the circulation will be cut off in the horse's lips. Figure 22 shows how the mouth rope looks on the off side of the horse's head, and the arrow at B indicates where the rope comes into contact with the under side of the horse's jaw. Figure 23 shows how the reins are attached to the noseband under the horse's jaw. They are looped around the noseband in the same manner that the reins are attached to a bridle bit, only they are passed around both strands of the noseband so they will have a firm pull on the jaw. The mouth rope serves as a bit in the horse's mouth and is easy on the mouth so that there is no danger of tearing it up should the horse fight his head. Also there is not the danger of bruising the back of the mouth with a mouth rope; it does not cause a hard mouth such as is produced by a snaffle bit, so the horse's mouth is kept light, which is much to be desired.

Figure P on Plate 34 illustrates how the rider handles the mouth rope to place it in the horse's mouth without any trouble. The two ends of the mouth rope are held between the thumb and first two fingers of the right hand; the little finger is hooked over the nose band and the rope is over the thumb of the left hand. Figure Q on the same Plate shows how the forefinger of the left hand is inserted in the horse's mouth, which makes the horse open same. The thumb helps to force the rope into the mouth. By using this technique, the rope can be put in a horse's mouth without any trouble whatsoever; a little practice will soon show how to handle it.

With the arrangement described above, when the reins are pulled on, the bronc's mouth and nose are both pulled. When the mouth rope makes contact with the under side of the jaw (Figure 22 at B on Plate 30) and the nose piece (sometimes a metal one) comes into contact with the bridge of the nose (Figure 22 at D), these points of contact will become very tender after the bronc has been pulled around during the first two saddles. And if the horse fights hard or tries to resist the pull on the reins during these first saddles, these places will become even more sensitive than is usual in handling a bronc. Then when the horse is being rode during the third saddle, he should give freely to the pull on the reins because of the pressure brought to bear—which is as it should be. The noseband should be set so it will be on the horse's nose in the position shown in Figures 21, 22, and 23; the metal piece should rest at the end of the bony part of the nose. The noseband should never be placed so low, however, that it will cut off the circulation of air through the horse's nostrils. If this were to happen, the horse would fight his head, and that doesn't pay.

When the hackalea, or the hackamore, is first put on a bronc, the mouth rope in the horse's mouth pressing against the horse's jaw should cause the spot where it makes contact to become softened as soon as possible. The more shock the mouth rope absorbs the better, and during the time the bronc is first being handled the pressure brought to bear upon the mouth rope and the bridge of the nose is such that it will have a decided effect upon the parts contacted and will help materially in making the bronc soften up and give to the pull upon the reins. The shock is usually more violent during the first two saddles than at any other time and should be taken advantage of.

It is not necessary to use any other sort of bit in the bronc's mouth than the rope while breaking him. When he is turned over to the owner as a broke horse, he will not cause any trouble when a bridle is put on him. The rest of his schooling depends on the man who takes over from there.

Figure 24 on Plate 30 shows the first step in saddling. When the horse has been well sacked over and has been convinced that he is not going to be harmed, the sack is thrown over his neck, as shown in the drawing. The saddle is then picked up in the manner indicated. The left hand holds the stirrup leather and the cinch so that they can be placed over the horse's neck without any trouble. Note the position of the rider: He is standing by the bronc's head in order to keep the animal from jumping ahead when the saddle is placed on him. In this position the rider is also out of the way of the horse's hind feet. The hackamore rope (*mecate*, often Americanized into "McCarthy") is placed over the left shoulder where it will be handy if wanted; it is not necessary to hold it in the hand while saddling a horse. If it is placed in this way over the left shoulder, the left hand is then free to handle the saddle.

Figure 25 shows the stirrup leathers and cinch being thrown over the horse's neck, or withers, and the saddle about to be set back onto the horse's back without causing him to move or flinch from the impact of the outfit. The old method of saddling a horse was to throw the saddle on the bronc without ever trying to check its fall or impact in any way; this naturally made the horse jump or whirl away from the rider. Handled thus, a horse will take some time to get used to having the saddle placed on him and will become unnecessarily fearful of being hurt.

Figure 26 on Plate 31 shows the rider taking a good hold on the *mecate* and the feador of the hackalea while saddling. He is standing in front of the bronc's shoulder. In starting to cinch up a bronc, the stirrup is placed over the saddlehorn, as shown, and then a loop is formed in the long latigo (the long strap used to fasten on the saddle) by doubling its end back. This looped end may be used to reach in under the horse's body to catch the end of the cinch so that the cinch can be pulled in under the horse and be easily grasped by the rider. When cinching up, take your time and do not jerk the slack out of the latigo, but take it out with a few firm steady pulls. By watching and timing the action of the horse's breathing, the cinch can be tightened whenever the horse's breath is going out and everything can be done without the horse making a move or humping up. The cinch should not be pulled too snug at first, but tightened up only when the rider is ready to mount the bronc. The stirrup is let down just as

PLATE 31   *Bronc Busting (Cont.)*

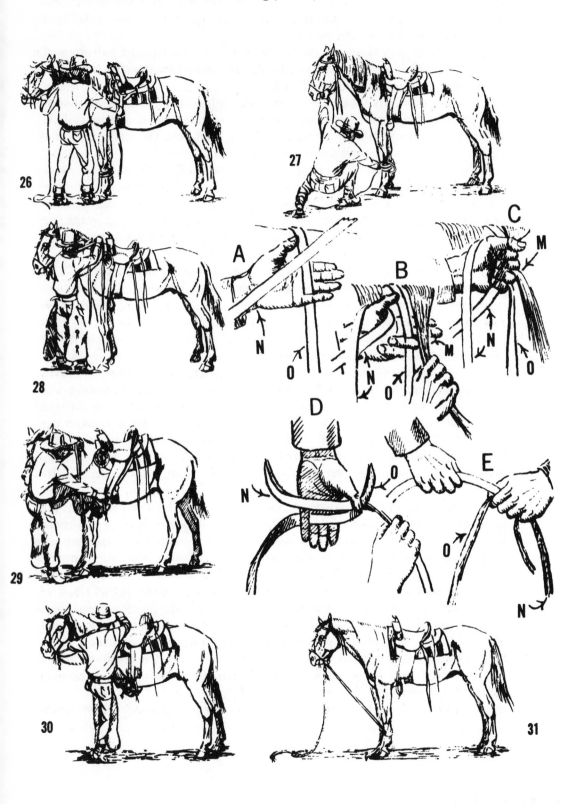

easily as the rest of the saddling was done, and the horse is in no way excited about the performance that has been going on because he has been convinced that nothing will be done to harm him.

Figure 27 on Plate 31 shows the bronc ready to be rode except for taking off the foot rope. The horse should be left to stand for a few minutes, while the rider is away from him preparing to make the ride, putting on chaps, etc. Meanwhile the bronc has a chance to investigate the rigging and to think things over. It is a good idea to pull the bronc around to one side to make him move and get the feel of the saddle while his feet are still tied. The rider should pull on the saddlehorn and put his weight in the stirrup to see if the bronc is going to stand when he is mounted. All this work should cause the bronc to stand properly when he is mounted after his feet are untied.

Untying the foot rope is done easily if the rider will assume the position shown in Figure 27. The hold on the hackalea will pull the rider up on his feet if the bronc should try to move and the rider will have a chance to get out of the way if necessary.

Figure 28 on Plate 31 shows the proper rein hold while mounting. This hold is an essential one; the right kind of control is important both to the rider and to the horse. A correct grip on the hackamore reins will insure a firm hold which cannot easily be shaken loose. The correct rein hold is shown in the detail drawings of the hands to the right of Figure 28. The rein indicated by N in the first of these diagrams (A) is the one next to the rider, called the near rein, and is drawn across the hand as shown. O is the off rein brought over the horse's neck and down across the hand. It is held between the third and little fingers of the left hand. In B (the second diagram) is shown how the rein, N, is brought around the thumb and how the two lower fingers are partly closed with the mane placed over the two first fingers. C (the third diagram) shows how the hand is closed on the reins and mane. It would be hard to break loose from this hold. The off rein, O in diagram C, is left slack and the near rein, N, is tightened in order to pull the horse's head close to the rider in the position shown in Figure 29. Pulling the bronc's head towards the rider will keep the animal from turning away in an effort to break loose from the rider starting to mount. If the bronc should decide to move, he should be made to turn toward the rider and to stand still by a downward swing of the elbow which takes more slack out the rein. This will make it easier for the rider to mount.

In Figure 29 the rider is in front of the bronc's shoulder with the ball of his foot in the stirrup. Never place the foot completely in the stirrup when mounting or dismounting because this can be dangerous. A bronc might whirl or jump or go backward, break the rider's hand holds, cause the foot to get hung up in the stirrup, and drag the rider down; this can lead to a serious accident. When only the ball of the foot is placed in the stirrup, the foot can be easily withdrawn if necessary. Safety first and always.

If a rider's foot does get caught in a stirrup and he is jerked down, it should be remembered that the best way to get the foot out is to make a sudden turn over, face down; this should turn or twist the foot so that the toe will be pointed down. In this position the foot will come out of the stirrup easily.

Figure 30 shows the rider ready to mount; with two good hand holds, it should be easy for a rider to go above (mount) a bronc any time he wants to. When he starts up, he should not hesitate unless he wishes to feel the bronc out by standing in the stirrup, going through the motions of mounting and dismounting in order to learn the bronc to stand. But in the majority of cases it is best to go on up when the rider starts the first time. When the bronc has been rode, the rider can and should get on and off to learn the horse to stand, always taking the rein and mane holds when dismounting as well as mounting. When the rider has mounted a bronc, the two first fingers of the reining hand (left hand) release the mane but retain the original hold on the reins.

Control is essential to the proper handling of any horse. Many riders do not know how to handle the reins after they are on a horse and seem to rely on the plow-rein method to control the animal. The sliding-rein method of handling the reins is a good practical way to control a bronc. The method permits the rider to give and take slack rapidly and at the same time to have two hands on the reins and be in a position to double the horse in an instant. A horse can be held directly on an object that he might booger at and can be forced straight up to (and even over) the object which has scared him. In diagram D of Figure 29 on Plate 31, is shown how the reins pass across the left hand, exactly as they do at A in Figure 28. That is the way the reins should be held in the rider's hand when the mane hold is released after he has mounted. Assume, now, that the rider is mounted and looking towards the horse's head with which the ends of the reins connect. Diagram E at the extreme right of Figure 29 shows the hands and reins when the rider is in this position. N indicates the near rein; O, the off rein. The right hand holds the end of N; the left, or rein, hand, slides up and down the near rein N. The near rein is held in the right hand all the time when pulling a bronc around to get him bridle wise. If the rider will really study and practice handling the sliding-rein method of controlling a bronc, he will be able to learn a horse how to neck rein as he turns. The sliding-rein method also causes the horse's nose to tuck in as the reins are being manipulated, and this is desirable for the head position.

Neck reining is the term used to describe a method of turning the horse by pressure of one of the reins on the horse's neck. The rider holds the reins in one hand, usually the left hand, and guides the horse in the desired direction by moving the rein hand (left hand) in the direction he wants the horse to take. This causes the rein to slacken on the side toward which the horse is to turn, and at the same time the other rein on the other side will press against the neck. This will tend to direct the neck towards the side to which the horse is to turn. In other words, the rein on the side opposite to the direction in which the horse is to turn is the one that presses against the animal's neck. In this technique, the horse is not pulled by the near rein in the direction in which he is to turn. The sliding-rein method described above is effective in bringing pressure to bear on the neck for turning. All cow horses are neck-reined, as this requires only one hand to control them.

Figure 31 on Plate 31 was inserted here because of lack of space elsewhere. The drawing shows how a bronc is anchored, or ground-reined, to learn him to stand when the reins are down. This is the most effective method the author knows of to learn a horse to stay put when he is not tied to a post or some other object. "Tying to the breeze" is a gamble which does not really give the rider assurance that the horse will be there when he is wanted; it is very seldom that a horse can be depended upon to stand for any length of time in one place with nothing to hold him but the reins hanging loosely to the ground. Some horses will stand without walking off to graze, but they are few and far between. A horse soon figures out that he is not tied and generally does walk off to graze or for some other reason. Also, the horse, when he starts walking, is apt to step on the reins, stumble, and hurt his mouth if he has a severe bit, although many horses soon learn to turn their heads and so keep the reins out from under their feet (mules are particularly clever in catching on to this).

In any case, the device of hobbling and tying the reins to the hobble is a very good way to anchor a bronc, or even a gentle horse, no matter where you may be. A pair of rawhide hobbles—or any other kind of hobble except a chain— is placed on the horse's forelegs and then the hackamore reins are tied to the hobble with a half-hitch between the horse's legs, as shown in Figure 31. The horse's head is pulled down to where he would normally hold it while standing and the slack is drawn out of the reins and tied as described. The hackamore rope, or *mecate*, is dropped on the ground in front of the horse so he can see it out there in front of him. If he tries to move or jump the reins will cause his head to be jerked down when his feet hit the ground and he will soon learn that it is best to stand where he was left by the rider. It makes no difference how wild or snaky the horse may be; if he is anchored in this manner he will always be there when wanted unless someone turns him loose.

The California method of learning a horse to stand without tying him up to some object is to tie a knot in the bridle reins and to loop them over the saddle-horn; this will cause a pull on the reins when the horse starts to walk and will keep him from going forward. When plaited rawhide reins are used, it is only necessary to place them over the saddlehorn and shorten them by moving the sliding rein-knot forward so the slack will be taken out of the reins, causing the horse's nose to be pulled back towards its breast sufficiently to prevent him from moving forward. This method was originated by the Mexican *vaquero* and is used by some American riders on the west coast, but it is very tiresome on the horse's neck.

Another way to make a horse stand is to tie the reins to a stirrup on the saddle. The tie should be made so the horse's head will be pulled a little towards the side he is tied to, which will cause him to turn around in the direction in which the head is turned. Another method is to tie the reins to the foreleg of the horse just above the hoof, that is, near his ankle. The head is about in the same position as that shown in Figure 31 and when he tries to walk off he is checked.

Figure 32 on Plate 32 and the succeeding drawings, illustrate the process of learning a horse to turn. It takes a lot of time and patience to learn a bronc to turn, or rein; when the bronc has been rode around the corral a while and is going freely, the rider starts in to learn him. When the sliding-rein method is used, one of the reins is brought against the side of the neck opposite to the direction in which the horse is to turn. This rein is *not* pulled. The horse's head, however, is turned inward by pulling his nose up with the other rein; this learns him to respond to the pressure of the first rein on his neck. This is the basic principle of neck reining. The rider takes a short hold on the near or left rein and gradually pulls the horse's head around to the near, or left side, as illustrated in Figures 32 and 33. When the horse responds to the pressure, or pull, or both, and turns, the reins are slackened and his head is freed. This procedure is repeated on the other side and continues, alternating a pull from one side with a pull from the other. This should be done only at intervals, however, because the horse will get tired if the process is repeated too often and will sull—become stubborn. Never go to extremes in educating a bronc or a young horse unless the horse fails—or simply refuses—to do the thing which he has been taught to do. In that case the horse should be forced to do the thing which he has failed in or rebelled against. He should be made to do the thing over and over until he does it willingly, so that the next time he is called upon to do what is wanted of him, there will be a good chance of his doing it without making a bobble.

In turning the bronc to the left (Figure 33 on Plate 32), the rider will often, in the beginning, have to reach down with the right hand and take a short hold on the near rein in order to get a purchase on the animal's head to pull it around effectively. While he is doing this, the rider should remember to keep his grip steady on the near rein all the time. But after the second day the horse has been rode, he will respond to a pull more readily because the mouth rope has made the under side of his jaw tender and a light pull will cause him to give, or respond. When a bronc fights against the pull of a rein, it is necessary to take more time with him and humor him to a certain extent because he is mad. But keep trying to turn him gradually, a little at a time and not too sharply.

The more a horse fights against a pull of the reins, the tenderer his jaw will be later on, and then he will be more willing to respond to the pull. When a bronc gets mad, he has to be given more time and must not be hurried. He should be rode and worked enough so he will know that he *has* been worked. (The use of the word "worked" in this section applies only to the general handling of the horse.) The next day will no doubt find him in better humor and he can be handled more freely. The rider must study the disposition of the bronc he is handling so he can work him in the right way. Every horse has to be felt out by the rider and different methods applied in each individual case. But the same general system as explained above should be closely followed and the results

PLATE 32 *Bronc Busting (Cont.)*

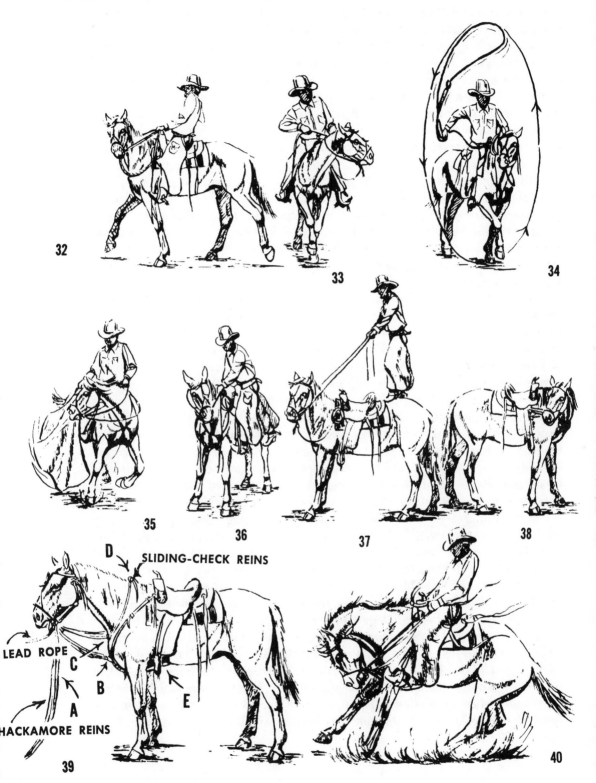

32

33

34

35

36

37

38

D → SLIDING-CHECK REINS

LEAD ROPE
C
B
A
HACKAMORE REINS
E

39

40

will prove favorable in the great majority of cases. Some horses will need more working than others, but it is nearly always a case of more time and more patience—applied with more hoss sense.

Figure 34 on Plate 32 illustrates the process of rope breaking a horse. This is one of the things which a cow horse should know. The first day he is rode, he should be made acquainted with everything pertaining to a cowhand's equipment that he will come into contact with in everyday work, and the catch rope is one of the tools he should know about. Handling a rope is really the second thing on the program of important things with which he must be made acquainted. Slicker breaking is the first thing the bronc should get accustomed to. (This maneuver is shown in Figure 35.) In rope breaking, the rope should be whirled, or rotated, slowly and be allowed to fall on the ground out in front of the bronc. The rope is then handled in every conceivable way that a rope might be placed while being used by a rider mounted on a horse. Be careful, however, not to let the rope hit the horse so as to make him flinch. Let the rope and the loop of the rope touch him all over gently, just as was done in sacking, to learn him that it will not hurt him.

Slicker breaking (Figure 35) is a procedure very similar to sacking (see above). An old slicker raincoat is best because it makes more noise. It should be extended out in front of the bronc by placing it on the toe of the rider's foot and should be dragged around on the ground, in front of him and behind him, and handled as though it was being put on during a wind storm, etc. In the northwest a rider packs a slicker on his saddle most all the time and a horse must become used to the slicker being worn by the rider. Whether the rider uses a slicker or not, the horse should be made familiar with one so that when the rider does have to wear a slicker the horse will not get boogered at it and try to shed his pack. A bronc twister generally hangs an old slicker or piece of blanket on the corral fence where it will be handy for him to reach for while riding the bronc around the corral. The bronc should not be whipped with the slicker or blanket, unless he should "break in two" and try to buck his rider off. In that event it is a good idea, if the rider can manage it, to whip the horse with the slicker while the critter is whoopen' 'er up an' tearin' up the scenery. Such a procedure would convince the bronc that it done him no good to object to being slicker broke. The rider should use a slicker or sack on the horse every time he rides the bronc in the corral to get him used to such things.

Figure 36 on Plate 32 illustrates the process of breaking to stand while mounting. This is an essential part of the bronc-breaking program. The rider gets a good rein and mane hold on the bronc just like the hold taken to mount which was illustrated in Figure 28 on Plate 31. His next positions is shown in Figures 29 and 30. The bronc's head is drawn around to the side (the left or near side) in order to keep him from turning away from the rider and attempting to kick him when he steps off the ground. (In Figure N on Plate 34 you can note how the rider prepares to *dis*mount, a maneuver which is explained on p. 137.)

Figure 36 on Plate 32 shows how a rider then stands in a stirrup to get up, setting down and around on a horse whether he is mounting or dismounting. Once mounted, the rider places his right leg over on the bronc's hips and then moves his leg out in front of the bronc and in every direction he is able to, so that the bronc will get used to the rider performing different stunts on him. It is a good idea for a rider to run his right foot down the hind leg of the bronc and attempt to pick up the hind foot with his own foot. This can generally be done easily. The more a rider circulates around on top of a bronc, the more gentle the animal will become. The bronc will gradually become convinced that a human is not going to do him any harm. Both sides of the bronc should be worked alike as much as possible.

Figure 37 on Plate 32 shows the rider making a stand on top of the bronc. This is a stunt which the author has often performed on a bronc after the horse had been handled about an hour, during the first saddle. This stunt is nothing unusual for some bronc peelers. The more the bronc is handled in such ways, the more dependable he will be in a pinch when he gets into a jack pot with his rider. It can be truthfully said that not one of the broncs which the author made a top stand on ever made a move to object to the stunt.

When a bronc continues to fight against turning to one certain side and is stiff-necked on purpose, it is a good idea to tie his head around to the saddle rigging (Figure 38 on Plate 32) or to his tail. If left tied to the side he refuses to turn to for several hours at a time, he will get to turning towards that side without having to be forced and later on will be willing to turn in the direction wanted when he is handled.

Figure D on Plate 33 illustrates the process of halterbreaking a horse. This is the last event on the program while working a bronc during the first saddle. When the bronc has been pretty well worked over during an hour's handling in the corral, the rider proceeds to learn him to lead. After the horse has been praised for having done well during his first lessons (this is done by rubbing his head and eyes and trying to make friends with him), the rider steps over to one side of the bronc with the *mecate,* or lead rope, in his hand. He gradually pulls the bronc's head over towards him until the horse is thrown off balance and has to take a step over in the direction of the rider. When he has taken the first step, the rider thanks him for it by rubbing his head and then steps over to the opposite side and repeats the operation there. Each time the horse responds, be sure to congratulate him for his good work. If the rider alternates the pull from one side to the other and tries to make the horse gradually come just one step closer each time he is pulled, the rider will find that eventually he can get the bronc to come towards him and follow him wherever he may go. If the rider is always generous with compliments and shows appreciation for the good work a horse does, the bronc will finally walk up to receive his applause and become friendly, which is just what is wanted. After the horse has got to coming up freely, the twister should start leading him around the corral and stopping every

PLATE 33   *Bronc Busting (Cont.)*

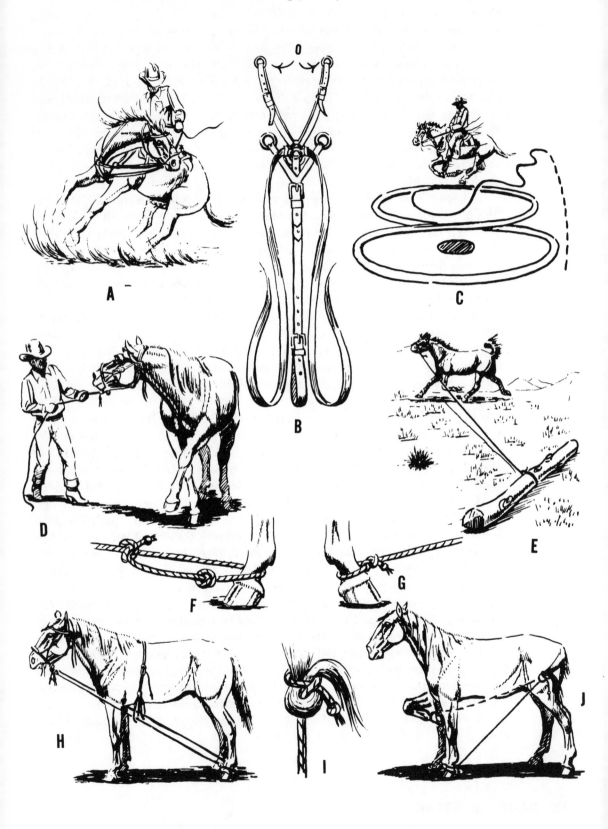

A

O

B

C

D

E

F

G

H

I

J

once in a while to pet him for his work. The bronc will eventually follow the rider without pulling on the rope.

When the bronc has been taught to lead, he is then held by the hackamore (or hackalea) and unsaddled. The rider should be careful to stand in front of the horse's shoulder, as is done in saddling (Figure 26 on Plate 31). The mouth rope should be untied before removing the hackalea, because a mouth rope is apt to hang up and cause trouble if it is left tied. The hackalea should be gently slipped off over the bronc's ears while the rider has one arm around the animal's neck; this is just one of the gestures showing the rider's gratitude and friendly intentions. The bronc must now be turned loose in a manner which will get him in the habit of not trying to jerk away as soon as the rider attempts to remove the hackamore. Never jerk a hackamore or bridle off a horse's head, or hit him with it to make him get out of the way, as some riders do. Take a few minutes time and make the horse feel you are his friend and interested in his welfare. The rider who acts in this way will be amply repaid for the pains he has taken to be right with the horse. Never try to scare a horse, especially a bronc that is being broke, because this will make him lose confidence in the rider; his confidence should never be betrayed. When a bronc has been turned loose, the rider should walk off from him, leaving him free to go away on his own. For further information on halterbreaking of horses, study the section below on the come-along, or force system of halterbreaking.

Figure E on Plate 33 illustrates stake breaking, or how to learn a horse to respect a rope and to stand tied. After a bronc has been handled in the first saddle, he is led out to a log which has been placed there for the purpose and the stake rope, a five-eighths-inch hemp rope about forty feet long, is tied to the log and the other end is tied to the bronc's halter. When the horse runs on the rope, the log will give as the bronc hits the other end, which often prevents the bronc from busting himself. If he were staked solid on a picket pin, he would loosen the stake and pull it up, and the result would be a bronc hightailing it for the wild bunch.

Stake breaking is practiced more in the northwest than in the southwest. Stake breaking means more work for the twister, for it often causes rope burns; such injuries have to be doctored to prevent them from causing the horse a lot of trouble. A bronc cannot be stake broke without getting skinned up to a certain extent.

The bronc twister who has eight or ten head of broncs staked out at one time has his hands full if he rides 'em all every day, waters them regular and changes their stake ground often. Horses do not do as well when they are being broke if they are staked out for too long, say ten days; they are bound to lose flesh and it takes 'em longer to get back to normal than a bronc that is *not* staked out. In the early days of the cow country it was common practice to stake horses out, especially at night when they were used as night horses.

The sliding check or safety-first rigging shown on the horse in Figure 39 on Plate 32 is a rig which the author originated for the purpose of stopping a stampeding bronc and preventing him from going into places that are dangerous, and also to learn him to slide on his hind feet in stopping and turning. At one time the author had to operate without a hazer—a rider who rides with a bronc twister to keep the broncs out of bad places. The region happened to be along Devil's River in Texas, pretty rough country, where the author had to work with no one around to help him to keep a mean bronc out of places he wasn't wanted in. In order to overcome the problem and prevent accidents, the author created this outfit. Figure B on Plate 33 shows the construction of the sliding check; the reader can see how it is arranged on a horse in Figure 39 on Plate 32. The outfit is based on the principle of a martingale (a breast collar used with a saddle) and draw reins, but it differs considerably from both of these. It will be necessary to refer to the construction of the hackalea (see p. 144 in Section entitled "Hackamores") to give the reader some understanding of how the reins of the sliding check are run through the pulley arrangement attached to the back end of the hackalea noseband. Meanwhile, turn to Plate 32: A in Figure 39 shows the regular pair of hackamore reins (shown hanging here, so as not to confuse the drawing) which are attached to the noseband. B shows where a second set of reins is attached to the sliding check. These reins are then run up through the pulley loop on the back end of the noseband under the jaw and back through the martingale rings, as shown at C, and then they are carried up both sides to the top of the horse's neck where they are tied together in a figure eight, or Spanish knot, as indicated at D. Before tying the knot, the slack is taken out of these reins so the horse will hold his head in a natural position and cannot carry his head too high, and also so that there will not be enough loose slack left for the horse to get his feet tangled up in the reins if he should take a notion to sink his head and try to slip his pack. The shoulder straps indicated at O in Figure B on Plate 33 are fastened to the front saddle strings, on each of which is a small snap. These snaps are fastened around the rings in the ends of the straps. The snaps are easily opened or fastened, which means that the straps can be quickly removed or attached. E in Figure 39 on Plate 32 shows where the cinch is run through the loop in the end of the breast strap. If the outfit is attached as described, there is no chance of it slipping out of place when a horse has his head down; it is always where it belongs, and no matter whether a horse pitches or falls, the reins are always in place. Some may think that a horse would get his foot hung up in the rigging while bucking, but it can be reliably said by the author that in all his experience with the sliding check, a horse never got his foot in the rigging, and there never was a time when the rigging was out of place or in the way of the rider or the horse.

To get extreme leverage on a horse, the breast strap, which attaches to the cinch, can be shortened up and the martingale spreaders can be lowered. The shoulder straps may also be lengthened so the breast part of the rigging can be lowered. The whole outfit can be adjusted to fit a horse as it should, that is, so that it will set fairly close to him. The sliding-check reins are left suspended on the horse's neck and are used only when the rider wishes to stop him.

Figure 40 on Plate 32 shows the rider setting back on the sliding check reins, or pulling on them. They are picked up in the hands with the other reins and as soon as the horse is checked, or stopped, they are dropped back on the horse's neck. He is turned back by the rider sliding his left hand down on the near rein, taking a short hold and pulling the horse's head around to place the horse's front feet back where his tail was. The rider helps the horse turn his rear end around by slipping a spur up towards his hip bone on the side the horse is being turned to.

On Plate 33, drawing A shows how the rider works to lift the horse around to head him back in the direction from which he has come. This maneuver learns a horse to slide and turn rapidly with his head down, which is the proper position for a horse to carry his head when working stock. His head should not be up in the air, stargazing, the way most horses hold their heads when turning. The sliding check is a good rigging for a high-headed, high-strung horse because it keeps his head down to normal where it belongs. The horse can be controlled more easily with this outfit. The rigging is placed on a bronc during the second saddle and he is rode with the outfit on during the rest of the saddles until he is turned over to the owner as a broke bronc. The rigging can be converted into a tie-down, or a martingale, when riding with a bridle, by removing the reins and martingale spreaders and using a short strap to connect with the breast strap and the noseband of the bridle. This make a good tie-down. If the reins only are removed, the rigging is converted into a martingale. The rigging can also be used as a breast strap on a saddle in mountain country or for roping purposes. It is a handy rigging for a bronc twister to have around.

The second saddle means the second time a bronc is rode. A bronc should be rode every day until he is ready to be turned over to the owner as a broke horse. If a rider lets a bronc rest a day or two while being broke, he will be harder to handle. So keep setting on 'em every day unless the weather is too bad to work—and that would have to be pretty bad to keep some hands, anyway, from handling 'em every day, especially if the broncs are being broke by the head, that is if the twister is being paid for each horse he breaks. Handling a bronc during the second saddle is very much the same as what has to be done during the first one, except that the whole process of forefooting described above should not be necessary unless the bronc is a pretty bad *hombre*. If possible, try to walk up to the bronc and catch him without roping him. However, it is usually necessary to rope him for the second saddle by the forefoot, but it should not be necessary after that if the bronc is alone in the corral. The bronc should always be cut off to himself, in a separate corral, before the rider tries to handle him. With no other horses to interfere, the bronc will naturally center his attention on the rider, and, if properly approached after the second saddle, he can be caught without roping. In some instances he can be caught that way even during the second saddle.

The approach is a big factor in catching a bronc without roping. When walking up to a bronc, a lot of riders extend one hand out towards the horse as if they were reaching for him, which makes him think that the rider intends to grab him. The hand should not be held out but should be down. With the hands down, the rider proceeds to walk up to the bronc in a leisurely manner, approaching from directly in front and talking to him at the same time. This will have a good effect and cause him to relax. Keep the hands down until the horse smells you to assure himself that this is the same *hombre* that handled him the day before. The rider should then place his hand on the bronc's head and slowly run the hand over the horse's eyes and handle him as described before. The loop of the catch rope is now slipped over the bronc's head and the hackalea is then put on him.

Figure O on Plate 34 shows how tying the forefeet together, the next step, is begun. The honda end of the rope is swung so it will wrap around the forelegs, and, as the honda comes around, the rider catches it on the toe of his boot, draws it up to his hand, and then passes the free end of the rope through the honda. Then he proceeds to pull the legs together and ties them. While all this is being done, the bronc is held as in Figure O. When the tie has been completed, the rider holds the bronc as shown in Figures 17 and 19 on Plate 30 and repeats the lessons he gave the bronc during the first saddle.

If a sliding check is used, it should be put on the bronc during the second saddle. It should be handled easily the first few times in stopping the bronc, until he gets used to it. After the bronc has been rode around the corral a while, he should be handled in a larger corral in order to give him more room to circulate around and to learn him to stop and slide with the sliding check. The bronc is loped across the corral and up to the fence, stopped with the sliding check, and suddenly turned back toward the other fence to make him turn sharply, as shown in Figure A on Plate 33. He is then walked back to the opposite side of the corral and again loped across the corral and stopped with the sliding check. Then he is turned as before and brought down to a walk in going back to the starting place on the opposite side of the corral. Do not overdo the sliding act (three times is enough at one setting) to avoid having the bronc take a dislike to the work.

For several very good reasons the bronc is not rode outside the corral until the third saddle. First, the bronc should be taught how to turn double—both ways—and should know how to stop when he is told to. The old method of breaking broncs was to ride the horse on the outside during the first saddle and this generally developed into a battle between the horse and rider which was hard on the horse no less than on the man. A hazer generally accompanied the bronc and rider to keep them out of jack pots and to help get the bronc back to the corral. The bronc usually got mad and had to be whipped and spurred to get him to go in the direction wanted. Riding the horse in the corral during the first two saddles and learning him to stop, turn and stand while the rider is getting on and off will do more good than the old method of handling. By pulling him around in the corral during the first two saddles, the top of the bronc's nose and the lower part of the jaw will become tender, so when he is rode during the third saddle he will be in better shape to respond readily to the pull of the hackamore reins. He is then well softened and ready to go outside for the first time.

During the third saddle the bronc is rode around the corral a few times and doubled and stopped and then he is taken outside. It is not necessary to have a hazer along to keep the bronc out of bad places because the rider now has the bronc under control. The horse should be rode off for some distance at a walk and should be turned in various directions once in a while. He should then be loped for a short stretch and then be brought back down to a walk. The rider should alternate the gaits by walking, trotting and galloping him in turn. This is easier on the bronc and learns him to travel like a saddle horse should. Each bronc should be rode on an average of about five miles per day, which is enough for the average horse being broke. He can stand up under that amount of riding and keep in good condition. A twister should always be watching out for the horse's condition while the animal is being handled.

Figure C on Plate 33 shows figure-eight work. This maneuver is effective in getting the bronc to turn. The figure eight is about thirty feet in diameter; lay it out on a good level piece of ground by walking the bronc around the course until the trail is visible so it can be easily followed. By working several head of broncs over the eight the first day, it will soon be a plain trail. The rider should approach the figure eight from a different point each day the bronc is worked out on the course, so that the animal will not get to know any particular entrance spot on the trail and try to turn off onto it. A bronc should be walked around the eight the first few times, then trotted around a few rounds, and then galloped the last few times. When making the turns at the end of the eight, the bronc should be made to feel the pressure of the neck rein; during the last few rounds the bronc should be moving pretty rapid and be made to turn in close by lifting him around with the reins. The last round, as the bronc is making the turn (at the point where the horse and rider are located in Figure C of Plate 33), the bronc is turned in towards the center of the circle and then turned from one side to the other as he is about to leave the eight by the trail indicated by the dotted line. The bronc is brought to a stop at the exit point and then walked for some distance in the direction of the dotted line. It is a good idea to work the bronc on the figure eight as soon as he is rode out of the corral in order to impress on him the discipline of turning and stopping as soon as he is out in the open. Then he can be given the long ride described above.

Figure H on Plate 33 illustrates the Upton side-line method of making a bronc break himself; this technique proves very effective in breaking a bronc, or at any rate in softening him up in a short time. The bronc breaks himself to turning and stopping. When it is necessary to break out a bunch of broncs quickly, this method works excellently. It would not do to use a hackalea on the bronc while he is being sidelined, as this would be too hard on him, but a common hackamore with a mouth rope used in conjunction with it will do wonders. After the side lines are taken *off* the bronc, the hackalea should replace the hackamore when the bronc is to be ridden.

Figure H shows how the side lines are attached to the hind feet and to the head of the bronc. A rope with guide loops to hold the side lines in place is run around the horse's body. The ropes used for the side lines and guide loops are common hemp rope about five-eighths of an inch in diameter. The outfit is put on a bronc while he is lying on the ground, after having been forefooted and thrown in the usual way. Or a blind can be used and the side lines put on while the horse is on his feet in much the same way as hobbling the hind legs, since it is fairly difficult to put the guide rope around the horse's body while he is down, but easy when he is standing up—even though it may require a longer time if the bronc is a salty one. The side-line ropes can be placed around the hind legs and the knots tied in the ropes which can then be slipped down in place without having to handle the hind legs; after this is done, the other ends can be tied to the hackamore. The side lines should be of equal length and care should be taken to prevent too much slack developing in the ropes. The hind feet should be together in a normal position and the head should be so tied that it will also be in a normal position when the bronc is on his feet. Generally speaking, the outfit should be put on the horse so that the position of the feet and head will correspond with the positions in Figure H on Plate 33. This method is a good one to use on a tough, spoiled horse and is great to soften or supple a cold-jawed animal.

Figure F on Plate 33 shows how the side-line rope is placed around the pastern (corresponding to the human ankle) of the hind leg to keep it from drawing up on the leg. Figure G shows how the rope will look when it is properly arranged. The granny knot prevents the loop from tightening on the pastern. The other ends of the ropes are half-hitched around the noseband of the hackamore. If necessary the side-line ropes can be adjusted after the bronc is on his feet. By using a blind it will be easier to adjust the outfit.

The guide loops are formed on the body rope by doubling the rope to form the loop and tying a plain or granny knot (see Figure H). The loops prevent the side lines from getting in between the horse's forelegs and burning the horse's breast and legs. Have the loops low enough so there will be no pressure on the horse's back.

When the horse moves, the action of the hind feet will cause the head to be pulled from one side to the other as the legs are extended out behind the horse. The rigging should be left on the horse for at least half a day. The bronc should be placed in a large corral where he will have plenty of room to circulate. When the horse is caught to remove the rigging, his forefeet should be tied together and then he should be handled as previously described in this section. The horse will have learned to turn and stop before he is rode, which will enable the rider to turn the bronc over to the owner several days sooner than if the side-line rigging had not been used.

Of the methods here described, it is up to the rider to decide which is the

PLATE 34 *Bronc Busting (Cont.)*

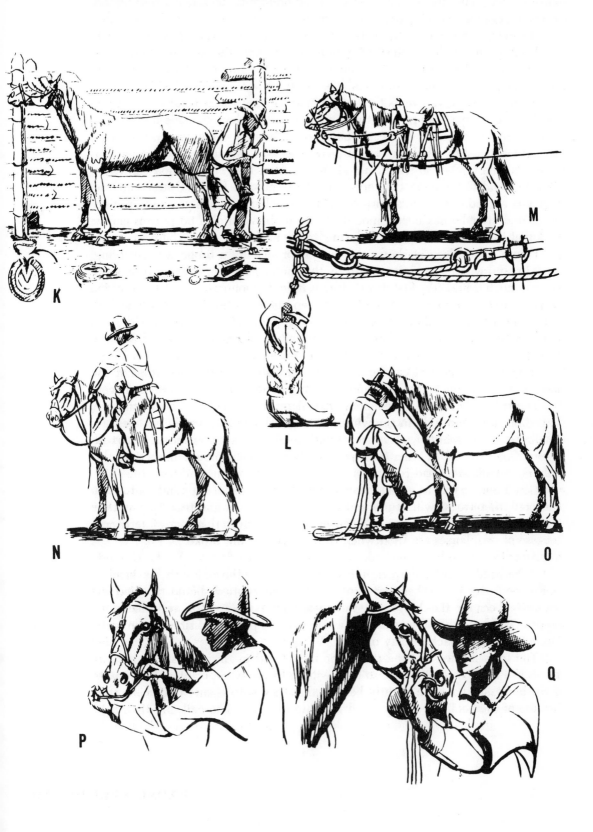

K

M

L

N

O

P

Q

most practical. The side-line method is a good one to use on a mean horse or an owlhead (a horse that refuses to be broke) that likes to stampede. It also takes the kinks out of a stiff-necked horse.

Figure J on Plate 33 illustrates the method for sidelining referred to in the Sections entitled "Mustanging" and "Working Wild Stock." Its purpose is to prevent an animal from running while being drove with a herd. The tail is tied to the forefoot, which prevents the foot from advancing and naturally checks the speed of the animal. Figure I on the same Plate shows how the side-line rope is attached to the bronc's tail. A soft hemp rope about five-eights of an inch in diameter is generally used for the purpose. The rope should be tied around the pastern of the foreleg so it will not tighten on the leg. The method shown in Figures F and G for tying the rope around the pastern for an Upton side-line rigging is a good one for this purpose. This type of side line is generally put on the animal after he has been roped and thrown but can also be put on gentle stock that is standing. This is a good thing to use on a horse that is hard to corral.

Figure K on Plate 34 shows the process of shoeing a bronc without tying a foot up and without any extra help. By this method a green bronc can be shod without much trouble the first day that he is rode. In mountain country it is often necessary to shoe a bronc's rear hooves to keep him from tearing up his hind feet and to learn him to slide on them. By shoeing the hind feet only, the forefeet will become tender and the horse will naturally pick them up and slide to a stop on his hind feet, which is the right way for a cow horse to stop. The horse that stops on his hind feet can be made to turn faster than one that stops on all fours; it is easier on both horse and rider if the horse slides on his hind feet.

The horseshoes used are generally flat plates, but sometimes heel corks are shaped on them and used in the winter months. The ends of the horseshoes are usually bent in towards each other, as indicated by the arrow in the insert of Figure K on Plate 34, in order to protect the heel. In some mountain sections the malpais (Spanish for "bad country") or lava rocks are porous and have the same effect on a horse's foot as a horseshoeing rasp. If the heel of the hind foot is not protected, these rocks will bruise and wear down the foot and tear it up so that it will be difficult for a horse to keep on traveling over this sort of territory. Because of this, horses are shod when they are first being broke.

After the bronc has been rode in the corral for the first saddle, he is blind-folded, his head is snubbed up high to a corral post, and the end of the hackamore rope is tied over to another post so it can be easily untied should this become necessary because the horse has fallen—although this is not very likely to happen. The head should be snubbed as close to the post as possible so the horse will not have any slack to play on.

The tools needed to shoe the bronc are placed in the rider's boot top, as shown in Figure L on Plate 34, so they will be handy when wanted. The points of the horseshoe nails are slightly bent so that they will be sure to come out on the side of the hoof when they are drove into the shoe. The nails are then held in the rider's mouth so they will be handy. With the equipment arranged as described, the rider is ready to work on the horse. The bronc is quietly but firmly crowded over against the side of the corral by placing a hand on his hip, or pin bone, and pushing him over. With one hand on the hip bone, the rider keeps the bronc crowded against the corral fence while he picks up the hind foot with the other hand. When the foot is picked up, it is held with both hands, the rider leaning against the horse to keep the animal crowded against the fence. The hind leg can then be held and, by using sense and time, the rider will be able to put a shoe on the foot. The shoe is fitted, to see if it needs to be widened or narrowed, before the foot is worked on, so that when the shoeing process is started it will not be necessary to let the foot down before the job is completed. As each nail is drove, its end should be twisted off so that it will not have a chance to injure the cowhand if the bronc should happen to try to get his foot loose. Chaps should be worn by the rider for protection. Practice will soon show how a bronc can be shod without much trouble and without tying up a foot.

Figure M on Plate 34 shows the rigging used in breaking a jerk-away horse. Horses that are in the habit of jerking away from a rider have to be convinced that this is a jerky habit that gets 'em in bad. It is necessary to attach a ring to the saddle rigging and one to the hackamore or bridle noseband, as indicated by the two arrows in the drawing. A catch rope is used and it is tied to the hackamore and then run through the ring attached to the saddle and is then brought back through the ring on the hackamore. The rigging shown in the diagram below the horse in Figure M gives an idea of how the rope is arranged. The rider holds the main line of the rope coiled in his hand and proceeds to go through the motions of mounting and dismounting to see if the horse will try to break away. The rider lets the horse make his getaway on purpose; to help him get a good start, the rider should run towards the horse as though he were trying to catch him. Then, when the horse is about at the end of the rope, the rider proceeds to bust the jasper by taking a hip lock on the rope. The experiment should be repeated over and over until the rider can run up to the horse as though in a hurry, without having the horse run off or try to make his getaway. A few good convinces with the above rigging will soon have the desired result.

Head-shy horses are a great source of trouble and if a bronc is handled properly he will not develop this undesirable habit. When a horse is broke with a hackamore (or hackalea), he seldom acquires the habit of trying to pull away from a man when he is being bridled or hackamored. Some broke horses refuse to take a bit into their mouths and have to be eared down to force them to take the bit. Some refuse to let a bridle be slipped over their ears. This sort of behavior generally results from their having had their ears twisted or chewed on by some ear-down man in a bronc-fighting contest during the bronc's first contact with a man. If a bridle is let out several holes before trying to put it on a horse, and if the bit is placed in the horse's mouth by first inserting a finger into the side of the mouth—in the same manner in which a mouth rope is put in the bronc's mouth (Figure Q on Plate 34)—then the horse will open his mouth freely to take the bit and the headstall can be slipped over the horse's ears without the rider having to take ahold of them. The rider should stand back alongside the horse's neck while placing a bridle or hackamore on him.

Figure N on Plate 34 shows the rider preparing to dismount. He takes the same rein and mane hold, with his left hand, as was shown in Figure 28 on Plate 31. The bronc's head is drawn towards the rider by taking a short rein hold, and only the toe (ball) of the rider's foot is in the stirrup so that it will not get caught when he steps off. The right hand has ahold of the saddlehorn. When the rider steps off, he does it slow and deliberate. He should hit the ground in front of the horse's shoulder and be facing toward the saddle; this will place him in the same position he was in when he was preparing to mount, as shown in Figure 28 on Plate 31. If it is necessary to quit a mean horse, the rider can hit the ground way out in front of the horse and be out of the way if the bronc should attempt to whirl and kick. But, generally, in the case of broncs there is no need for a rider to try and get away from the horse and he should get off and on in a leisurely fashion and hold the horse so the animal cannot get away.

Figure O on Plate 34, tying the forefeet together, is referred to and explained above (see p. 131).

Driving horses by using a not altogether broke bronc for the purpose is sure *not* a good idea, because it puts crazy notions into the animal's head which will be hard to get out again later on. Some cowmen think it is a good plan for a bronc twister to keep up a half-broke bronc to wrangle horses on in the morning, or any other time, for that matter. But if they had to handle the bronc for long under such conditions—especially in rough country—they would soon change their minds about this subject. A bronc will try to get too close to the horses and when the rider tries to hold him back, he will get mad, cold-jaw, and charge into 'em regardless of what happens. This is apt to end up in a battle that will take some long forgetting and be the cause of a good horse going wrong. So the advice given here is to keep a bronc away from loose horses if good progress is to be made in breaking him.

Using the come-along (see Plate 36) to halterbreak horses requires time and patience if good results are to be achieved. This is a force system and should be resorted to only when coaxing and kind treatment fail. A horse can be halterbroke by this method in less time than by any other method employed by bronc busters and the effects will be just as lasting as those obtained through any other type of handling. But only when a horse is mean and stubborn should it be necessary to use a force method to learn him to lead. There are times when a well-broke horse may refuse to lead through a gate or into a stock car, and he is especially apt to balk at an auto trailer. When anything like this happens, the come-along will be equal to the emergency.

When the come-along has been placed on a horse as shown in Figures 1 through 5 on Plate 36, it should be adjusted so that the nose piece will be at the end of the boney ridge of the nose and will sink into the soft surface in the same way that the noseband on the hackalea does (Figures 21, 22, and 23 on Plate 30). Under no circumstances should the rope be placed so low that it will stop the circulation of air through the. horse's nose. If the rope should slip around on the nose while it is being used, it should be readjusted and placed in the proper position as shown in Figures 4 and 5. The rope is easily adjusted by giving and taking slack with the main line. To proceed with the operation of the come-along, the operator walks in a leisurely way over to one side of the horse as though he intended to halterbreak him in the manner explained above (see p. 127). After he has come to within a distance of about twenty feet of the horse—this gives the rider plenty of room to play in— the rider proceeds to take up the slack in the rope. He should pull on the rope in a slow deliberate manner, always taking up more slack and never giving. The rope is not jerked but is vibrated after a certain length of time. Everything is done as though the rider had all day to do the job. Remember what has already been said about time and patience! After about five minutes of steady pulling, if the horse has not responded to the pull and seems to be going to sleep on the job, the rope is struck with the open hand which causes it to vibrate violently. The horse will come to life suddenly and advance a few steps toward the operator, causing the rope to loosen on his head. The bronc is then given time to consider why the rope stopped pinching him so suddenly. The rider did not move out of his tracks while the horse advanced, thus giving him all the slack in the rope that he had created by coming forward. A little friendly talk on the subject should be indulged in by the rider at long range while he proceeds to walk over to the opposite side of the horse to repeat the process of hoggin' the slack. Again the rider gradually takes up every bit of slack in the come-along and after a while he again strikes the rope with his hand and gets the same sort of response as before.

While the horse is thinking it over, it is a good idea to go up to him and slowly adjust the come-along on his head, and while near him it is well to rub a hand over his head and eyes as a friendly gesture to help break the tension. A little friendly conversation will help to divert the bronc's mind from the bad ideas he has been associatin' with. The pulling process is now repeated until the horse decides it is best to respond. Never fail to congratulate the bronc when he does the thing wanted of him; this will convince him that a human is a decent animal after all. In a few minutes time the rider can have the horse following him around the corral on a trot by pulling the rope lightly but firmly as he jogs around the corral. The rider should do this to show the horse that he can lead when he's asked to. And if at any time the horse should have a lapse of memory and seem to forget how to lead, another application of the come-along will restore his memory *muy pronto*.

Ten days is the average time required to handle a bronc so he will be in good shape to turn over to another rider to handle. Much, of course, depends on how the bronc was handled by the bronc buster. A twister who knows his business can break ten head of broncs in ten days, or, on an average, thirty head per month. Not all the ten head of horses will be rode on the first day, but they will all be well started by the end of the second: about seven head can be handled the first day, and the second day the ten head can be rode; that is, seven head of broncs will be rode for two saddles and three head for one saddle each. In ten days seven head will have been rode for ten saddles and three head for nine saddles. (Each day that a horse is rode is counted as a saddle.) The day lost in getting the last three head started can easily be made up by devoting some extra time to each saddle they are rode. More time will have to be spent on some of the broncs than on others, and the rider must work them accordingly.

After the first four saddles, the work will be easy and it will just be a matter of riding the horse a certain length of time, on the average about one hour per day to each horse. One hour will be all that is necessary for the average bronc, as in that time he can be rode five miles and handled sufficiently in other ways to let him know that he has been worked. A bronc rider will average sixty miles of riding per day under these circumstances, and this is a good day's work. The amount of riding given each horse every day will keep the horse in good shape and he should be in as good flesh when he is turned over as a broke horse as the day he was first caught. However, he must get enough feed to hold him up while he is being broke. Only five head, or half of the bunch of ten broncs being handled, should be held up at one time. After one is rode, he is turned out so he can graze. If handled in this manner, none of the broncs should have to stand in the corral very long; when horses are held in a corral for any length of time they naturally begin to lose flesh.

Some broncs are only rode seven saddles before being turned over as broke horses. Much can be done during seven saddles and if the horse is properly handled he can be well started on his way. And if he is handled right by his new rider he will get along all right and do good work.

Some owners demand that a bronc be rode with a bridle before being turned over as a broke horse. In such cases, the bridle is put on over the hackamore (or hackalea) and the horse is rode with double reins during the last two saddles. When the bronc is broke with a mouth rope, there will be no trouble in handling him with a bridle.

A description of how a horse was actually broke of the "falling-back" habit may prove helpful to bronc twisters. A bronc that does this is called a cinch binder. The horse in question was quite devoid of intelligence, as could easily be noted by observing his long narrow head, glassy eyes, pin ears, narrow chest, ewe neck and long running gears. He had a faraway look much like that of a locoed horse, and probably he was locoed, but he had apparently been born that way. When the cinch tightened on his belly, he threw a fit, fell over backwards and proceeded to stay there regardless of every effort to get him up. The saddle had to be removed in order to get him on his feet. Every time a cinch touched his belly, he would fall over and lay there for hours until the saddle was removed. The same thing would happen when a riding surcingle* or a rope was tied around him.

After a week of such performances, he was placed in a separate corral and given an opportunity to repeat his previous stunt; then, as soon as he hit the ground, his four feet were tied so closely together that he was unable to move them. The bull rigging which had been placed on him was cinched up and he was left there to himself to think things over and to rest while the rider went off to ride out a bunch of broncs. Every time a horse was rode, the rider pulled off his chaps, sneaked up to the horse that was tied down, and proceeded to give him a good scare and also a good chapping from head to tail, as well as to let out a few blood-curdling panther squalls. The horse would make every effort to get up, but not a chance. After each horse was rode out, the process was repeated. Eventually the recalcitrant horse tried to get up even when no one was chivying him, but he found that he couldn't shake a leg.

When he had had a good long rest, his feet were untied and he was more than willing to get up, as you could tell by the way he shook himself and licked his lips, a sure sign he was ready to surrender. He was now led to the round corral, the rigging was removed and the saddle was put on him, a proceeding he almost seemed to enjoy. The rider mounted and worked him out in the corral, though he had to push on the reins owing to the fact that the horse was light in the upper story. But the horse was broke, contrary to all predictions that he could never be made to follow a cow. He was never again known to fall when he was cinched up. "The Camel" was the name wished on him by the outfit, and he certainly looked and acted the part.

Opinions differ as to the age at which a bronc should be broke to get the best results. Some maintain that a colt should be broke at two years old, but three years old is the average age at which the majority of range horses are broke. A horse can be broke when he is a year old, but it is sure necessary to humor or favor him to keep from riding him too much. A three-year-old can be rode and do a lot of work. At that, a rider should be careful not to ride him like he would an older horse, because a young animal cannot stand up under hard riding. The four-year-old is developed enough to stand up under the average work required of a cow horse and if broke when he is three years old, he will be able to do his part then, too. It is much harder to break a bronc after he has reached the fifth year because it is necessary to cover more territory with him when handling him in order to tire him so he will know that he has been set on. In other words, the older the horse, the more riding is necessary to bring him down to where he will handle decently.

A horse that carries his head high in the air is often referred to as a stargazer. This head position is caused generally by two things that have happened to the horse. One thing is the rough handling of the bit in a horse's mouth, which

* Bull rigging, *i.e.* a strap with a handhold on top, usually used for riding bulls.

has caused him to throw his head up to break the leverage on the bit when the bridle is pulled on; by doing this he tries to protect his mouth from injury. This is one way to turn out a stargazer. The other reason why a horse may become a stargazer is that he is by nature of a nervous disposition and highly excitable; he has been that way since he was foaled and this nervousness and excitability cause him to carry his head too high. However, the majority of stargazers are made, not born, and have been made stargazers by rough usage at the hands of some rider who did not possess as much horse sense as any horse has been foaled with. Jerking, riding with tight reins and a steady pull on a horse's mouth with no give and take, and so forth, cause a bit, especially a severe bit, to cut and tear the animal's mouth and tongue to such an extent that the horse will naturally be forced to carry his head high while working, in anticipation of the mishandling of the bit.

Horses that are broke with a bridle instead of a hackamore are generally stargazers. The use of a stiff bit, or port bit, or a snaffle bit (see Section on bits) in the mouth of a green bronc when he is first being broke will almost always cause the mouth to become very tender or sore. Next to cutting his wind off, the use of a bit in breaking a bronc has caused more horses to fight back, cold-jaw, and stampede than any other procedure. It is difficult to break a bronc with a bridle without injuring the mouth.

Once a horse becomes a stargazer, it is difficult to break him of the habit of holding his head too high with a bridle. A tie-down (standing martingale) is used on a horse to hold his head down to normal position, together with a straight-bar or a low U-port bit. The tie-down, or standing martingale, is a strap attached to the noseband of the bridle, then run down between the forelegs of the horse and connected to the cinch like an ordinary martingale.

Much depends on the rider in controlling a high-headed horse. One rider can handle a horse with good results, while another would not be able to get along with him at all. Patience is the most important factor in attaining success in handling a horse. The tender-mouth horse has to be handled with a light pull which generally means *pushing* (not pulling) on the reins. However, the hard-mouth horse has to be handled with a firm give and take, by a steady pull all the time he is being worked.

The best method to handle a stargazer, at least in the opinion of the author, is to place a hackalea on him, with a mouth rope, as was shown in Figures 21, 22 and 23 of Plate 30. This mouth rope is used in conjunction with the sliding check in exactly the same way as was described above (see p. 144). Generally the horse will get to carrying his head down to normal and will work better with this rigging than he ever did with a bridle. The reins of the sliding check should be tightened as much as is necessary to hold the horse's head down to normal position and the horse should be taught to slide with the rigging so as to learn to turn with his head down. With his hind feet shod and the front feet rasped down so that they will get tender, the horse will soon learn to slide as was described above.

16

HACKAMORES

Three types of riding hackamores (probably from the Spanish, *jáquima*, "head-stall") are shown on Plates 35 and 36. The old style of hackamore shown in Figure 1 on Plate 35 is the one most generally used for all-around purposes. It is used as a halter, and also, by attaching a pair of reins to the noseband underneath the horse's jaw, as a riding headstall to handle broncs with.

The various parts of the hackamore are designated by the letters A, B and C in Figure 1 on Plate 35. A indicates the headstall, consisting of a brow band and the cheek pieces; it is generally made of either saddle strings or latigo leather, which is a pliable oil-tanned leather. C is the feador, often called "theodore," which is generally made of a good grade of medium-weight sash cord about five-sixteenths of an inch in diameter. Small strands of hair or hemp rope are also used when the sash cord is not procurable. B designates the noseband which is generally made of plaited rawhide.

Rope nosebands of three different designs are shown in the center at the top of Plate 35. Figure 2 is practically the same as the noseband shown on the hackamore just described. Figure 3 is a type of noseband designed for riding purposes only. The two large smothering knots are intended to help cut off the flow of air through the horse's nostrils. This type of noseband did not become popular because those who tried it out found that it did more harm than good since the cutting of a horse's wind makes him fight his head—and when that happens he is apt to do anything to get rid of the rider. It only served to make the bronc mad and that always causes trouble.

Figure 4 is a double-strand noseband made with one continuous piece of rope, as shown by the two loop ends. The double strands make a wider noseband than the single strand. The single-strand is more popular than the double-strand, due, perhaps, to the lower cost and because of the construction of the end, which, being solid, is more substantial.

The bosalea (from the Spanish *bozal,* "muzzle") shown in Figure 5 on Plate 35, is strictly a riding headstall for breaking broncs and is not intended to be used in tying a horse up to an object, as can be done with the hackamore or a hackalea (Figure 7). A flat metal nose piece forming the front part of the noseband is indicated by the double arrow between Figures 5 and 6. Figure 6 shows how the noseband is constructed. The two B's indicate the rings to which the reins are attached. They give added leverage on the horse's head when he is being turned. The metal nose piece, which is about five-eighths of an inch wide and one-eighth of an inch thick, is secured to rings on the side of the noseband, which is adjustable. The bosalea is constructed so as to cause the horse's nose to become sore or tender from the pressure brought to bear on it by the pull of the reins. This will naturally force the horse to give or respond to the pull. Because the noseband is not stationary, it generally slips around on the horse's nose when the reins are pulled, causing the metal nose piece to cut into the surface of the nose and making a scar across the bridge of the horse's nose. By this scar a rider can easily identify a horse which has been broke with a bosalea. Such a bosalea is more effective in handling a bronc than the old-style hackamore. To get a horse used to a bit in his mouth, a bridle is often used in conjunction with a hackamore, and the same thing is often done with the bosalea.

The hackalea in Figure 7 on Plate 35 is a type of hackamore that was devised by the author. In order to follow the description of the hackalea given below, the reader must refer to Plates 30 and 32 pertaining to bronc busting, as well as to Plate 35. The outfit will become much clearer when one notes how it is put on the horse in, for instance, Figure 21 on Plate 30.

Note first how the tasseled strands that are left hanging in Figure 7 on Plate 35 are tied into the upper loop of the feador to make a throat latch in Figure 21 on Plate 30. (See Figure 15 on Plate 75 for the method of making the tie.) Then note how the nose piece of the headstall and the nose piece of the noseband form a V, and how the rest of the noseband brings the lower end of the feador in under the front of the horse's lower jaw. There a mouth rope is tied to it and inserted in the horse's mouth like a bit. The under part of the noseband acts like a curb (see p. 187). The bottom loop of the feador is now in position to take the lead rope. (See Figure 16 on Plate 75 for the method of tying on the lead rope.)

Next, note Figure 39 on Plate 32: This shows the martingale, at B, looped at one end around the cinch, at E. The other ends of the martingale are attached to the front saddle strings on both sides of the saddle and form a V on the horse's breast. The sliding-check reins (see below) shown in Figure 39 are

PLATE 35 *Hackamores*

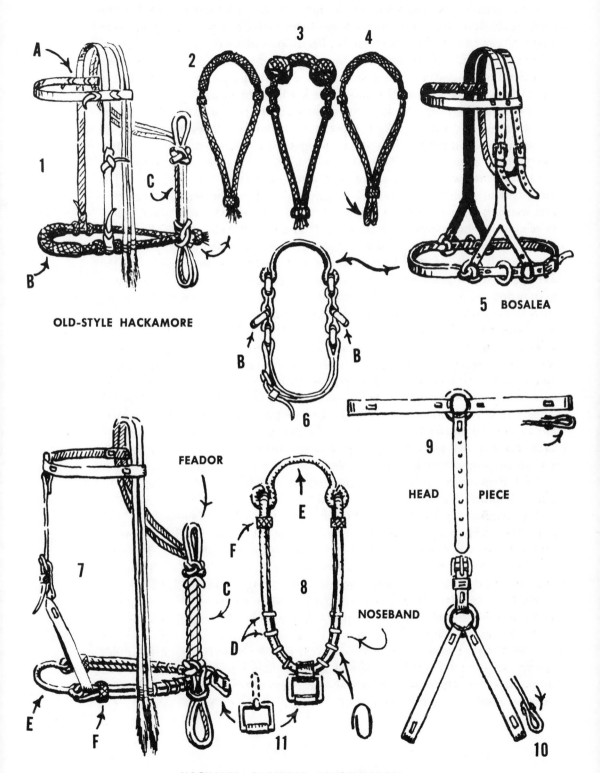

A

C

1

B

2

3

4

5 BOSALEA

OLD-STYLE HACKAMORE

B   B

6

FEADOR

9

HEAD   PIECE

7

E

C

8

F

NOSEBAND

D

E

F

11

10

HACKALEA, SHOWING CONSTRUCTION

attached to the front of the martingale, passed over the roller on the hackalea, under the horse's jaw, and then are brought around and up both sides of the horse's neck. The rider thus has leverage that will keep the horse's head down easily. He can't buck if he can't get his head up, and he is easier to handle in other ways as well. This drawing also shows a lead rope attached to the hackalea. This operates the hackalea somewhat as in a come-along (see below). It can be detached or tied around the horse's neck when not in use.

The principles of the hackamore and bosalea are combined in this hackalea with other features which make it superior to any style of hackamore designed for use in breaking broncs. It is the outfit first explained on p. 117 and shown in Figures 21, 22 and 23 on Plate 30. The headstall is more easily adjusted than the old-style hackamore. The metal nose piece (Figure 7 at E on Plate 35) is firmly held in place and the ends are attached to the rope forming the noseband, causing it to be held in place as shown. The metal piece never moves out of position but is always stationary. It is made of heavy galvanized steel wire about one quarter of an inch in diameter and is rounded and has no sharp edges; it will sink into the surface of the nose easily but not cut or scar the nose badly. It is placed at the end of the boney structure of the nose but it should never be placed so low that it will cause the horse's wind to be cut off, which will invariably make a horse fight his head.

Figure 8 on Plate 35 shows how the noseband is built. D and O indicate pieces of galvanized steel wire clamped around the double strands of rope to hold them together. The ends of the wire loops are lapped beside each other in order to hold the rope firmly. Two plaited knots are placed at F to hold the doubled rope together and to keep the V-shaped nose piece of the headstall in place. The rope used is heavy sash cord of the best quality and measures three-eighths of an inch in diameter. A piece of three-eighths-inch braided cotton rope like that used for trick roping is best for the purpose, as it is stronger than ordinary rope. The two ends of the rope are brought together at the back end of the noseband. They are concealed by the leather piece holding the buckle (Figure 11 between Figures 7 and 8) as indicated by the arrows. This is a roller arrangement in the end of the noseband, made from a one-and-a-half-inch roller buckle with the tongue removed. It is the buckle used for a pulley in conjunction with the sliding check or safety-first rigging shown on Plate 32; the reins of the sliding check are run through the buckle from the bottom and back down through the spreader rings on the rigging, as shown in Figure 39.

Figure 9 on Plate 35 shows the top part of the headstall of the hackalea and Figure 10 indicates the bottom part. All the ends are looped, as indicated by the arrows. One-and-a-half-inch rings are used for the headstall, and the straps are three-quarters of an inch wide. (It is not necessary to put the roller or pulley arrangement in the noseband if the sliding check is not used.) The hackalea used with the mouth rope is an outfit very effective in breaking broncs, as will be proved once it is tried out.

PLATE 36 *Rope Hackamores*

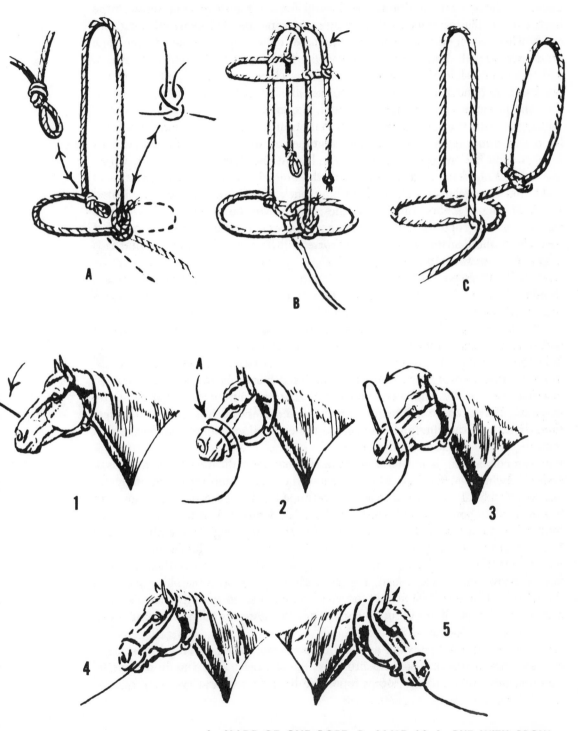

A, MADE OF ONE ROPE. B, SAME AS A, BUT WITH BROW-
BAND AND THROAT-LATCH ATTACHED. C, THE COME-ALONG,
PUT ON WITH CATCH ROPE, AS SHOWN IN 1, 2, 3, 4 AND 5.

Rope hackamores, shown on Plate 36, are easily made and often used for halters in tying up either broncs or gentle horses. Figure A is a simple rope hackamore or halter made with one piece of rope about fifteen feet long and one-half to five-eighths of an inch in diameter. The loop is formed in the rope on the off side, as shown in the enlarged detail drawing to the left of Figure A, and the bowline knot is tied on the near side, which forms the front half of the noseband and the head piece. The dotted line indicates how the free end of the rope is run around and down through the loop on the off side.

Figure B is the same as Figure A, but strands of rope are used for a brow band and throat latch which are tied together as shown in the drawings. This type of rope hackamore is one which will generally make the horse on which it is used stand tied, because it pinches the animal's head in such a way as to make him change his mind about pulling back after he has thoroughly tested it out. The more a horse pulls back, the more he will be pinched, and when he slackens on the rope the whole hackamore loosens up; when he finds out that this is how the hackamore works, the horse will be quickly convinced that it is best to humour the outfit.

Figure C shows the come-along, illustrated in greater detail in Figures 1 through 5. The come-along's construction is based on the same principles as that of the hackamore in Figure B, but it is more effective. It is made with the catch rope and is a temporary arrangement put on a horse that will not lead and after ordinary procedures have failed to produce satisfactory results. The name come-along was given to it because it *does* make a horse "come along." Very few riders know how to put this hitch on a horse's head, but it is the most effective method for making a horse lead that the author has ever seen. By using it a horse can be halterbroke in fifteen minutes and in some cases in less time than that. Knowing just how to use the come-along to get the best results requires experience in handling one.

The come-along is put on a horse in the manner indicated in the five numbered drawings on Plate 36. Figure 1 shows how the catch rope is brought up on the off side of the horse's head and wrapped around the nose, as shown in Figure 2. Note how the rope is placed above the wrap at A in the drawing. The bottom wrap is drawn out as is shown in Figure 3 by giving slack with the main line of the rope and is placed over the horse's ears as shown in Figure 4. There are no twists made in the rope, just one wrap around the nose and then the rope is placed over the horse's head. Figure 5 shows how the come-along looks on the off side. It is self-evident that after the rope is placed over the horse's head, a pull on the main line (Figure 4) will tend to tighten the head loop and will act as a powerful persuader.

A soft-surfaced rope is not as suitable for a come-along as a hard-twist rope, because the former will not slip properly. A hard-twist rope should always be used for best results, though other ropes can be used if necessary.

17

EDUCATING

THE

COW HORSE

Much depends on the cowhand who handles a fresh-broke bronc as to whether the horse will be given a chance to develop into a first-class cow horse or not. The horse may have been properly handled by the bronc twister and have shown every indication of being a real saddle horse when first turned over to the outfit as a broke horse; but if he is not handled right by the rider to whom he is assigned for future use, he may, in spite of everything, never develop into a good cow horse. The green-broke horse must be given time to learn the work he is expected to do. He should be handled with a firm but friendly hand and he should not be overworked. Slow, steady work will produce better results than fast work because the horse that is worked slowly will have no reason to get excited and do things which will develop into unruliness. The best place for a young or green-broke horse is behind a cow, because following a cow is slow work that lets him take things easy and settle down into the gaits of a well-broke horse. He learns to follow a critter, which is one of the principal things that will be required of him, and he learns to respond more naturally to the pressure of the neck rein in turning.

When the bronc is first introduced to the ways of a cow horse, the rider should make it a practice, while doing every-day range riding, to cut a critter out of a bunch of stock in a leisurely manner, proceed to drive it off away from the bunch and then walk the horse back to the cattle and repeat the process several times—just as if he really intended to cut the cattle out and drive them back to the ranch. If he takes the time to do this sort of work whenever possible, the horse will soon become interested in the job and will learn to watch a cow and turn with every move of the critter. Always turn the horse toward the cow when turning a critter back; never turn the horse tail-end toward the animal. Cutting horses are developed in this way and the more practice a horse gets, the better he will work. Some horses will turn out to be better cow horses than others because they are more intelligent and because of the manner in which they have been educated.

Horses, like people, are of varying intelligence; some, naturally, are smarter than others. But whether a horse turns out to be a good cow horse or a poor one depends to a great extent on the intelligence of the human being that handles him. There are few really good cow horses among the many working on the ranges. In the majority of cases the riders who handle them are to be blamed for the poor quality of the horses. Some bronc busters, however, can take an average bronc and in ten saddles develop him so that he will out-turn and out-work the average horse. Such riders know how to handle a horse much better than the ordinary run of cowhands. A good bronc buster knows much more than the average hand about horse psychology and control. He has gotten his knowledge the hard way, by close study of the horse's behavior under various conditions and the horse's reactions to various stimuli.

Roping is another phase of cow work which the young horse has to learn if he is to become an all-around cow horse. He knows what a rope is, but he does not know how to handle himself on the end of a rope. His first lessons in rope work should be with young stock. While working around stock, the rider should drop a loop on a medium-sized calf and dally his rope until he learns how the horse is going to react to the new work. The rope is then dally-tied to the saddle-horn, and the rider steps off the horse and proceeds to tie the bridle reins to the catch rope so the horse will have to keep his head turned towards the calf; this will at the same time hold his head down so that he won't run off after the calf. The rider then goes down the rope as though he intended to flank the calf and tie it down, but instead of taking ahold of the calf, he goes through a series of scary motions to induce the calf to try to break loose. Naturally the horse will become real interested in the commotion and will set back on the rope, holding it taut without allowing any slack. This, of course, is what the rider wants. The calf should be allowed to circle around the horse several times with the rider in close pursuit, as though he really wanted to get ahold of the calf and throw it. The more the rope is vibrated by the action of the calf, and by the rider, the more this will induce the horse to set back on the rope and try to hold the calf. The bridle reins which are tied to the rope will also vibrate and make the horse stay back where he belongs. After fifteen minutes of instruction in the art of rope work, the rider jerks the loop off the calf's head and turns him back with the wild bunch. The rider then, in leisurely fashion, coils up the catch rope as he advances towards the horse, talking all the time to the horse about what has just been happening. (Yes, talking does have a good effect on the horse.) When the rider has reached the horse, he shows his appreciation for the good work done by congratulating the animal.

The horse's next experience when he is ridden again will consist of a repetition of the performance just described. He will finally become accustomed to holding a calf and it is a good idea at this point to try and get him to lead the calf for some distance when it is first caught. This should be attempted after he has had a few lessons in holding a calf. It will learn him to pull by the saddle horn as if he were dragging a calf out of a herd to be branded. If a little time, whenever the horse is rode, is devoted to giving him a lesson in this kind of work, he will soon develop into a real cow horse.

By tying the honda in a loop so it can't slip and close the loop, the rider can rope grown stock to further train the horse to do rope work. The loop will come off the critter roped because it is held open and it will not be necessary for the rider to take it off. In this way a horse can get a lot of practice and no harm will be done to the animal roped. When two men work together, they can indulge in a little team roping (see p. 117 and Plates 50 and 51) which will be good for the horse. The rider working on the young, or green, horse should rope the cow by the head and hold it while the other rider does the heeling. When the critter is stretched out, the rope is taken off its head while the rider on the other, experienced horse still holds the critter down with the rope that is on the hind legs; then the animal is let up.

The more a rope is handled on, off or around a horse, the more he becomes used to it and the wiser he will get to be about handling himself on the end of a rope. It is a good idea to rope weeds, pull them up, drag them on the end of the rope and up to the horse, and then take them off the rope. Dragging a log or pole or some other heavy object is a good way to learn the horse to pull by the saddlehorn. When giving a young horse his first lesson in rope work, some riders start by roping a grown cow; then they step off the horse to observe the results. Of course, the rope has been tied hard and fast to the saddlehorn and therefore will stay put. Not knowing what it is all about, the horse naturally gets jerked down, and as fast as he tries to get up, he is jerked down again. When the horse finally gets up on his feet, he naturally braces himself to keep the cow from jerking him down once more. In the meantime the rider is standing off to one side watching the show. This method of breaking in a young horse to hold an animal is a rough way to teach him to handle himself on the end of a rope, but it is a method which will make a horse watch his step when he is doing rope work.

Learning a horse to back up when a critter has been roped and the rider is on the ground is taught to horses being schooled for rodeo or contest work as rope horses. In calf-roping work, especially, the horse that will back up on the rope, while the roper is on the ground going to the calf, will help the roper materially; the horse causes the calf to be pulled towards the roper while the latter is trying to get ahold of the critter to throw it. It saves time to have the calf pulled towards the roper and helps him to do faster work. In training the rope horse to back up, the rider learns the horse to do this freely while he is on the horse, whether he is doing rope work or not. And while backing the horse, the word "back" is spoken as a *command;* and when the horse is stopped, the word "whoa!" is also spoken as a command. The horse will get accustomed to a spoken command in backing and stopping for roping purposes, and the roper will be able to control the horse by giving the commands even when he is on the ground working.

To learn the horse to back with a rope, a hogging rope or any other short piece of rope is tied around the horse's neck close up to the head. The catch rope is then run through this neck loop and the end of the catch rope is turned back and tied to the saddlehorn. The roper proceeds to run the horse and goes through all the motions of roping a calf, though the calf is imaginary at this point. As soon as the catch rope is thrown out in front of the horse, the rider steps off and runs to the end of the rope, picks it up and throws his weight against the rope, meanwhile commanding the horse to back. If the horse does not back up, the roper slaps the rope up against the horse's neck in such a way that it will *make* the horse back up. The roper must be careful not to let the rope hit the horse's eye as this may injure it. When the horse responds to the command and does the work wanted of him, the roper should make it a habit to show his appreciation by petting him and talking to him.

In steer-roping work the horse should be taught to pull on the rope with his head turned away from the critter roped while the roper is on the ground working (see the drawing at the bottom of Plate 46). It is necessary for the horse to throw his weight against the rope in order to keep it taut enough to hold the steer down while the latter is being tied. If the rope is not pulled on, the steer will struggle and give the roper trouble and cause loss of time in tying. This applies to range work as well as to contest roping. A good steer-roping horse is not always good for calf roping, however, and vice versa. It is generally necessary to tie a rope around the neck of a good steer-roping horse to keep him from dragging the calf while the roper is trying to tie it down. Contest rules generally state that a rope shall be tied around the horse's neck to prevent the horse from running off with the calf.

The bridle reins are generally dropped on the ground in calf-roping work; but in steer roping the reins are tied together so they will *not* drop on the ground. If the reins should be on the ground, the horse might step on them and then he might stop pulling on the rope, which might cost time (and prize money) in contest work. (For the part played by the horse in both calf and steer roping, see the Section entitled "Ropes and Roping" and Plates 42, 45, 46, 48, 49, 50 and 51.)

In training the horse for contest or rodeo steer-roping work, it is often necessary for the roper to strike the horse across the rump with the open hand or with a small stick after stepping off the horse to run to the steer that is lying on the ground. He hits the horse in this way to keep the horse pulling on the rope while the rider is running to the steer to hog-tie it. The horse is not halted while the rider steps off, but is kept in action so the rope will not be slackened. Some horses are trained to bust (throw) a steer after the rider has stepped off. When the horse has been turned off to bust the steer, the rider steps off onto the ground while the horse is going to the end of the rope; he does this in order to be closer to the steer when the critter hits the ground. The idea is, of course, to save time, since the rider has some ground to cover to reach the animal that the horse is busting. The training of a rope horse requires a lot of time, patience and actual steer-roping work in order to get the horse to manipulating properly.

18

ROPES
AND
ROPING

If you try to backtrack the history of the lariat, *la reata,* beyond the time of its introduction to the early Mexican rancheros, you would have to follow a long, cold trail difficult to trace. *La reata* was a long rawhide rope used by the early Mexican *vaqueros* and was no doubt first introduced into Mexico by the Spanish conquerors. The *reata* was first made of twisted strands of rawhide cut from green buffalo or cow hides. Because of the difficulty in twisting the strands so they would remain closely laid and straight, the *reateros* (ropemakers) discontinued making them from rawhide and took to using plaited or braided rope. It is seldom that a good twisted rawhide *reata* can be found nowadays, but there are still a few *reata* builders who can turn out a first-class hide rope. Four, six and eight plaits (strands) were used in plaiting the ropes. Twisted rope, however, made the best type of *reata* when properly built because of its superior strength and smoother running surface. The twisted rope *reata* is cheaper than one of plaited rope because it is more easily made than the braided kind when one knows how to build it.

The *reata* was the most useful tool of the Mexican *vaquero* and he was highly proficient in handling it. The dexterity displayed by the Mexican ropers impressed the early American cowhands and the *reata* was quickly adopted by them, as were other items of equipment used by the *vaquero.* The rawhide rope is not designed for tying hard and fast to a saddlehorn as are the grass (vegetable-fiber) ropes used by present-day cowhands; tied hard and fast, it will not stand up so well against the weight of a roped steer. The leather *reata* is dallied (wrapped) around the saddlehorn so it can give when something hits the other end of it. The early Texas cowhands were all *reata*-and-dally men until the hard-twist rope made its appearance. The Manila rope is a great deal cheaper to make than the rawhide rope and can be tied to a saddlehorn without much danger of breaking it. The rawhide rope is still used in California, Nevada and Oregon, but the silk Manila rope is also used there.

Rope terms employed by cowhands are unfamiliar to the general public which does not know the ways of the cow country. It is therefore necessary to explain the how and why of this nomenclature before going into detail on the subject of ropes and how they are used.

LARIAT is an Americanization of *la reata,* Spanish for "the rope."

LASSO is the *lazo,* meaning in Spanish a noose or snare. The term is not used by the cowhand to designate a rope with which to catch stock, in other words, a catch rope, nor does he use it as a verb meaning to catch stock. A tenderfoot is identified by his use of this word in either of these meanings.

Lazo reata is a Spanish term meaning snare rope.

CATCH ROPE, THROW ROPE, SADDLE ROPE, GRASS ROPE, TWINE, WHALE LINE, HARD TWIST, LASS ROPE, and ROPE are all used to designate a catch rope.

Reata is from the Spanish *reata,* meaning rope, as noted above, but the American cowhands use it to designate a rawhide rope.

REATA MEN are hands who use a rawhide rope and they sometimes refer to this rope as a lass rope.

Roping terms used by the cowhand are: ROPE, meaning to throw a rope; ROPED, meaning to have caught something with the rope; ROPING, the act of catching; and LOOPED, meaning caught.

Ropes of various types are shown on Plate 37. These drawings will help give the reader a clearer idea of how the ropes are constructed. Figure 1 shows the rawhide *reata* which is generally about sixty feet in length. The *reata* can be thrown farther, with the use of less energy and retaining a more perfect loop, than any other type of rope on the market, bar none. But because it will not stand up under the shock of tying hard and fast when a half ton of meat hits its further end, and also because it costs so much more than Manila rope, this type of *reata* has more or less lost out. A good rawhide *reata* retains its vitality far longer than any other type of rope, but it is more easily damaged than other kinds; consequently it is necessary to use precaution in handling such a rope. It is made in three sizes, designated as light, medium and heavy. Light weight is for calf roping, medium for all-around roping, and heavy for hard, rough work. The rawhide *reata* should be kept pliable by greasing with tallow, which makes it waterproof and preserves it as well.

Figure 4 on Plate 37 shows a silk Manila, or yacht line, a hard-twist rope that is the most popular and widely used catch rope of them all. It costs less than other types of rope and is the most dependable all-around type for roping pur-

PLATE 37 *Ropes & Hondas*

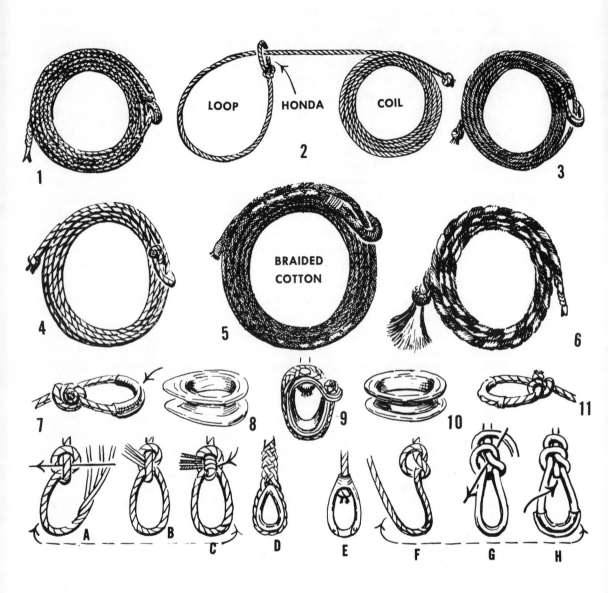

LOOP HONDA COIL

BRAIDED COTTON

1 2 3 4 5 6

7 8 9 10 11

A B C D E F G H

poses. Silk Manila catch rope is made in six different sizes ranging in weight from light to medium to heavy as follows:

1. A scant 3/8″ in diameter—a light rope used for calf-roping and for trick-roping purposes.
2. Exactly 3/8″ in diameter—the regular size used for calf-roping work.
3. 13/32″ in diameter—a light, medium-weight rope used by many for all-around purposes on light stock.
4. Exactly 7/16″ in diameter—the size most used for general roping work.
5. A full 7/16″ in diameter—the standard size for heavy work. It is used extensively in steer-roping contests.
6. Exactly 1/2″ in diameter—slightly heavier than Number 5 and recommended for the heaviest rope work.

Linen ropes, twisted like a hard-twist Manila rope, have come on the market and are said to be excellent for roping purposes; indeed, it is said to be the strongest rope made for roping. The cost is about double that of the silk Manila type of catch rope, but it will last longer. It is also said to be a smoother-running rope than the silk Manila, and it is waterproofed. It comes in 3/8″ and 7/16″ sizes.

Mexican *ixtale* ropes are similar to maguey rope (see below), but they have a longer and finer fiber. They are a good light rope for calf-roping work in the 3/8″ size which is also used by trick ropers for catches.

Figure 3 at the top of Plate 37 shows a maguey rope, also Mexican-made, fashioned from the fiber of the maguey plant, similar to the century plant. It is a 3/8″ rope, good for calf roping and for making horse catches in trick-roping work. It is a light rope but will stand up under general rope work if it is dallied to give slack and so prevent a break under heavy strain.

Figure 5 shows a braided cotton rope known as spot cord; it is especially useful for trick and fancy roping and is an ideal rope for exhibition work. The rope is made in various sizes: light weight for small loops in spinning, medium weight for general big-loop work, and heavy weight for special loop work. It is not a practical rope for regular range work and is not used for that purpose.

Figure 6 shows a hair rope, or *mecate*, used for a hackamore tie rope and for reins. Hair ropes were used to some extent for roping purposes as well, but because of their size and weight they were found to be inferior to the other types. They were eventually used mostly for tie ropes on hackamores, halters, etc. The ropes are made from mane and tail hair taken from horses. The mane-hair ropes are generally softer and silkier than those that are made from tail hair. The *mecate* is usually made in lengths of fifteen to twenty-five feet.

Figure 2, in the center at the top of Plate 37, shows the make-up of a catch rope. The terms used to designate its component parts are the loop, the honda and the coil. Tassels on a rope are decorations generally eliminated in ordinary roping operations and are merely for show. A tassel on the honda is more of a nuisance than anything else as it generally gets tangled up in the honda. It is also a wind-resister and slows up a rope when a loop is thrown.

A honda is the eye in the loop end of the rope through which the main line of the rope passes to form the loop. Several types of hondas are shown and the method of tying a honda in the end of a rope is illustrated in Figures A, B and C at the bottom of Plate 37. This is the type of honda generally used throughout the cow country. Figure C shows, at the arrow, how the loose ends are wrapped around the main line; this keeps the end from pulling out without having to tie a knot in it. (However, sometimes a knot *is* tied in the end of the rope to hold it in place.) This is the same honda as that shown in Figure 7, except that the latter has a leather covering on the loop end to keep the honda from cutting out with wear and tear. The same honda is shown in Figure 11, this time with Hogue's patented honda protector clamped on the loop end. This protector is made of aluminum which is light in weight and is easy to put on.

Metal hondas are shown in two different shapes: egg-shaped in Figure 8 and oval in Figure 10. These hondas are made of brass, generally, and some are nickel plated. They are all right for some purposes, but they are not essential to practical roping work. When the metal honda was first introduced, it was widely used but its popularity was short-lived. It is seldom that a cowhand can be found today using one of them in his catch rope. One reason for not using the metal honda is that it has to be spliced into the rope as shown in Figure D. This takes some time to do and not all stockhands are good at splicing rope back. The metal honda is too free running and because of its weight it has a tendency to close up a loop too fast. Moreover this type of honda is hard on the eye of an animal which it happens to hit. As a general rule the metal honda in the end of a rope identifies the owner as somewhat of an amateur cowboy; metal hondas are not used by cowhands any more than "lasso" is used by them as a word for a catch rope.

Figure 9 shows a rawhide honda used mostly in rawhide ropes, although it is sometimes used in Manila ropes, too, but not often. The end of the rope is run through the hole in the top of the honda.

Figure E, the Ward patent practice honda, was designed by the author. This honda is so constructed that it will release the rope when the loop tightens on the object roped; this eliminates the trouble of taking it off when practice catches are being made.

Figures F, G and H illustrate the central-draft honda, a type not generally known to most cowhands. But it is a good honda, nevertheless. Its main feature is that it hangs straight from the end of the rope and it is somewhat heavier than the regular type because of more rope in the knot. Figures F, G and H show how the knot is tied; actually, this knot is similar to a single-bow, or slip knot, only the end passes over the main line, as is shown in Figure G, and drops down through the center, as shown in Figure H. The knot is pulled down by inserting a stick through the honda and then standing on the stick with the honda between your feet. Then you place the rope around your hips while in a squatting position and pass the rope back around the main line in front of you. Then, holding on to the rope tightly, you straighten up your legs; the leverage thus applied tightens the honda. The end of the rope is now cut off, as shown, so that it will not interfere with the smooth running of the rope through the honda.

New ropes should be stretched right after the honda and knots have been tied in. It is a good idea to stretch the rope between two posts on the side of the corral. Be sure to untwist all the kinks while you do this, for to get them out of the rope is the main purpose of the operation. A pole is generally used for a lever to take the slack out of the rope. This is done by placing the pole at about the center of the rope, running one end of the pole between the corral poles, pulling the other end down on the rope, and then fastening it down so it will keep the rope taut. Leave the rope on the fence overnight, or even longer. When the rope is taken off the fence, it will be in condition to handle.

Waterproofing ropes is seldom done by cowhands as it makes a rope greasy to handle. Also, a rope so treated will tend to collect dirt and become discolored. Ropes have been soaked in linseed oil and also lubricated with tallow, but generally nothing is ever used to waterproof Manila and other types of grass ropes. Rawhide ropes, of course, need several applications of tallow every year in order to keep them pliable and to give them longer life.

Rope lengths vary according to the type of rope and the country in which the rope is to be used. Thirty-three feet is the average length used in Texas where the rope is tied to the saddlehorn, as well as in New Mexico and Arizona where it is also tied to the saddle. In Montana, Wyoming, Idaho, Canada and the Dakotas, thirty-five to forty feet is the length most generally used, as in these states the rope is dallied more often than it is tied hard and fast. In Oklahoma, Colorado and Utah they tie *and* dally and cowhands have compromised on the average length of about thirty-five feet. Forty to forty-five feet is the length mostly used in California, Nevada and Oregon, where a rope is generally dallied. And in these states, the rawhide rope is from fifty to sixty feet long.

Dally is a word taken from the Spanish *dar la vuelta* (dar-la-wel-ta, Americanized to dally-welta) meaning to take wraps or turns around an object, literally, "give her a turn." Dallying a rope is easier on stock being roped, and on the saddle horse too, than a rope tied hard and fast. The give in a dallied rope eliminates the sudden stop. Then, too, in case of an accident, the rope can be turned loose if necessary, whereas, if tied, the rope must be cut loose.

Tying hard and fast is referred to as tying, and tied means tying the rope securely to the saddlehorn so it will not slip off. Anchoring a rope to the saddlehorn means making sure that the animal will be held under any and all circumstances, except when the rope breaks. More cowhands have been crippled-up because of tying a rope than by dallying. This should be taken into consideration when doing rope work. Both methods of handlin' a rope have their good points and are about stand-off when the subject is really analyzed. A lot depends on the cowhand who is handlin' a rope as to whether it is best to tie or dally. Generally the hand who dallies knows how to handle a rope better than those that always tie. Now that statement may cause a lot of hands who tie to rear up an' fall over backwards. To back up this statement I will refer 'em to the Mexican *vaqueros* who are dally hands and the *hombres* who showed the old-timers how to handle a rope. When it comes to handlin' a rope and makin' all kinds of catches, the average cowhand is out-classed by the *vaquero*. (But when it comes to roping against time, the American roper is supreme.)

Mexico is a dally-welta country, as is clearly shown by the type of saddle-horn used there which makes an excellent snubbing post to dally a rope on. The larger the saddlehorn, the more surface comes in contact with the rope and the easier it is to hold a wrap. The small metal saddlehorn is not a suitable surface to dally on and it is very difficult to hold the wraps on it because of the extremely short turns that have to be taken and because of the slick surface. Such small saddlehorns are best for tying to and for gettin' a strangle-holt on when a hand is forced to play safety first to keep from gettin' busted if a bronc hangs his head.

Rope catches are made in many different ways, but the average cowhand is limited to using about six different methods of making a catch. These catches vary according to the kind of work to be done. The methods which are generally used in range work are described below so that the reader will be able to understand how rope catches are made. Practice, and plenty of it, is necessary for anyone who wants to become proficient in the ways of handlin' a rope and he should not be discouraged if he should happen to miss a catch once in a while, as they *all* spill a loop occasionally, regardless of how good they are.

The overhead swing is the commonest method for making a catch. The loop is carried around in a horizontal circle above the roper's head and is thrown at the head of an animal in the manner shown in the drawing on Plate 46. This is the method generally used in roping stock from off a horse, but it is seldom used in roping from the ground.

The hoolihan catch (Plate 39) is a catch used when roping from the ground and is used in catching saddle horses in a corral; but it is also used in roping calves around the neck from off a horse (Plate 38). A hoolihan loop can be placed in a greater variety of positions than any other method of roping. The positions range from vertical to horizontal loops. This is why the method is used in picking out a horse's head from among several that are close together. The loop can be placed in a diagonal position also, so that it will fall over a horse's head when he is at close quarters. The catch is shown in the drawing referred to above (Plate 39) which shows how the loop is held on the left side of the roper to start the action described by the circle and the line figure. The loop makes one revolution, generally. More can be made if necessary, although this is seldom done.

The pitch catch is simple and used mostly in roping when the roper is on the ground. The loop is spread out behind the roper as in making the slip catch (see Figure 1 on Plate 40), but in this case the rope is pitched (tossed) over on the head of the animal to be roped, as in the overhead swing described above. The loop is not rotated but is thrown direct from the starting position; how this

PLATE 38

HOOLIHAN CATCH

is done is shown by the dotted line in the drawing illustrating the slip catch. This drawing also shows how a loop is dragged behind the roper.

The difference between the slip catch and the pitch catch is that the loop travels in a vertical position when thrown in the slip catch and in a horizontal position when thrown in a pitch catch. When a roper drags a loop behind him, he is in a position to make a slip catch, a pitch catch, or a whip catch, and all are done without ever making a single revolution with a loop. All are catches made from the ground when the roper is afoot and are the catches generally used by all cowhands and bronc peelers.

The slip catch which is shown in forefooting a horse on Plate 40 is the best method of catching a horse by the forefeet and is used just as effectively in roping a horse by the head. It is only necessary to raise the loop higher in front of the horse so he will run his head into the loop. It makes no difference from what direction the horse runs by the roper, the roper is instantly in a position to throw for a catch at any time if he is looking for a chance to do so. Forefooting a horse, as shown on Plate 40, is easily done if the roper will only use a little judgment in placing the loop in front of the running horse. The loop should be timed so it will be well opened up in front of the horse when he hits it; it should be placed about three feet in front of the horse to have time to open up. The bottom of the loop should be close to the ground and the top of the loop should reach well up on the horse's breast, as can be seen in the illustration. If the roper will

PLATE 39

HOOLIHAN CATCH

place the loop as shown, and at the right time, success is practically certain. Always strive to see how easy a loop can be placed, and how pretty and how well, if a good job of roping is to be done.

The heeling catch, shown in the drawing of heeling a cow on Plate 41, is used to catch cattle or horses by the heels (hind legs) and is done in roping calves to drag 'em up to the branding fire, or in heeling an animal that has been roped by the head, in order to string, or stretch, it out on the ground. The loop is rotated around in a vertical circle in slow motion and is slowly slipped in under the critter as its hind leg is on its way back. This will cause the opposite, or left hind leg to advance and enter the loop first. The roper holds the loop up and open so it will catch both hind legs. If the loop is whipped in under the cow too fast, the loop is apt to close and catch accidentally, if at all. Slow precision will get best results in heeling. Taking time and working easy will not chouse (excite) the stock and a roper can get in closer to the animal wanted and get a chance to place a loop decently. The dotted circle on Plate 41 shows how the loop hand is carried on a level with the shoulder; the hand is rotated by wrist movement instead of by the whole arm. When the right opportunity presents itself, the loop is slipped in under the cow and jerked up when the legs are in the loop. A small loop is used for calves and a larger one for grown stock. But too large a loop gets in the way and is slower to take up the slack, which may cause the animal to make its getaway.

The forefooting cattle catch at the top of Plate 42 is one that does not hold

PLATE 40

1. FOREFOOTING: PLACING SLIP CATCH IN FRONT OF HORSE

2. FOREFOOTING: BUSTING HORSE

the animal caught. It is used to stop and turn back a bunch quitter that has broke out of the herd with the idea of quittin' the flats. The roper carries the loop above the head in a horizontal position similar to that in the overhead catch (Plate 46). The roper must be up alongside the steer to place the loop correctly. The loop is turned over the steer's shoulders so the top of it is turned down; this causes the loop to turn half over and swing around in front of the running steer so as to catch both its forelegs. To turn the loop over is as simple as turning the hand upside down; it is done with a forward motion of the wrist only. This naturally throws the top of the loop down and the bottom up (see Plate 42). A large loop is used so it will catch the forelegs high up. As soon as the catch is made, the roper turns off at a sharp angle, as is indicated by the arrow in the diagram, and when

PLATE 41

HEEL CATCH (HEELING)

the horse hits the end of the rope, the rope up-ends the steer and leaves him in a position headed back in the direction from which he has come. The loop, having been high up on the steer's legs, is flipped off the legs when they are raised and this turns the steer loose, leaving him free and also placed between the rider and the herd. Seeing the herd in front of him and the rider behind him, with the possibility of being hoolihaned (turned over, end for end) if he should try to get away again, the steer most generally decides to head back for the herd. Sometimes it takes several convinces to change the ideas of an old brush snake, but this catch generally is effective and makes 'em stay put.

The six methods of making a catch described above are the ones generally used by the American cowhand. But not all cowhands are good at making all six catches. Often, because of lack of practice, they are awkward in carrying through one or more of them. The experienced Mexican *vaquero* can make more different catches than the American cowhand because the *vaquero* practices more and takes great pride in making difficult and artistic catches. The difficult catches perfected by the Mexican ropers have been used as a basis for the trick and fancy rope stunts which have been developed to a very high degree of perfection. This has been demonstrated by the work of the top trick and fancy ropers in the game.

PLATE 42

FOREFOOTING AND HOOLIHANING

BACKHAND SLIP CATCH

The backhand slip catch, made from off a horse, is one developed by the Mexican *vaquero* and is shown in the drawing at the bottom of Plate 42. The roper is making the catch as the calf ducks in behind him. When a calf is on the opposite side of a cow (that is, with the cow between the roper and the calf), the roper heads off the cow by riding around in front of her. This causes the cow to turn in back of the roper and gets the calf in between the roper and its mother. Then, as the calf passes in behind the horse, the roper slips the loop up in front of the calf, as shown in the drawing. The loop is handled the same as in the heeling catch (Plate 41), only the action is reversed so that the loop can be placed in back of the horse. This method of making a catch is a good one for a roper to practice and it should also give him an idea as to how to place an animal in position to make a catch.

Backhand forefooting is also a Mexican type of catch. A community loop (large loop) is used in making the catch and the roper does not turn loose (let go) of the loop entirely but releases the honda end of the loop and retains the main line in his hand, as can be seen in Figure 1 on Plate 43. The roper stands facing the running horse and swings (rotates) the loop in backhand motion (left to right). When the horse is almost directly opposite him, he spins around to the right and rolls the loop out in front of the horse, as indicated in Figure 2. Note that the loop is upside down. The loop is so large (which throws a lot of slack into the honda end) that it is not necessary for the roper to turn loose from the main line to make the loop reach the horse and still stay large enough to make a clean catch. By retaining the main line in the hand, the roper can jerk up the slack as soon as the horse hits the loop. In this way the roper can prevent the loop from catching the hind foot or from coming off.

Swinging a loop as described above is not generally recommended in roping horses by the forefeet or by the head when a roper is on the ground; this method of roping is for exhibition work more than for practical purposes. For exhibition purposes also, the Mexican roper often ties the end of the catch rope around his body and often half-hitches the rope around his leg too, during the tying process, the idea being that he can release the rope held in his hands when the horse reaches the other end of the rope and then can let his own weight throw the horse. The roper is generally jerked down and dragged some distance, but the horse is almost always thrown.

The sneak catch shown on Plate 44 was developed by the author and is a very practical catch when forefooting horses. It is a surprise catch and is done instantly before the horse knows what is going on. Generally a bronc, when by himself, will stand, or can be made to do so, and face the roper. The roper proceeds to advance slowly towards the horse with the loop already cocked for action. When he gets within throwing distance, twelve to fifteen feet, the loop is slipped up alongside of the horse's forelegs, as shown in Figure 1. Then the horse is made to jump into the loop as soon as it has reached its destination; the roper makes the horse do this by suddenly stepping over to the right and scaring the horse into the loop by his sudden movement. It is as soon as the loop leaves the

PLATE 43

1. FOREFOOTING: START OF BACKHAND CATCH

2. FOREFOOTING: COMPLETING BACKHAND CATCH

PLATE 44

1. FOREFOOTING: PLACING THE SNEAK CATCH

2. FOREFOOTING: COMPLETING THE SNEAK CATCH

roper's hands that he steps over towards the right side of the horse. Just two motions are made which are actually blended into one, and if they are properly timed and the distance is properly estimated, the horse can be caught on the first move he makes. The loop should be placed within about two and a half feet of the horse's forelegs so it will not be too far away to make a clean catch. The rope is handled in the same manner as in making the slip catch (Plate 40) and is called a sneak catch because the roper does have to *sneak* up to within throwing distance of the horse in order to make the catch successfully.

Roping and tying down cattle in everyday range roping work is much the same as contest or rodeo work described in this section. The only difference is that in professional contest roping every part of the equipment and every move made are planned for fast work and every second saved may mean the difference between winning and losing. Therefore the contest roper arranges every detail of his equipment so there will be no hitch in his plans and so every move to be made will accomplish some definite objective. Just a certain number of moves or manipulations constitute a complete act or job. The speed with which he is able to accomplish or complete an act depends upon how he has arranged his equipment and upon how well he has planned out his work. He is always trying to figure out how to eliminate certain movements in order to cut down their number as much as possible so that they will merge into each other in such a way as to increase speed and efficiency and save time. The equipment must be of the best so it will be dependable under any circumstances. The rope horse must be well trained and fast. A top rope horse is a very important factor in the success of a good roper. Much can be said about what a good rope horse can be trained to do to save time for the roper in his work.

The equipment of the contest or rodeo roper (not to mention his horse and saddle) generally consists of two catch ropes and two hoggin' ropes or piggin' strings (tie-down ropes); these are carried under the roper's belt as shown at the bottom of Plate 45. A piggin' string is carried on each side of the roper, so that if anything should happen to cause one of the ropes to become lost in the deal, he will be sure to have another one to tie the animal down with. The rope is so arranged, you will note, that it will slip out from under the belt without becoming tangled or fouled when the roper draws it out. The front part of the loop is grasped just above the honda, by the right hand, while the other hand holds the foreleg of the steer.

The two catch ropes are tied to the saddlehorn so they will be anchored when used. The extra rope is for an emergency, in case the roper should miss the first throw. If the first loop is wasted, the roper instantly drops it, takes down the extra rope and makes another attempt to catch the steer. The first rope is left to drag behind the horse. The extra rope is generally fastened to the saddle in such a manner that it can be quickly released when wanted. Some ropers tie this rope to the front saddle string by a single bow-knot, so it will be easily untied. Another method is to have the horn string, or rope strap, so arranged that the rope will be instantly released when the roper slips the loop off the horn of the saddle. A good method of arranging a quick-release horn string is shown in Figures 1, 2 and 3 on Plate 53. Some ropers are also in the habit of carrying a loop half-built in the extra catch rope so the loop will be easy to shake out (open up). Various techniques for carrying ropes for fast work are shown in the other drawings on Plate 53, and these should enable the reader to understand how the ropes are handled. (See also p. 180 and p. 184 of this Section.)

The contest or rodeo steer roper generally starts from the right-hand side of the chute from which the steer is to be released. In this position the roper will be able to cut in behind the steer at an angle as he proceeds to rope and bust the animal. Cutting in behind the steer (going from the right side to the left side) will give the roper a better chance to whip a loop onto the steer's horns from the right side as he passes in behind the steer, because by doing this he will cause the steer to turn outward to the right and thereby present a better position for the roper to make a catch. If the right horn is caught first, the loop will whip over the left horn as well, thus making a clean horn catch; whereas, if the roper rode directly behind the steer in making his catch, as is generally done in range roping,

PLATE 45 *Flanking*

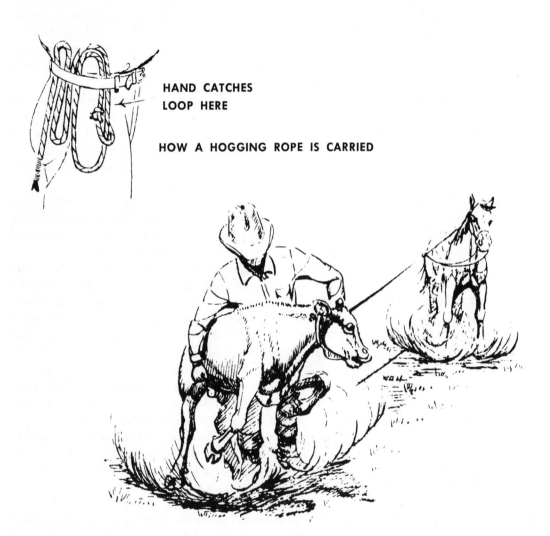

HAND CATCHES
LOOP HERE

HOW A HOGGING ROPE IS CARRIED

the loop would be very apt to fall down over the steer's nose and would naturally result in a whole-head or neck catch. This would make it more difficult for the roper to bust the animal because of lack of leverage.

When the loop has reached its destination, the roper's loop hand (right hand) makes contact with the main line when the hand is drawn back from making the throw and, almost automatically, jerks the slack out of the loop and tightens it around the steer's horns. Then, the slack in the rope having been thus jerked out as soon as the catch was made, the roper whips the main line to the right side of the steer's body. The rope will naturally fall behind the steer as the roper rides to the left of the animal to bust him (see "Busting or Throwing Critter" on Plate 46). As soon as the steer is thrown, the roper quits his horse and runs to the steer with hoggin' string or tie rope in hand and proceeds to tie the steer down while the horse holds the steer, as shown in the drawing "Start of Tying Critter Down" on Plate 46. If the horse is properly trained, he will keep the rope taut so that the steer will not be able to get up. The roper slips the loop of the hoggin' string on the top foreleg, usually the left, and jerks the slack out of the loop to tighten it around the leg. Then, as he steps back behind the steer, he passes the rope in under the hind legs; this will place the hind legs on top of the foreleg when the foreleg is drawn back. The foreleg is now pulled back as far as possible and the two hind legs are pushed forward with the left hand and held in this position, to a certain extent at least, by the roper's left leg which is placed behind them, as shown on Plate 46.

The diagrams on Plate 47 show how the three legs are crossed and tied; this is called hog-tying. The position of the hands shown on Plate 49—but more clearly at A on Plate 47—indicates how the roper starts in to make the ties. The left hand grasps the rope down close to the legs in order to hold them in place and also to hold the slack in the first wrap so there will be room to pass the free end of the piggin' string in under the wrap when completing the tie. B on Plate 47 shows slack held in the left hand, and the arrow in C shows how the end of the rope is brought through in under the first wrap. In D is shown how the rope is brought across the three first fingers of the left hand that holds the slack when the second wrap is being completed. The little finger holds the slack while the other fingers are receiving the end of the rope (D). When the rope crosses the three fingers, they automatically close on the rope and the little finger releases the slack; then the end of the rope is pulled through the loop formed by the slack in the first wrap, as shown in E. When the end of the rope is pulled through in under the wrap, the right hand grasps the rope below the left hand and the slack is pulled out of the wraps in order to tighten them so they will hold the end of the rope securely. This will prevent the steer from kicking loose and getting up before the tie is inspected by the time judge.

The time is scored from the moment the steer crosses the starting line (about thirty feet out in front of the chute) until the roper signals his completion of the tie. In the majority of contests the steers and calves are given a thirty-foot

PLATE 46

OVERHAND HEAD CATCH

UNDERHAND HEAD CATCH

BUSTING OR THROWING CRITTER

START OF TYING CRITTER DOWN

PLATE 47 *Hog Tying*

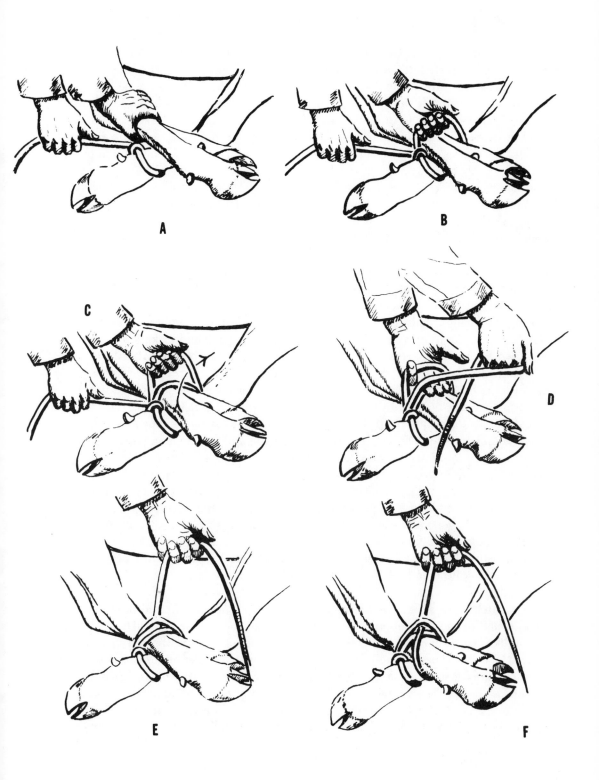

A

B

C

D

E

F

start on the roper to allow the animals a chance to get into action before the roper catches them.

In steer roping the critter generally falls on its right side when the roper busts him from the left side, or the side a right-handed roper would naturally go on. If the steer is thrown high in the air and turned completely over, he will generally land on his left side with his feet out to the right, as was shown in the drawing "Start of Tying Critter Down" on Plate 46. But if the steer is roped around the neck, he is not likely to be busted hard enough to turn him completely over because the roper cannot get sufficient leverage on the head. If the main line should happen to drop down too low alongside the steer when the rope is whipped over to the opposite side of the animal as the roper goes to the end of the rope to bust the steer, the critter will not be completely turned over either. The rope should drop down about midway along the side of the steer, just above his hocks, in order to throw the animal properly. The speed of the horse and the weight of the steer will to a great extent determine how hard the critter is thrown. Light cattle are more easily thrown than heavy stock, of course.

In everyday range work the roper generally ties the critter more securely than is customary in contest work. Three or more wraps are taken and the end of the hoggin' string is half-hitched around a leg several times to hold it securely. The extra wraps are to prevent the animal from gaining slack and kicking out. In contest work it is not necessary to tie a critter so securely because it will be untied immediately after the tie judge has inspected the tie. In range work it is best to tie the bottom foreleg instead of the top one because the animal will not be able to set up as he might do with the top foreleg tied. When the steer finds out that he can't straighten up, he will not be likely to struggle much, which helps to eliminate the possibility of his breaking loose and making a getaway.

Calf roping in contest work is done in practically the same way as on the range, with the rope tied to the saddlehorn. However, more wraps are taken in making a tie in range work in order to hold the calf more securely. The calf roper in contest work carries two piggin' strings (tie ropes) that are shorter and lighter than those generally used in steer tying. These piggin' strings, for contest purposes, should be made of smooth hard-twist rope as this rope will slip more easily when the slack is pulled out of a tie than soft rope will. A hard-surfaced rope will sink into the flesh of the critter better and this will tend to hold the tie more firmly.

Two catch ropes are allowed a roper in the majority of contests and they are generally tied to the saddlehorn unless the rules call for a loose rope. The calf roper, unlike the steer roper, generally starts from the left side of the calf chute because the calf is roped around the neck and not busted on the end of the rope as in the case of a steer. A rope is tied around the horse's neck (this is called a neck rope), and the catch rope is run through the loop to keep the horse's head turned toward the calf while the roper is on the ground. This prevents the horse from dragging the calf and choking it. The calf is generally given a thirty-foot

PLATE 48

LEG OR TRIP HOLD

start on the roper, except in cases where a shorter or longer distance is necessary because of the type of arena or enclosure the contest is held in.

As soon as a catch is made, the roper quits his horse which he at once brings to a standstill. Then he runs to the calf which is playing at the end of the rope out in front of the horse, and proceeds to flank or trip it (Plate 45 and p. 59) in order to throw it. The trip hold is shown in the drawing on Plate 48. The roper reaches under the calf, grabs the opposite foreleg with his right hand and up-ends the calf so that the critter will fall on its back and will be turned completely over. The calf will now be on its left side, as shown in the drawing entitled "Start of Tie on Calf" on Plate 49. This method of throwing a calf places the foreleg in a position where the roper will have it in his hand when he starts the tie. The piggin'-string loop is slipped over the leg and the slack is jerked out. The rope is then passed under the hind legs while the roper holds the calf down with the pressure of the left knee. The calf's hind legs are held up in place by the roper's right leg while he proceeds to wrap and tie, as shown in the second drawing on Plate 49. The tie is made in exactly the same way as in steer roping explained above and as shown in the diagrams A, B, C and D on Plate 47. Be sure to note the position of the roper in making the tie; this is very important in holding a calf while making a tie. If the rope is also in the correct position, there will be

PLATE 49

START OF TIE ON CALF

COMPLETING WRAPS

no chance for the calf to get up and the roper is placed so that he is over the calf while making the tie. When he straightens up to pull the slack out of the tie rope, he can easily turn the calf over on its other side to comply with the contest rules which prescribed this procedure so that the tie can be tested. When the calf is turned over, it will naturally struggle to free itself and if the slack is not drawn out of the tie properly the calf may kick loose and get up. When the calf is turned over, the foreleg which is tied is thereby placed next to the ground which prevents the calf from getting a foot hold during his struggle. A little practise in this method of making a tie will give the reader an idea of the why and how of the fast time made in contest calf-roping work. Each move and act merges into the other with clock-work smoothness. It is important to eliminate all excess motion down to the one-hundredth part of a second. It is not unusual for a good roper to rope and tie a calf in less than twenty seconds. Fast? Try it and judge for yourself.

Team roping in contest work is practically the same as team roping on the range (see Plate 50). Two ropers work together. They are supposed to catch the steer by the head and heels (hind legs), stretch the critter out on the ground and tie a hobble rope around its hind legs. When the tie is made the roper who done the tying signals that the tie is completed. The two ropers are stationed so one will be on each side of the chute at the start. The steer is generally given a thirty-foot start and when he crosses the deadline the ropers take to him. The roper who is to catch the steer by the head is in front of the one who is to do the heeling. If the roper in front fails to catch the steer at the first throw, he drops back and builds another loop while the other roper takes his place and proceeds to catch the steer by the head; the steer is then heeled by the first roper. The roper who catches the steer by the head stops his horse in order to stop the steer so the heeler can heel the animal. If the steer doesn't move when the heeler places his loop in under the critter, the other roper proceeds to pull the steer into the loop. When the heeler catches, he goes to the other end of the rope and stretches the animal out so it will fall on the ground. In the meantime the other roper has quit his horse and has run to the steer. If the steer is not down, he catches it by the tail as shown on Plate 50 and tails him down. As soon as the steer falls, the roper proceeds to tie (hobble) the two hind legs together with a piece of rope about two feet long. This rope is generally made of hemp. The hobble rope is merely passed around the legs of the steer and tied in a square knot. The tie judge is on hand to inspect the tie which is removed immediately after it has been inspected. The head rope is removed from the animal first and then the rope on the hind legs is slackened and the steer is let up to be put back into the wild bunch.

Tailing down and team roping on the range, which is shown on Plate 50, is practically the same as team roping for rodeo work. The chief difference is that in contest team roping, the roper on the ground who has ahold of the heel rope would be on his horse stretching the cow out while the other roper tailed the critter down.

Range team roping, while practically the same as contest work, does differ

PLATE 50

TAILING DOWN IN TEAM ROPING

in another respect: no rope is tied around the steer's legs except when the cow-hand wants to hobble the critter, which may be the case when handlin' wild mountain stock. Cattle are roped and stretched out on the ground for various reasons: to pick a brand; to doctor the critter for an injury; or for other reasons too numerous to list. If the cow is caught by only one hind leg, as shown on Plate 50, the other roper often helps to tail her down but generally one man can tail down alone. The drawing was made to show how two men throw a critter when it is roped in the manner shown. The man on the tail jerks the cow over towards him, and as the cow is thrown off balance the man on the heel rope jerks the hind feet out from under the critter; this causes her to fall on her left side. If the cow were caught by the right hind leg, the men would have changed positions to throw the animal correctly.

The hip or standing-loop catch, shown in the drawing on Plate 51, is used for heeling when a critter happens to sull and refuses to move. The roper who does the heeling throws a large loop over the hips of the animal; the other roper, meanwhile, slackens the head rope and this causes the steer to back up into the loop which is then immediately jerked up on the hind legs. Then the critter is stretched out as in team-roping work.

Tailing, or Mexican hoolihaning, is another way in which an ox is thrown by the tail. The drawing at the bottom of Plate 51 shows how the Mexican *vaquero* tails 'em down. He rides up alongside the running critter, grabs its tail which he dallies around the saddlehorn, and then throws his leg over the tail in order to pull the ox in close to the horse so he can hoolihan the animal, *i.e.* up-end it or turn it over head first. The tail hold is turned loose when the critter has been up-ended, which leaves it headed back in the direction from which it came. This method of throwing a critter has the same objective as does forefooting an ox (see above). Mexican hoolihaning leaves the animal headed back towards the herd it has quit and helps to take some of the snaky ideas out of its head. The American cowhand does not throw his leg over the critter's tail when he tails an ox from off a horse, and therefore he is not as successful in throwing the critter

PLATE 51

HIP OR STANDING LOOP

TAILING DOWN (HOOLIHANING)

properly. There is generally a good reason for doing a thing in a certain way; this fact is often overlooked by those who try to duplicate a maneuver by some other method and therefore they often fail to arrive at the desired results.

Jerking slack out of a rope after making a catch is the stunt which the contest roper is likely to be more proficient in than the average cowhand. Knowing how to handle a rope *after* a catch is made is important in roping work. No more slack than is absolutely necessary is given a loop as it travels to its destination. The hand holding the coils of a rope closes as soon as the loop reaches its objective. The loop hand (free hand) catches the main line of the rope when it is drawn back after throwing the loop and automatically jerks up the slack out of the rope in order to tighten the loop around the horns (or it may be the neck) of the animal. In roping, whether from the ground or from a horse, the roper continues to hold the main line of the rope with his loop hand from the moment he jerks the slack out of the rope to tighten the loop on the animal until the animal is either busted or turned loose. Control of the slack in a rope after a catch is made should be practised as much as the process of making the original catch.

On Plate 52, entitled "Some Catch-Rope Pointers," directions are given that are essential to successful practical rope work. The proper way to hold the coils of a rope is shown in Figure 1. As indicated there, the little finger holds the end of the rope separately and the other fingers hold the coils which are in proper order so they will slip out of the hand freely. In Figure 2 the hand is closed to prevent any coils from being released. When the coils are being released in order to give the loop slack when traveling to its destination, the three fingers holding the coils are slightly opened so the coils can slip out of the hand. The thumb of the coil hand acts as a guard or brake to stop the rope or give it slack as necessary. The roper automatically opens or closes the hand as necessity demands.

The coils should be well opened and not kinked, so that the rope may function freely. One should be sure that the coils are in proper order so that they will not become tangled when leaving the hand. Figure 3 on Plate 52 illustrates how the loop is held in the right or loop hand. The honda, indicated by the arrow, is some distance from the hand, which is as it should be. On an average, the honda end is dropped down from the hand about one-third the length of the loop. This is done to give slack in the main line of the rope. When the loop is thrown, this slack helps to prevent the loop from closing. When the loop is traveling through the air, it has a tendency to revolve; if there is no slack when the loop is being built, the loop will be checked in its flight and will have a tendency to close. The slack in the honda end of the loop also gives weight to the loop and this is a help in throwing.

Note how ropers hold a loop when ready to make a catch and you will see that the honda end is nearly halfway down the loop from the hand (see Plate 53, Figure A). It is easy to tell a green hand by the way he handles a rope, for poor handling of a rope is an unfailing sign of inexperience.

In Figure 4 on Plate 52 a dally, or wrap, is shown being taken around a

PLATE 52   *Some Catch-Rope Pointers*

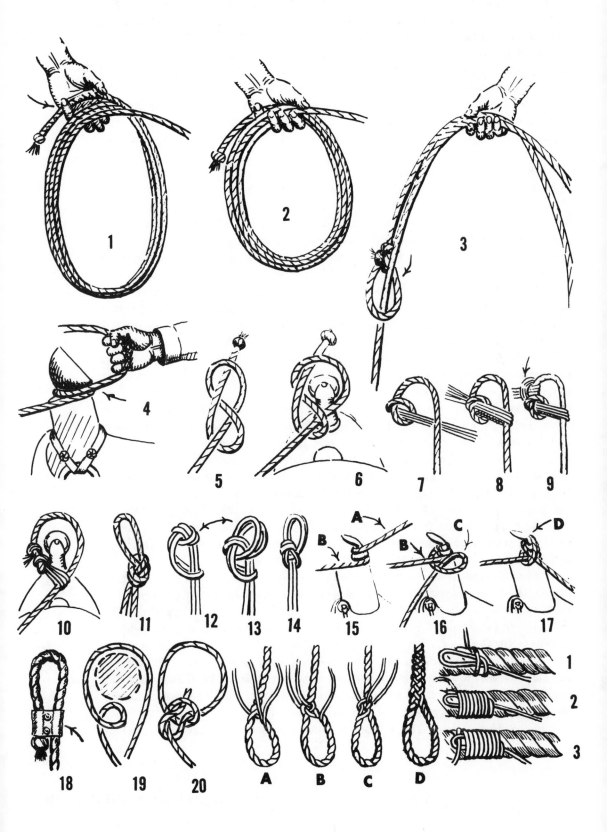

Mexican saddlehorn; the latter is especially designed for dallying purposes. One wrap around such a saddlehorn will hold as well as three wraps or more around the average saddlehorn in general use. The horns used for general dally work in the U.S.A. are wrapped with a wide leather saddle string to make them larger around so the rope will have more surface to contact, as shown in the drawing of the California and Oregon type of saddlehorn (see Plate 56, Figure 8).

By dallying, a critter can be turned loose at any time by the roper—in case of an accident or for any other reason. Dallying is necessary in handling a rawhide rope or *reata*, for it is necessary to give slack to prevent the rope from breaking.

Horn knots in general use are shown in the following diagrams: The figure-eight knot is shown in Figure 5 on Plate 52, and in Figure 6 it is shown being placed over the saddlehorn. This is a temporary knot, often used, and is easy to remove. How to make a permanent horn loop, or knot, is shown in Figures 7, 8 and 9. The end of the rope is untwisted and a common granny knot is tied at the base of the untwisted strands. The strands are then passed around the main line of the rope and brought back through the center of the knot, as shown in Figure 8. The ends are half-hitched around the rope, back of the knot, as indicated by the arrow in Figure 9. After the granny knot has been pulled down and the half-hitch has been drawn up close to the knot, the ends are cut off within an inch of the rope. A slip loop is thus formed which is placed over the saddlehorn when the roper wishes to tie his rope to the saddle, as shown in Figure 10. The loop is generally left on the horn, unless the rope is wanted for roping to be done on foot.

The take-up horn loop is often used when it is necessary to shorten a rope for close work. A horn loop is formed where it is wanted in the rope by doubling the rope and tying a plain granny knot near the looped end, as in Figure 11 on Plate 52. The loop thus formed in the end is turned back over the knot, as shown in Figure 12, and the loop is pulled back through the knot, as indicated by the double arrow between Figures 12 and 13. A double loop is thus formed in the end, as shown in Figure 14, and this is slipped over the saddlehorn. The double loop does not close up but remains loose around the saddlehorn. The take-up horn loop is used by ropers when catching calves in a corral. It is quickly made and easily untied and can be placed wherever it is wanted.

The dally-and-tie is illustrated in Figures 15, 16 and 17 on Plate 52; these Figures show how to tie a dallied rope when it is necessary to get off a horse to work on the ground while the horse holds an animal on the end of the rope. The dallied end of the rope, A in Figure 15, is passed under the main line, B, as shown in Figure 16. C shows a loop formed by a half-hitch which is slipped over the saddlehorn and pulled down tight, as indicated at D in Figure 17. The rope is securely tied and is easily removed. There are other styles of horn knots or loops which are not in general use; those shown are the practical ones for daily use by the majority of cowhands.

Figure 18 on Plate 52 is another type of horn loop that has been used by

PLATE 53 *Carrying Ropes & Loops*

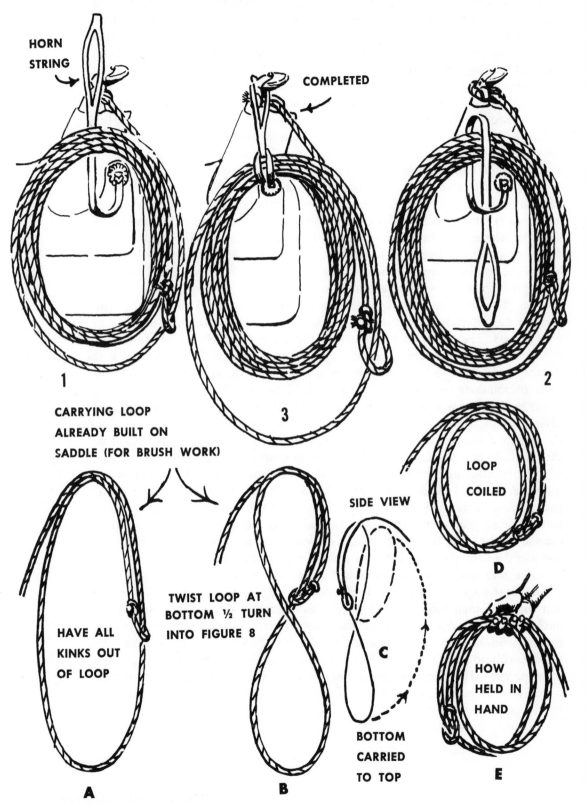

HORN STRING

COMPLETED

1

CARRYING LOOP
ALREADY BUILT ON
SADDLE (FOR BRUSH WORK)

3

2

HAVE ALL
KINKS OUT
OF LOOP

A

TWIST LOOP AT
BOTTOM ½ TURN
INTO FIGURE 8

B

SIDE VIEW

C

BOTTOM
CARRIED
TO TOP

LOOP
COILED

D

HOW
HELD IN
HAND

E

some cowhands but is seldom seen nowadays. The arrow indicates a piece of leather which is wrapped around the rope and securely riveted in the center to hold it firmly. The leather is about one and three-quarter inches wide and must be heavy and strong. The loop is slipped over the saddlehorn and drawn up tight. It is easily removed.

Figures 19 and 20 show how a bowline or necking knot is tied. This is the type of knot used mostly by cowhands and bronc busters in tying a rope around a horse's neck. It will not slip and is easily untied.

A, B, C, and D at the bottom of Plate 52 show the various steps in turning the end of a rope back and splicing it to form a honda. This splicing method is adopted when a metal honda is used in a rope (see Figure D on Plate 37).

Figures 1, 2 and 3 in the lower right-hand corner of Plate 52 show how to whip or bind the end of a rope when the roper does not want to make a knot in it such as is put in the end of a hogging string or tie-down rope. In completing the whip, the end of the loop through which the other end of the cord is run is drawn down so the loop will be just in under the edge of the last wraps (see Figure 3), and both ends of the cord are cut off close to the wraps. If the cord is wrapped tightly it will make a neat job.

On Plate 53 is shown how ropes are carried for fast work in catching wild stock in the pinnacles; these techniques are also adaptable to contest purposes (see above). The brush loop is shown in Figures A to E. Figure D shows how a built loop is doubled up to carry on the saddle; Figure E shows how it is carried in the hand to keep the loop from catching or hanging up on a limb or bush. By releasing the bottom of the loop, held by the two first fingers, the loop opens up without a kink in it and is instantly ready when the roper wants to make a catch.

Figure 3 on Plate 52 shows how a loop is carried half-cocked so it will be easy to shake out; this is the way most contest ropers carry the loop.

The quick-release horn string, located on the front saddle-string button and shown in Figures 1, 2 and 3 on Plate 53, is used by some brush hands. "Sonora" Jack Francis is credited with the idea. The string was designed to save time in getting a rope into action when a brush snake was jumped in the roughs. When slipped off the horn, the string instantly releases the coils of the rope when it is taken in the hand. The quick-release holds a rope just as securely, if not more so, as the regular method of using a horn string for tying the coils of the catch rope.

Horn strings located on the front saddle-string button are more convenient and practical than those located on the saddle fork, because they are placed farther in front and are out of the way. Also, when the catch rope is carried in such a position, wear on the fork and on the leg of the rider is eliminated. The constant rubbing of a saddle rope carried on the fork wears the leather out where the rope rubs. This decreases the value of the saddle and spoils its appearance.

19

BRIDLE
HEADSTALLS AND
BRIDLE BITS

Bridle headstalls were in use even before the development of the saddle. The history of the bridle (*freno* in Spanish) goes back into the dim past and cannot all be told here. In this section only a selection of plain and fancy types of bridle headstalls is described. Some of them were made for hard service; others were, or are, intended to be showy and admired for their fancy appearance.

The parts of a headstall are indicated in Figure 1 on Plate 54. This piece of equipment is a good all-around outfit. It is a fine piece of workmanship and is an excellent example of the best in modern headstalls; it was made by S. D. Myers. The stamping is in the latest two-tone style. The various parts are: A, the crown; B, the brow band; C, the curb strap; D, the throat latch; E, the cheek piece; and F, the noseband.

Figure 2 shows a strong, serviceable outfit in wide use. Figure 3 is a good type of one-ear headstall, popular in the northwest. It is strong and serviceable. At A in Figure 3 is indicated a pair of reins, sometimes referred to as split reins, meaning two reins that are not fastened together. Figure 4 shows a California type of split-ear headstall equipped with bit hooks attached to the bottom of the cheek pieces; this type of fastener is seldom used. Figure 5 also shows a California type of double, split-ear headstall; it is silver mounted like the one shown in Figure 4 and is not intended for rough use. Figure 6 shows a good type of ear headstall with a throat latch attached to prevent the horse from shedding the outfit.

PLATE 54 *Bridle Headstalls*

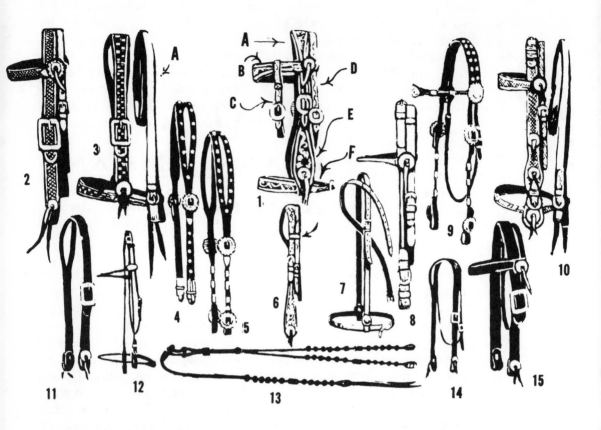

The headstall shown at Figure 7 is a combination ear and throat-latch outfit. The ear piece is formed by the throat latch which can be moved up or down to adjust it to the horse's head. This is a light and very serviceable affair designed by the author. Figure 8 shows a serviceable and light-weight outfit that is very popular. The round cheek pieces and round brow band make it a neat job. Figure 9 is a representation of a California style of headstall richly silver-mounted and decorated with silver *conchas* and spots, all of which make it a pretty showy piece of equipment. Figure 10 illustrates the Texas type of outfit, an old favorite, strong and serviceable. With the reins, it is a very complete outfit. Figure 11 shows a plain split-ear headstall made of latigo leather and used by a great many riders. It is simple to make and is a good headstall. Figure 12, depicting a full round headstall, is very light and therefore a nifty outfit for light work. A pair of rawhide, plaited reins, with *romal* (quirt) attached, is shown in Figure 13. This is a typical California product and is generally used with the California type of headstall. The reins are made with four, six, eight and twelve plaits of rawhide and are decorated with plaited knots as shown in the drawing. Figure 14 shows a combination split-ear and throat-latch headstall made of latigo leather on much the same lines as the headstall illustrated in Figure 11; it is used by a good many cowhands. Figure 15 also shows a plain latigo-leather headstall which is long on durability and mighty serviceable. It is built for rough work and is widely used.

Headstalls are often made of plaited rawhide and woven hair; this makes very attractive outfits but they are not as serviceable as those described above. Such outfits are complicated and difficult to repair once they are broken. Hair headstalls are made in a wide variety of colors and are very purty to look at, and also very expensive, for a great deal of time and patience are needed to build one. They are generally made by folks doing time in a state institution for the unruly. Such outfits are for show purposes and not for every-day range work.

Ear headstalls such as those shown in Figures 4, 5, 6, 11 or 14 are much lighter than full-rigged outfits and are easier to put on and take off. The only objection to them is that a horse can rub them off his head if he tries hard enough. Actually, there isn't much danger of this happening and they are a popular type of headstall.

Some basic explanation may make clearer the following descriptions of bridle bits and the drawings on Plate 55. It will be noted that the bit in Figure 1, used by the conquistadors, was a snaffle—that is, the mouthpiece was split in the middle. It had no other hardware in the mouth to hurt the horse. It did have a curb chain, the uppermost of the three chains shown in Figure 1. (The other chains were there simply to make a pleasant jingling and to have ornaments hung on them.) The curb chain fits under the horse's lower jaw. When the reins which are attached to the rings on the bottom of the cheek pieces (see descriptions of the parts of bridle bits below) are pulled, leverage is exerted that causes the curb chain to press against the horse's jaw. As the pressure is increased, the pain to the horse's mouth will increase. To avoid this, the horse submits to control. This is more efficient than simply exerting a pull back on the corners of the lips as is done with a simple snaffle or bar bit.

The more severe bits were developed in the course of cow work where instant obedience by half-wild horses was essential. The ring bit is an extreme application of the curb principle. The spade bit forced the horse's mouth open and if he didn't respond, it could be pulled far enough forward so that it would stick into the roof of his mouth, hurting him and in some cases even cutting. A horse that didn't respond immediately with one of these bits in his mouth was in for serious trouble. The theory is that fear of application of these severe bits trains a horse to the split-second stops and turns that are so spectacular and essential in working cattle efficiently.

The trend has been for a long time toward easier bits. As more time became available for training a horse, less cruel bits could be used. When a cowboy can pick and choose a good cutting horse and take his time about training him, the bit becomes a secondary matter. A good horse enjoys his work and takes pride in outwitting the cows.

PLATE 55 *Bridle Bits*

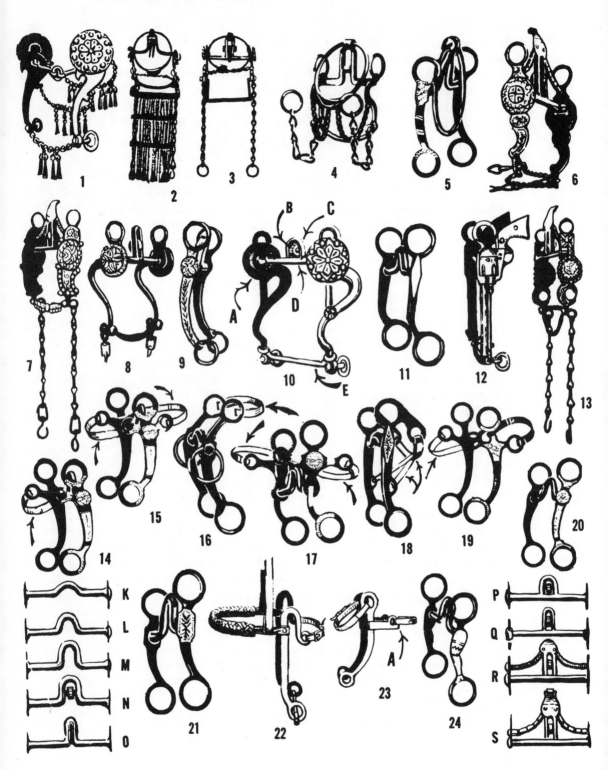

The port in a bit is the raised part on the mouthpiece. This acts in a much milder way than the spade. But when it is tightened, it does give some pressure on the roof of the mouth which, together with the pressure of the curb chain or strap under the jaw, causes enough discomfort so that under ordinary circumstances a horse will stop or slow down. Ports range from high in Figure 8 on Plate 55, to low in Figure K. The roller inside the port is merely to give the horse something to do with his tongue and to relieve him of tension, as with a human chewing gum.

Bridle bits have been in use for many centuries and no attempt is made here to trail their history any farther back than the time of the Spanish conquest of Mexico. The various parts of a bit are shown in Figure 10. They are as follows: A, the cheek piece; B, the cricket, the small roller inside the port, C, which makes a chirping noise that amuses the horse; D, the mouthpiece; and E, the bottom bar.

The bit shown in Figure 1 on Plate 55 is the type used by the conquistadors, and from it the various types of cowboy bits have been developed. The bit shown in Figure 2 dates back to the seventeenth century and the Figure 3 bit is an eighteenth-century product. Both Figures 2 and 3 are ring bits, and the port (raised part of the mouthpiece) of these bits is really a pendant put there to entertain the horse by making a noise when he is standing by himself. The Spanish riders were long on noise, which accounts for the long bit chains and gadgets that are suspended from the bottom bar and the curb rings. The chains kept up a constant clanking as the horse moved. The more noise made by bit and spur, the better they liked it. After all, what rider still doesn't like to hear those same fascinating sounds? The clank of rowel and chain are dear to all real cowhands. However, more practical considerations have caused the unessential gadgets to be discarded. But the *vaquero* still keeps a firm hold on those old-time noisemakers.

The west-coast buckaroo favors Spanish or Mexican types of equipment and is the principle user of the spade bits shown in Figures 6, 7 and 13. In Figure 4 is shown a ring bit of the nineteenth century; it is a close copy of other ring bits mentioned and is still used today by some riders. Figure 5 represents the modern type of ring bit, a typical twentieth-century product. It was developed by those well-known bit and spur makers, the Crockett brothers. It is a good bit for cold-jawed horses,* and is light in weight to boot. The ring bits when they are pulled on are severe enough to stop any horse and are only used on horses that are hard to hold.

Spade bits are a typical California product and are seldom used outside the west-coast territory. The bit shown in Figure 6 is made with a seldom-used type of hinged mouthpiece. The riveted mouthpiece shown in Figure 7 and the type of hinged mouthpiece shown in Figure 13 are in the style most generally used in such bits. Some have chain bottom pieces and some are equipped with solid

* A cold-jawed horse is one that keeps his jaw closed and is likely to get the bit in his teeth and run away with it.

bars, as shown in the illustrations. All three bits (6, 7 and 13) have high spades with crickets, or rollers, in the ports and they have rich silver mountings.

The army style of bit shown in Figure 8, when silver mounted as shown, is a good-looking bit and a very serviceable one for general use. The cheek pieces (side ports, not to be confused with the mouth port) are long and give a great deal of leverage on a horse's mouth. Figure 9 shows a very good type of bit for general use; it has a Montana-type port and long cheek pieces. It is a popular bit.

The bit shown in Figure 10 is known as the Visalia humane bit and is a recent development in bits. The mouthpiece is hinged to the top of the cheek pieces which can be turned half around, since the bottom bar is also hinged to the cheek pieces below. This is a good all-around bit, easy on a horse, with a fairly long type of cheek piece to give it good leverage.

Figure 12 shows a bit with a novel type of cheek piece that is attractive and is a good copy of a pair of Colt six-shooters. The handles are mounted with mother of pearl and the whole surface of the cheeks is overlaid in silver.

The bits shown in Figures 14 through 18 are special types which are patented by the makers. They are designed for more leverage on the horse's mouth or nose, as the case may be, and yet they are easy on the horse's mouth, as can be noted by the U-port in all of them.

Jaw straps, or curb straps, and nose straps (smothering straps) are drawn in in Figures 14 through 19 in order to show how they are attached to the bits and to give the reader an idea of how the action would be on a horse when power is applied to the bridle reins. The bit in Figure 14 is made so that the headstall rings will remain stationary when the shanks, or cheek pieces, are in action. This arrangement allows more power to be applied to the curb strap when the reins are pulled on. Figure 15 shows a bit built on the same principle as the one in Figure 14, but smothering rings are added so that a nose strap can be used; such an arrangement has the effect of a hackamore on a horse's nose. Figure 16 shows a bit built so that the curb rings will provide more leverage on the curb strap; the principle on which the whole bit is constructed is similar to that employed in the bit shown in Figure 14.

In Figure 17 is shown Crockett's hackaree bit, constructed with the nose strap and curb strap, which form a noseband, so placed that this noseband will set in the same position as a hackamore noseband. This eliminates the possibility of the nose strap cutting the circulation of air through the horse's nose. When the nose strap on a hackaree bit is placed too low, it is very apt to cause a horse to fight his head when power is applied. The headstall rings and the mouthpiece of the hackaree bit are made so they will remain stationary when the cheek pieces are in action. This makes a fine bit to use on a bronc to accustom him to a bit while he is being educated to the ways of a saddle horse.

Figure 18 represents a bit that is easy on a horse's mouth; it is made with plenty of leverage but has the same action on the curb strap as the ordinary run of stiff-port bits.

The Texas type of bit is shown in Figures 20, 21 and 24. They are the kind of bits most generally used by cowhands. They are made of one piece of steel, have short-shanked cheek pieces, are light-weight and easy on a horse's mouth.

Hackarees are shown in Figures 19, 22 and 23 and are designed to take the place of a hackamore on a horse. (See p. 143 for the description of hackamores.) They give the rider more purchase, or leverage, on a horse's nose and enable him to stop the animal more easily than can be done with an ordinary hackamore. Figure 19 shows a hackaree made by Crockett. It has a steel nose piece that is much like the one used on a bosalea and has the same effect on a horse's nose. Unless the edges of this nose piece, when they come in contact with the nose, are rounded a lot, they will have a tendency to scar the horse.

In Figure 22 is shown the Savage hackaree which is a recent development in this type of bit. It has a plaited leather nose piece which is exactly like that on a regular hackamore noseband, and the cheek pieces are so designed that more leverage is brought to bear on the horse's nose, thereby enabling the rider to stop the animal even more easily than with the ordinary type of hackaree. There is no danger of the nose piece injuring the nose of the horse. A loose bottom bar connects the shanks, which prevents them from spreading; this is an added feature. Figure 23 shows another type of hackaree which has practically the same action on a horse's nose as that effected by the bit shown in Figure 19. At A is indicated how an extension on the smothering rings holds the metal nose piece up so it cannot drop down on the horse's nose. This extension also makes it easier to put the outfit on a horse.

Bit mouthpieces are shown down in the right- and left-hand corners of Plate 55 in Figures K through S. These will give the reader a good idea as to what styles of mouthpieces are generally used in stiff, or port, bits. K is a low U-port; L, a medium U-port; M, a high U-port; and N, a Montana port which is really a high U-port with a cricket in it; O is a closed U-port. In P is shown a low half-breed port and in Q is shown a regular half-breed port. All half-breed ports include crickets. Note the hinged, or clinched, mouthpiece which is sometimes used with high-port mouthpieces. The cheek pieces are loose and a chain is used in place of a bottom bar. These types are naturally easier on the sides of a horse's mouth but will wear out where a riveted mouthpiece will not. When a bit is made of one piece of metal, there is naturally no possibility of the cheek pieces becoming loose.

In Figure R is shown a typical spoon-spade mouthpiece, easier on the horse's mouth than other types of spades. The spade is rounded and not so high as in the regular type shown in Figure S. The port braces are wrapped with copper wire. They are really tongue guards to keep the horse from getting his tongue over the top of the spade, which would injure the tongue. In Figure S is shown a regular spade mouthpiece, but with a roller top to prevent the edge of the spade from injuring the roof of the horse's mouth. The roller rolls on the surface of the mouth, whereas the spade without the roller will scrape. The port braces are covered with copper rollers which keeps the cricket company when it comes to making music.

The mouthpieces on the left side of the Plate (bottom) are types which are most commonly used in the majority of cowboy bits and they are easy on the horse's mouth. The last three mouthpieces shown on the right are severe types and if they are *properly* handled can be used effectively without injuring a horse's mouth. It all depends on how a rider handles the reins.

In Figures 2, 3, 4 and 5, already described, can be seen the differences in the structures of mouthpieces for ring bits. Figures 2 and 4 are very similar. The ring fits over the lower jaw of the horse and is a curb; it takes the place of a curb strap. It has more effect on the horse's jaw than a curb strap and, attached to a high port, it is the most powerful type of bit made. It is very effective on cold-jawed horses. It will drive their tails in the ground when plenty of power is applied. They will be easy enough on a horse if properly used; otherwise, not!

20

SADDLES

The stock saddle ridden by the cowhand of today is the end product of a long evolution and its history dates back to the dawn of civilization, which is a mighty long ways back. No attempt is made here to trace the development of the saddle any farther back than the Spanish conquest of Mexico in 1519 when the saddle was first introduced on the American continent by Cortes and his conquistadors. The type of saddle rode by the Spanish invaders had a high pommel (fork) which curved forward like that shown at A in Figure 1 on Plate 56. Some of these Spanish forks were shaped like a horse's head as shown in this Figure. The cantle (the hind part of the saddle in Figure 1) was also high and curved backward.

From this Andalusian saddle the modern saddle has developed. For more than three hundred years after Cortes and his followers had conquered Mexico, this type of Spanish saddle used by the early *hacendados* and rancheros remained practically the same.[*]

The wooden framework of the saddle is known as the tree, and over the tree rawhide is shrunk to give strength before the leather parts are added. The early trees, as is apparent in Figures 1, 2 and 3 on Plate 59, were made all in one piece. It was not until the beginning of the nineteenth century that the metal saddle-

[*] In order to follow more easily the discussion of various types of saddles in this Section, the reader who is not already somewhat familiar with the subject is referred to the list of the parts of the saddle on p. 202 and to Figure 6 on Plate 56.

horn and fork were built (bolted) onto the saddle tree. This development began in California. Otherwise the saddle tree remained practically the same; even the cantle stayed, although it was made lower than in the old-style saddle, as can be seen in Figure 3 on Plate 56 and in Figure 2 on Plate 59.

The early type of saddle was quickly adopted by the Mexican *vaqueros* and was used for many years throughout Mexico. Eventually the gourd horn, as is it often called, was evolved; this is the type of horn used on the great majority of Mexican saddles today and it is shown in Figure 3 on Plate 56. A few years after the gourd horn came into being, a new type of horn was created by those same Californians; it was a horn with a low flat top like that shown on the saddle in Figure 4. A different design of cantle was also built onto the tree; it was not nearly as thick as its predecessor and handholds were made in it, as can be seen in Figures 4 and 5. Saddle skirts, or coverings (*bastos*), were first used on this tree and large saddlebags (pockets) were part of the outfit. One-piece box stirrups replaced the old Spanish type. This saddle replaced the gourd-horn Mexican saddle used by the Texas cowhands in the early days.

Figure 5 on Plate 56 shows the first type of saddle covering used on the Spanish-American tree (as it is often called). It was made of one piece of leather and was split at both ends to fit around the horn and cantle. Straps with buckles were attached to fasten the ends together. This covering was called a *mochila* (mo-chee-la) and often was also called a "macheer" by old-time cowmen. The corners were weighted with lead-filled ornaments that were generally silver plated or else made of solid silver. These weights helped to keep the corners from curling up.

Figure 6 on Plate 56 illustrates the old-style Texas iron-horn saddle. (The drawing of this saddle is the one used as an example for the descriptions of the various parts of a saddle on p. 202). This is the type of saddle that was used by the majority of old-time trail drivers and it will be noted that the cantle and bindings consisted of a roll-type covering. The front rigging* is known as the Sam Stagg rig and was a popular style of rig while it lasted. Very few saddles are made with this rig today. The stirrups are the old-style Visalia type—wide, with a bolt through the top part to hold the sides together. On this saddle the double rig first made its appearance and was known to the cowhands of the northwest as a rim-fire rig. There were no buckle tongues in the cinch rings and so the latigos (7 in Figure 6 —long straps used to hold the saddle on) are tied in the cinch ring as shown. There were four latigos, two on the off side and two on the near side, tied in what was known as latigo ties. The side jockeys, shown at 4 (protective pads on the front, rear and sides of some saddles), were separate pieces and were fastened

---

* The words "rig" and "rigging" are used with various meanings. This should not confuse the reader. They may refer to a type or style of saddle or to its various parts. More specifically, "rigging" refers usually to the cinches, to the manner in which they are attached to the saddle, and to how they are placed. A double or single rig refers to the number of cinches used—two or one. Spanish, three-quarter or center-fire rigs refer to the placing of cinches. By extension, a cowboy may refer to the design or placing or material of any part of the saddle as "such-and-such a rig." See Sections entitled "Cinches" and "Trees and Riggings" for further details on rigs.

PLATE 56 *Saddles*

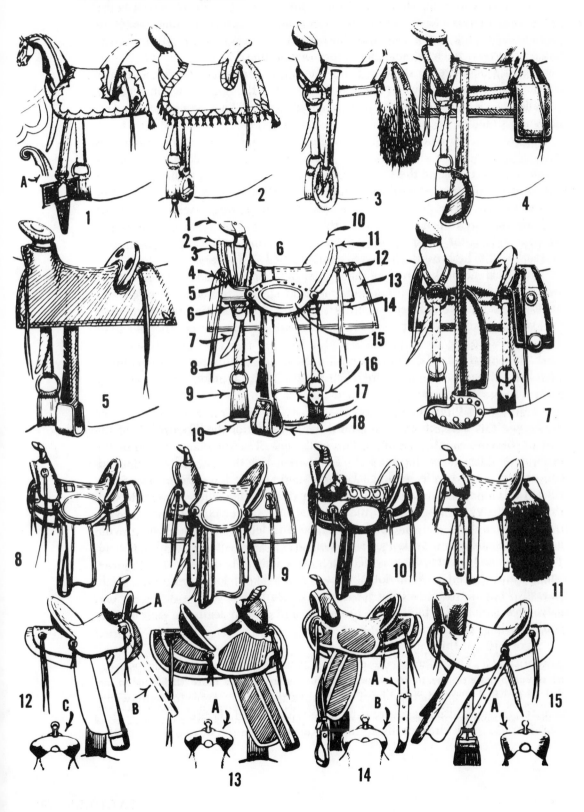

on with screws and with two short saddle strings. The horn, shown at 1, was the first steel horn used on a saddle and had a large head about four inches in diameter. The neck of the horn was short and thick; it was attached to the tree with screws very much as most metal horns are fastened to the trees today. Figures 6 and 7 on Plate 60 show in detail the horn when it is covered and as it appears before it is attached to the tree. The head of the horn shown in Figure 7 is smaller and is the size used on modern saddle trees. The fork was narrow and the cantle straight.

Figure 7 on Plate 56 shows the modern Mexico saddle. The only difference between this saddle and the old-style Mexican saddle is that fenders (17 in Figure 6) are attached to the stirrup leathers (8 in Figure 6) and that the saddle itself is made with a double rig. The old-time gourd horn is still used by most of the Mexican *vaqueros*. Because the back end of a saddle rigged with the Spanish single rig is easily tipped up when the rider is roping off it, this rig is becoming less popular and the *vaqueros* have begun to use the double rig so popular in the southwest. The brush taps (see Section entitled "Tapaderos") on the saddle in Figure 7 extend back more than the regular bulldog taps used by the American cowhand. The American styles of equipment do not greatly influence or change the styles of the Mexican riding outfits, but no doubt in time the American rigs will become more popular and will eventually supersede the old-style Mexican saddles.

Figure 8 on Plate 56 shows a typical early-day, California-Oregon saddle much like the one shown in Figure 27 on Plate 57. This type of saddle was used in the northwest cow country a great deal. It is also very similar to the saddle shown in Figure 10 on Plate 56.

Figure 9 on Plate 56 shows a typical Texas saddle of the 90's used in many parts of the cow country, including the southwest. The fork is narrow and the cantle is straight, as in the old-style Texas tree, but the roll has disappeared from the fork and cantle binding. The seat and side jockeys are made in one piece. The fenders and stirrup leathers are wider and the skirts are longer and deeper. The rigging rings are leather-covered and the cinches are made with buckle tongues (not shown) so they can be buckled into the long latigos on the near side and into short latigos on the off side. These features are all identical with their counterparts of today. The tree was long (sixteen inches) and the seat was not shaped to fit a rider but was much like a log to ride on, which generally kept the rider shifting from one side to the other to ease up on the seat of his pants. The tooling on the skirts and stirrup leathers, etc., of this saddle is wheeled and creased.

Figure 10: In this saddle, bucking rolls attached to the fork and a quilted seat are shown. The riders of these saddles were the ones who set the pace in the development of the modern saddle. The bucking rolls were the forerunner of the swell fork. Note that the horn is wrapped to make it larger for dally-welta purposes; the rider usually covered the horn with rawhide himself.

Figure 11: This drawing illustrates the next step in the development of the modern saddle; it is made on the old Billings tree. It has a dished (concave) cantle and is equipped with hair saddle pockets.

Figure 12 on Plate 56 shows a bronc-riding saddle on a Tipton tree. This type of bronc saddle has been popular and is still used by many bronc riders. Note the high fork and high, straight, deep-dished cantle on this tree. The fork is cut under and the tree is short, which places the rider up close to the fork. This tree was designed in 1913 especially for contest riding, but the fork was not cut under at the time as much as is shown in this improved Tipton tree. The rider could get his feet up into a horse's neck with this outfit. The leather is put on the tree with the flesh side out, which eliminates the slick surface of the grain side of the leather that is most generally turned to the outside. Many bronc riders have their hulls built with the flesh side of the leather on the outside. Turned this way, the leather does not easily peel up and the rider can stick with it more easily because there is more friction to the surface.

This saddle shown in Figure 12 is a three-quarter rig outfit with the stirrup leathers set well ahead, as they should be on a bronc-riding saddle. This type of tree is generally made in a thirteen-and-a-half or fourteen-inch seat for the average-size rider. Bronc-riding trees are almost always an inch or two shorter than the average stock saddle because the bronc rider always rides with his feet well forward. Also, he rides with a much shorter stirrup to enable him to hold them and to give him enough play to break the jar when the horse hits the ground. The stirrups should be short enough to allow the rider, when he stands up in them, to clear the seat of the saddle by about three or four inches. If the rider has his feet placed well forward, he will always be in a position to meet any jump that a horse might make and will naturally be able to make connection with his tree when the horse tries to shed his pack.

Figure 13 shows a Hamley form-fitter bronc-riding saddle. This tree is especially designed for riding broncs and is a very popular type for that purpose. It is just what its name implies, a "form fitter." The rider's legs are set forward so that they will automatically make contact with the fork. The cantle is of medium height and is deeply dished and shaped to conform to the body of the rider. The horn is set well forward to be out of the way of the rider when he leans forward. The seat, side jockeys and front jockeys are made of one piece of leather. The stirrups are again set well forward as they should be. In this position they give the rider more leg action and permit him to get his feet up into a horse's neck when necessary. The saddle is three-quarter rigged, the style of rig used by the great majority of bronc riders. This is a full-flower stamp saddle and high-class in every detail.

Figure 14 illustrates the Rodeo Association bronc-riding saddle. This is the regulation style of saddle used by all bronc riders in contests conducted under the management of the Rodeo Association of America (R.A.A.). The main idea behind this standardized saddle is to eliminate the possibility of any one bronc rider having an advantage over another because of a difference in the type of saddle he might be using. Since this particular style of saddle has been officially adopted, many bronc riders have discarded the saddles which they were accustomed to riding and have adapted themselves to this new style.

The tree on the Association saddle is a good all-around type suitable for roping as well as bronc riding. It has a medium-height cantle, sloped back and dished just enough to make for easy riding. The fork is well shaped and is cut under enough to give a rider a chance to make connections with it. The seat, side jockeys and front jockeys are in one piece, which naturally gives the stirrup leathers a chance to work high in front. Note the fact that the stirrups are set well forward and that they are buckled so they can be quickly and easily adjusted. The stirrups are of the narrow-bottom, ox-bow, bronc-riding type.

This is a three-quarter "E Z" rig with a flank strap (see A in Figure 14), also called a kitchen strap, attached to the back end of the saddle. This rig is designed to make the horse get high behind and usually makes the average bucking horse about fifty percent harder to ride. The strap is placed as far back in the flank as possible and then is tightened up, since at certain stages in a horse's bucking career the flank strap has a tendency to jerk the saddle back, which may become interesting.

The standard measurements of the Association saddle are as follows: fork, 14 inches wide; cantle, 5 inches high; seat, 14 or 15 inches long (but it is made in the length wanted by the individual for his own personal use); weight, about 30 pounds. The saddle is generally basket stamped when made for rodeo committees. This saddle used to be called a committee saddle, but is now generally known as the Association saddle. It was originally designed by Hamley of Pendleton, Oregon.

Figure 15 illustrates the Ward special bronc-riding tree. It was developed in 1914 and was especially designed by the author for riding broncs without stirrups and for contesting. The fork of the tree is shown in Figures 8 and 21 on Plate 59 and Figure I on Plate 60. It was made so the fenders and skirts could be easily removed to strip for action. It is a very popular type of tree for the purpose for which it was designed and is still used by a great many riders. The cantle is so shaped that it conforms to the rider's body and it slopes back from the rider much more even than appears in this illustration.

The four bronc saddles just described are the outstanding types of saddles used for settin' above the rough ponies.

Figure 16 on Plate 57 illustrates a fine example of modern saddle-making. It shows clearly the modern two-tone, hand-carved decorations in this S. D. Myers product. The black background of this stamping makes the designs stand out in bold relief; this type of decoration is far more attractive than the old style of stamping. This saddle is built on a Myers special tree, a good all-around type of tree. The saddle has a low, sloping cantle and a medium-wide swell fork which slopes well forward. The seat is built high in front and is well shaped for riding comfort. The stirrup leathers pass through the loop fenders, as shown in the drawing. The saddle is double rigged and is built for service. This outfit is one of the finest pieces of saddlery the author has ever located and is ultra modern.

PLATE 57   *Saddles (Cont.)*

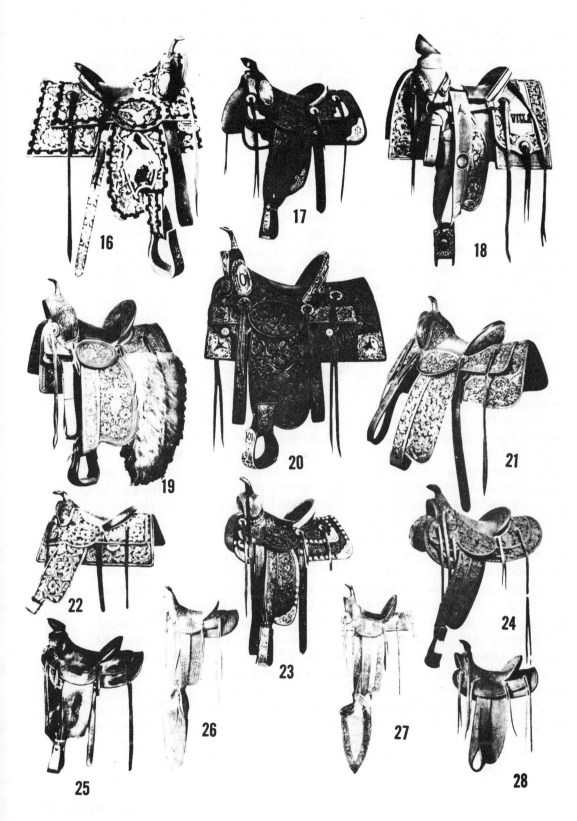

Figure 17 shows a Hamley low-boy roper tree, another fine specimen of the modern type of saddle, with lavish silver mountings and finely hand-carved leather. The saddle is built for roping purposes and has a tree similar to that shown in Figure 16. The horn is a half-breed Mexican type and is a good one for dally work. It is double rigged and is a fine piece of workmanship. It was especially made up for a prize saddle to be given to the winner of the steer-roping contest at the Pendleton, Oregon, roundup.

Figure 18 shows a modern Chihuahua Mexico saddle. This saddle is shown because it has a type of tree different from the one shown in Figure 7 on Plate 56. This saddle is also made by Myers, in the U.S.A., but the tree is made in Mexico and is called the Chihuahua tree. The horn and cantle differ in shape from those of the old-style gourd-horn tree. The cantle is dished and the horn is lower and has a thicker neck than the old-type horn. Note the silver-inlaid, steel, box-type stirrups, and the silver-inlaid rigging buttons and rings common on Mexican saddles. This saddle, like the majority of other Mexican hulls, has the old-style Spanish rig. The seat is half covered, but the fork is uncovered, like all such saddles. This saddle is a copy, so it is said, of the saddle rode by the famous Pancho Villa, as indicated by the name on the saddle pockets. The workmanship and material in this outfit are high class and the hand carving is in the modern, two-tone relief style.

Figure 19 on Plate 57 shows a Colorado type of saddle popular in the beginning of the twentieth century. It is the first of the modern saddle types. The nickel horn, swell fork, dished cantle, quilted seat and large angora-hair saddle pockets were all combined in the majority of saddles used in the northwest. This made a rig that weighed between forty-five and fifty pounds. The skirts and fenders were made large. These saddles set the range afire for several years, but eventually the cowhand began to lighten his pack by eliminating the large saddle pockets and the wide fenders and skirts. These saddles were also all the rage in the southwest, but the hair pockets were seldom used there. The stamping on the leather is the regular flower stamp, hand-carved, as is all flower-stamp work on saddles that are shop made.

Figure 20 shows the 101 Ranch $10,000 saddle made by S. D. Myers, although the illustration does not really do the saddle justice, for this is the finest fancy saddle ever built, at least so far as the author has ever been able to learn. This saddle was made for the Miller brothers of the famous 101 Ranch who were also owners of the once celebrated 101 Ranch Wild West Show. The saddle has been displayed throughout the U.S.A. and in foreign countries. It is mounted with fifteen pounds of gold and silver in which are set 166 diamonds, also 120 sapphires, 17 rubies and 4 garnets. The horn is fine silver and gold, inlaid, and the stirrups are bound with silver, gold-overlaid. The stamping is fine hand carving and is in the flower design.

Figure 21 depicts an all-around stock saddle. It can be said that this style of saddle, generally speaking, is a good example of the make-up of the saddle rode by the majority of cowhands in the cow country today. It is popular in the north and south and the only alterations that would be necessary to please some of the riders of the north would be the changing of the double rig to a single rig, and the square skirts to skirts in the round style. But even without any change, it will suit the majority of southern cowhands and a great number of riders in the central part of the range. The cantle and fork are of medium height and width, making a well-designed tree. The stamping adds up to a fine piece of hand carving and the whole outfit is a good piece of work.

Figure 22 shows an ultra-modern type of saddle. It was designed for contest or rodeo bulldogging and roping work. The extremely low, narrow fork and cantle make this saddle an easy one to get out of when a rider is bulldogging a steer or roping for fast time. The tree sets low on the horse and reduces the leverage on the horn to the lowest point of resistance possible from a roping saddle. Note that the seat, side jockeys and front jockeys are made all in one piece. The cantle has an old-style roll binding which is used more often on the modern type of trick-riding saddle than on any other type of present-day outfit. The fenders and the stirrup leathers are also made in one piece. The style of stamping is that of the modern, two-tone, bold relief in the hand-carved flower design. This is a double-rig saddle.

Figure 23: Here is another example of the saddler's art, a Porter product. It is built on an improved Tipton tree and is covered with black leather. The elaborate silver mounting makes a pleasing contrast to the black leatherwork. This is a fine piece of saddlery and demonstrates effectively what can be achieved in the building of quality saddles.

In Figure 24 you have a Porter saddle on a Lee Robinson tree. This is a modern roping saddle which has been very popular among contest or rodeo ropers. The tree was designed by the late Lee Robinson who was himself a prominent rodeo roper, bulldogger and all-around cowhand,

> *Who has crossed the Great Divide,*
> *And is driftin' down the slope,*
> *Gone where they always ride*
> *And where they always rope.*

This Porter saddle is made with a twelve-inch swell fork and a two-and-a-half-inch cantle which slopes back. The saddle has a shaped seat and a low horn. The skirts are of a neat, round pattern. It is double rigged and weighs about thirty-two pounds. It is full-flower stamped in the modern two-tone style and is a dandy job. It is used by many bulldoggers as it is well designed for the sort of work they do.

Figure 25, the Guadalajara, a modernized old-Mexico type, bids fair to become so popular that it may supersede the old gourd-horn style of saddle used in Mexico today. The fork and horn are of the type used on the Guadalajara saddle tree of Mexico and the bars (sides) and cantle are of the American type. In other words, this is an Americanized Mexican saddle. It is a Visalia product and is made with a flat-plate, three-quarter, double rig. It is a well put up outfit and will no doubt find favor with many of the *vaqueros* across the border, as well as with many riders in the U.S.A. It is essentially a dally-welta saddle, but it can also be tied to.

Figure 26: This saddle has practically the same tree as the saddle shown in Figure 27, but it has a narrow swell fork, a slightly lower cantle, and the skirts are a little deeper. The full, double, California-style stirrup leathers are in evidence on this center-fire rig. The taps that protect the rider's feet are long, round-tipped, one-piece, monkey-nose, and the stamping is in a checkerboard style very similar to a basket stamp. This type of rig has been popular on the west coast (California, Nevada, and Oregon) for a long time and is a good all-around outfit.

Figure 27 depicts the Oregon type of saddle of the 90's. The skirts shown in this illustration are square, but round skirts were most generally used with this saddle. The tree is short (fourteen inches), the horn is high and full sloped, and the cantle is high and straight. The stirrup leathers are of the full, double style and twisted; this has been characteristic of west-coast saddles. This particular Oregon type is center-fire rigged and the stamping is known as a flower-border stamp. The taps are of the long, one-piece, monkey-nose style. The seat is quilted like the one shown in Figure 19. (The quilted seat originated in California, however.) This saddle, like the ones illustrated in Figures 26 and 28, has the famous D. E. Walker hull.

Figure 28 illustrates an old California saddle which became popular in the 90's and is still hitting the high spots. The fork and horn are low and the cantle is dished, slopes back with a full slope and is low, which makes an easy riding seat. This is a loop seat because the stirrup leathers are exposed in the seat. The fork is narrow and the stamping is a basket stamp. The skirts are of typical California style, small and round. This saddle also has a center-fire rig.

Parts of the saddle: In Figure 6 on Plate 56 the various parts of a saddle are indicated by numbered arrows. 1, the HORN, which in the later American saddles was made in a separate piece and bolted down onto the fork; the American cowboy uses this horn to tie one end of the catch rope to when roping. In dallying, of course, the "home" end of the rope is not tied to the horn. 2, the FORK, which corresponds to the pommel in other types of saddles, is part of the tree (the frame of the saddle). 3, the FORK BINDING. 4, the FRONT JOCKEY; the jockeys are leather pieces or pads placed on the saddle skirts (see 13 below) at the front, rear and side (see 12 and 15 below). 5, the RIGGING, known as the Sam Stagg style of (double) rigging. Here the reference is to the straps to which the rigging rings are attached on either side of the saddle tree (see Figures 13 and 19 on Plate 59). 6, the RIGGING itself, showing the rigging ring and how the latigo (see

7) is tied to it. **7,** a LATIGO; this is a long leather strap that is fastened at one end to the rigging ring and at the other end to the cinch ring. The latigo holds the cinch tight under the horse (see **9**). **8,** the STIRRUP LEATHER. **9,** the FRONT CINCH, this saddle being a double rig with two cinches, one front and one rear; many saddles have only one cinch and are known as single rigs (see Figures 17 and 18 on Plate 59.) The cinch is a broad band with a metal ring at either end; it stays fastened to the off latigo. It is passed under the horse and the latigo on the near side is run through the cinch ring and pulled tight and tied securely (see Section entitled "Cinches"). **10,** the CANTLE. **11,** the CANTLE BINDING (the binding shown here is the old-style roll binding). **12,** the BACK JOCKEY. **13,** the SADDLE SKIRT, or *basto,* a leather plate resting on the horse's back, under the saddle proper. A saddle pad is placed under the skirt to protect the horse's back (see below). **14,** a SADDLE STRING; there are usually several saddle strings hanging from the front and rear of the saddle, on either side. They are used to tie necessary equipment, such as a slicker, onto the saddle. **15,** the SIDE JOCKEY; this pad protects the rider's leg from chafing. **16,** the FLANK (rear) CINCH. **17,** the FENDER, or leather shield, fastened to the stirrup leather; it serves to protect the rider's leg from the horse's sweat. **18,** the STIRRUP (see Section entitled "Stirrups and Tapaderos"). **19,** the CINCH HOBBLE, or connecting strap (see Section entitled "Cinches").

In addition to these parts of the saddle, there is the short latigo which is not shown in Figure 6 because it is located on the off side of the rigging; this is a latigo which is double and about eighteen inches long to which the cinch is buckled on the off side of the rigging. Also not shown here because it is located on the off side is the rope strap or HORN STRING. This is a short latigo used to fasten the catch rope to the saddle on the off side of the fork.

Saddle pads and blankets: A good saddle blanket or pad is a very necessary article of the cowhand's equipment and is essential to protect his horse's back and to keep it in good condition. But no matter how good the blanket is, the horse's back can be easily hurt by an improperly constructed saddle or an old, worn-out, weather-beaten hull which has been warped out of shape. Also, much depends on the rider and the way he sets in the saddle. If he is constantly sitting half-cocked, riding on one side with most of his weight thrown on one stirrup, this is very likely to hurt a horse's back and the rider shouldn't be surprised if this happens. A rider should keep himself straight up in the saddle with his weight evenly distributed on the tree so the pressure will be equalized on the horse's back.

In Figures 1 through 6 on Plate 58 are shown different types of saddle pads:
1. The Corona saddle pad made of heavy carpet and leather-trimmed and bound. It is utilized as a cover for a sweat pad like that shown in Figure 2 and is used under the California type of saddle. It protects the saddle skirts from sweat.

PLATE 58 *Saddle Pads & Blankets*

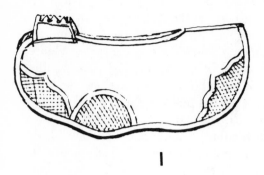

1

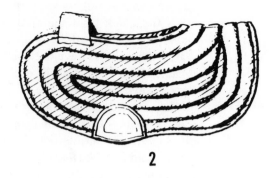

2

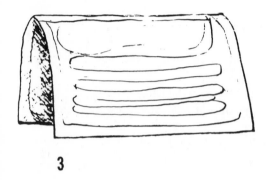

3

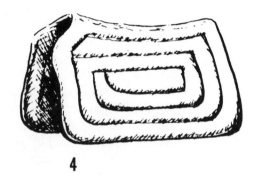

4

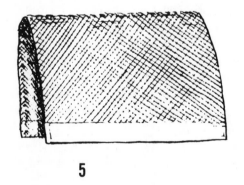

5

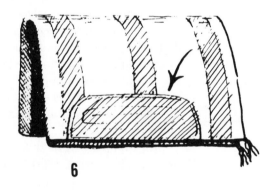

6

2. The Corona hair pad which is leathered and is made to be used in conjunction with the pad shown in Figure 1. It is a dandy sweat pad of good thickness and should be used with round-skirted saddles.
3. The old-style saddle pad, filled with hair or felt which was once used by some riders.
4. A saddle pad made of ducking, filled with deer hair and a good pad for general purposes.
5. A woven hair blanket that makes a good sweat blanket to place underneath a regular saddle blanket because it is very porous, is cooler on the horse's back and is more springy than the common types of saddle blankets. A good hair pad or blanket is the best type of sweat blanket.
6. The popular Navajo saddle blanket which is doubled and made of wool in a combination of different colors and designs. This type of blanket is perhaps used more than any other as it is good protection for the horse's back, will absorb sweat well, can be washed and will last much longer than most blankets. Some riders use a small single blanket underneath the Navajo to serve as a sweat blanket; this helps protect the Navajo and makes it last longer.

Another common type of saddle blanket used by many riders is very like a bed blanket, only not so large. It is folded so that it will be double and is used generally with a sweat blanket underneath it. Most of these blankets are made of cotton, although some are part wool and part cotton. They generally have one or two contrasting stripes as a border.

There is also a woolen blanket, made in Mexico, known as the *carleitas* blanket. It is very similar to the Navajo but it comes in a solid color, generally white. It is an excellent saddle blanket much used in the southwest.

Saddle blankets are sometimes made of mohair—goat's hair—and these are greatly superior to the woolen variety but they are more expensive. Nevertheless, they are now in general use.

Saddle blankets should be washed once in a while to free them from the dirt that they naturally accumulate. This will prevent them from getting hard and give them longer life. Caution is always necessary to be sure that the blanket is free from wrinkles or the bunches of hair that rub off the horse's back and knot up under the blanket. Any other foreign matter that may cling to the blanket should be brushed off. It is important to avoid any unevenness of surface which may cause the horse's back to be injured while he is being rode.

Saddle blankets should be leathered (see the arrow in Figure 6) to protect them from the wear caused by latigos and stirrup leathers. Saddle blankets will last much longer if the surfaces that take the most friction are protected with wide pieces of leather. This leather can be sewed to the blanket.

PLATE 59 *Trees & Rigs*

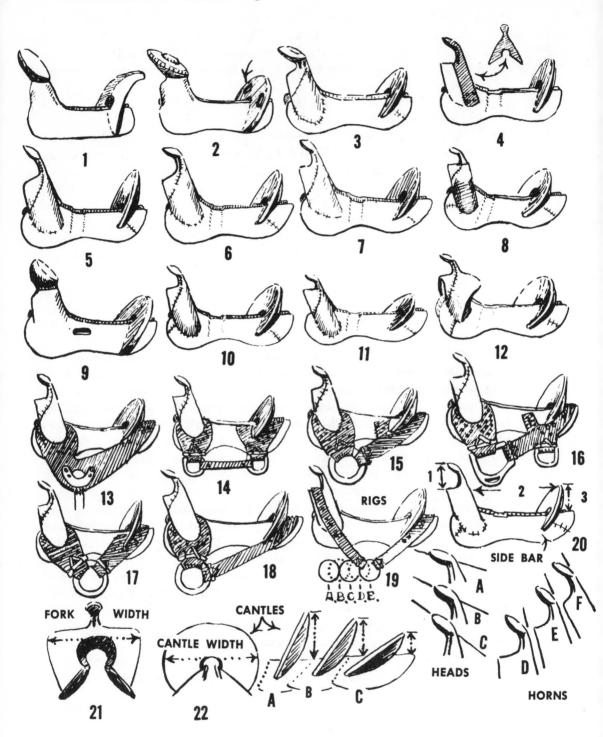

1

2

3

4

5

6

7

8

9

10

11

12

13

14

15

16

17

18

19

20

RIGS

A.B.C.D.E.

1

2

3

SIDE BAR

FORK WIDTH

21

CANTLES

CANTLE WIDTH

22

A B C

A
B
C

HEADS

F
E
D

HORNS

21

TREES

AND

RIGGINGS

The saddle trees shown on Plate 59 will give the reader some idea of the development of the stock-saddle tree. Some of these have already been described in the Section on saddles and therefore they will be only briefly described here.

Figure 1 illustrates the first Spanish-American stock-saddle tree with the original saddlehorn and the Andalusian style of cantle. This tree is made of one solid piece of wood and is covered with rawhide to strengthen it, as is done for all stock-saddle trees as well as for other types of saddle trees. This rawhide covering helps to hold the shape of the tree and prevents it from warping. The material used in many of these first saddle trees was hard wood, and some of them were not covered with rawhide but were often inlaid with pieces of wood of different colors and then were highly polished like a fine piece of furniture. But the majority were covered with rawhide. (The reader is referred back to Figure 3 on Plate 56 to note the second stage in the evolution of the saddle itself.)

Figure 2 on Plate 59 illustrates the next step in the development of the Spanish-American saddle tree. This type of tree was created a short time after the one illustrated in Figure 1 had been built, and it shows the large flat-top horn which was so popular with the *vaqueros* of those early days. The top of the horn often measured seven inches in diameter; it had a short thick neck. The cantle is made with handholds cut into the sides, as shown. This tree was also made of one solid piece of wood and was covered with rawhide.

Figure 3 on Plate 59 shows the original Texas iron-horn tree. The horn and fork and cantle are low. This tree is made of four pieces of soft pine covered with rawhide. The present-day saddle trees are not made out of hard wood. It is the prevailing opinion of many who are familiar with the structure of the stock-saddle tree that hard wood is too heavy and too difficult to work.

Figure 4 shows the steel-fork, Sam Stagg tree which was the next innovation in the development of the saddle tree. The horn and fork are made in one piece. The arrows in the Figure point to the side and back views of the horn and fork. This new type of equipment was called the steel fork and the name is still used by many saddle-manufacturing concerns in the eastern section of the U.S.A. to designate the steel-horn saddles made up by them and classified as cowboy saddles. The steel fork was riveted to the side bars (sides) of the tree and because it formed only one half of the fork, the front half was made of wood, as can be seen in the drawing. The horn was much smaller than the old Texas iron horn, and higher. This style of fork enjoyed only a short period of popularity because it would work loose when it had been put to the test of heavy roping. Therefore it was discarded in favor of the improved type of Texas iron horn shown in Figure 6 of Plate 60. The cantle on this tree (Figure 4 on Plate 59) was made higher than in other types of saddles, but it was straight. This tree, of course, was covered with rawhide.

Figure 5 illustrates the Visalia tree and is typical of the old-style California and Oregon type of tree. It had a high steel horn and a cantle which was slightly dished (concave). This was, and still is to a certain extent, a popular type of tree manufactured by Walker of Visalia. All these old trees were made on short side bars and this tended to hurt a horse's back. The trees that are used today have sides that are better shaped and longer; they extend well back of the cantle and this has eliminated the tendency to hurt the horse.

Figure 6 shows the Nelson tree which was popular in its day. It is very similar to the old Ladesma tree that was also an old favorite.

Figure 7 illustrates the Taylor tree, in the same class as the Ladesma, Nelson and Visalia trees, all of which were popular types in the 90's. These same trees are still popular but have been much improved and are not the same today as they were some fifty or more years ago.

Figure 8 shows the original Ward special bronc tree designed especially for bronc-riding purposes. It is a slick bronc-riding tree with a medium cantle shaped to conform to the rider and it is a popular type of bronc tree. The fork of this tree is shown in Figure 21 at the bottom of Plate 59 and in Figure I on Plate 60.

Figure 9 on Plate 59 shows the modern Chihuahua Mexico tree which is also shown in the modern Chihuahua Mexico saddle in Figure 18 on Plate 57. It is a type of tree that differs from the old-style Mexico saddle illustrated in Figure 7 on Plate 56. The cantle is shaped and dished and the horn is low and thick necked.

Figure 10 shows the Association tree used in the Rodeo Association of America contests. It is the regulation bronc-riding tree of the Association saddle already described in the Section entitled "Saddles."

Figure 11 on Plate 59 shows the modern roper type of tree, similar to the Lee Robinson tree and the Hamley roper, etc. The fork, horn and cantle are low and sloping, a construction especially suitable for contest roping work in rodeos.

Figure 12 illustrates the Hamley form-fitter tree and is a bronc-riding tree. It has a cut-under fork and the cantle is deeply dished so it will conform to the shape of the rider. This is a popular type of tree and has been copied to a certain extent by many tree makers.

Six of the most popular types of riggings used on a stock saddle are shown on Plate 59. Although there are several patent types of riggings and rings, those shown here are the principal ones that have made good. In these rigs improved methods of construction have been employed which are superior to those used in the old style illustrated in Figure 19 of Plate 59.

Figure 13 illustrates the Hamley flat-plate, three-quarter rig (patented). It is made of heavy leather with a flat crescent-shaped metal plate attached to it like that shown in the drawing. It lies flat and eliminates the lump which is usually formed in under the stirrup leathers by the other style of ring rigging; this type of rig also permits the stirrup leather to swing freely over the top of the rigging, which is an improvement on the regular three-quarter rig shown in Figure 15. It makes a rider feel like he was really setting down next to his horse, which is to be desired.

Figure 14 shows the double rig used with two cinches. It is generally called the Texas rig and is called the rim-fire rig by the northern cowhand because the flank cinch is used (see Section entitled "Cinches"). It is the type of rig put on modern roping saddles and is the style most popular in the southwest.

Figure 15 depicts the three-quarter single rig, the favorite rig of the northwest and the type used on the majority of bronc-riding saddles because it sets better on a horse than most single rigs used for bronc riding. It is the style that is used in dally work by most riders. The stirrup leather underneath is run through the rigging ring which has a flat surface and is made of stainless steel. This is a popular type of rigging ring used on the majority of single-rig saddles.

Figure 16 illustrates the three-quarter double rig with the Hamley "E Z" rigging ring in the three-quarter position. A flank ring is attached so that a flank cinch can be used if wanted. This is the best all-around type of rigging, is very popular in the northwest and is becoming more popular in the southwest too. It can be used either as a three-quarter rig without the flank cinch, or as a double rig, as desired, which is a good combination. The stirrup leather has more play in this "E Z" ring.

Figure 17 shows the center-fire rig. This is, and has been for a long time, a favorite type of rig on the west coast. It is generally called a California rig because it is used so much by the California buckaroos. The rigging ring is placed in the center of the tree, which gives it an even leverage on the front and back of the tree. Riders who use this style of rig are almost always dally-welta men, because a saddle with this equipment will not set down on a horse's back like a saddle with a double rig. The stirrup leathers work in front of the rigging ring. This type of rig permits a saddle to rock on a bucking horse; it will set farther ahead, or forward, on a horse's back and is easier to ride in than the double-rig outfits.

Figure 18: In this drawing you see the Spanish rig, a style of rig most generally used on Mexican saddles. The rigging ring is placed in the same position as the front rigging ring on a double-rig outfit. This type of rig has a tendency to let the back of the tree kick up behind when a critter has been roped in front of the rider. Because of this drawback Texas riders converted the rigging into a double rig by having a flank ring placed near the back end of the tree; the flank ring held the back end of the saddle down.

Figure 19 shows the positions of the rigging ring in the different styles of single rigs. The rigging shown is the center fire, indicated at E, and is the old-style method of attaching the rigging onto the old-time saddle. The letters indicate the positions of the various rigs: A is the Spanish rig; B, the seven-eighths rig; C, the three-quarter rig; D, the five-eighths rig; and E, the center-fire rig.

Saddle makers will rig a saddle to suit the rider. Some riders prefer to ride with a five-eighths rig while others prefer the seven-eighths rig. But the double rig, the three-quarter rig, and the three-quarter double rig are the set most generally used in the cow country today. The center-fire rig is popular only on the west coast and the three-quarter rig is fast replacing this old California stand-by.

Figure 20 shows tree measurements. The height of the saddlehorn is measured from the top of the fork to the front edge of the head, as shown at 1 in this Figure. The length of the seat is measured from the top of the inside edge of the cantle to the back of the fork, as indicated at 2. The height of the cantle is measured from the top of the side bar to the top of the cantle, as indicated at 3. The side bar of a tree is indicated by the arrow at the bottom of the tree.

Figure 21: This drawing shows a saddle fork and how it is measured across the front or back, as indicated by the dotted line. The measurement is taken from the extreme outside edges of the fork.

Figure 22 shows a cantle board which is measured across the cantle from the extreme outside edges, as indicated by the dotted line.

Figures A, B and C under the heading "Cantles" indicate the different slopes of a cantle. A shows the high straight cantle, 5½ to 6 inches high; B shows a medium height and slope in a cantle 4½ to 5 inches high; C shows a low, full-slope cantle 3½ to 4 inches high. Extremely low cantles are fully sloped and are 2½ inches high. The full-slope low cantles are the type used on contest roping saddles.

Heads of saddlehorns, showing their different slopes, are shown in the drawings labeled "Heads." A is a one-half slope; B, a medium slope; C, a full slope. The drawings labeled "Horns" show: D, a straight horn; E, a half-slope horn; and F, a full-slope horn. Horns are also sometimes made with different widths of heads, but the standard width is the one most often used. There is no need to say anything further in this connection, since the widths of the heads are accepted "as is."

22

HORNS

AND

FORKS

Almost all of the horns shown on Plate 60 have been described in the Section entitled "Saddles" and it is therefore not necessary to go into great detail at this point concerning the subject.

Figure 1 on Plate 60 shows the type of front (pommel) used on some of the Spanish saddles of the conquistadors in 1519. The front was high and curved forward and was wide at the base, acting as a shield for the rider's legs. Some of these horns were fashioned into the shape of a horse's head, as shown in the drawing.

Figure 2 shows the original Spanish-American saddlehorn evolved from the Andalusian saddle of the conquistadors (Figure 1). It was developed in the early part of the nineteenth century in California.

Figure 4, depicting the low flat-top horn, was developed from the horn represented in Figure 3. This horn (Figure 4) made its appearance a few years after its predecessor shown in Figure 2 was evolved, and it became the popular type of horn in the region north of the present Mexican border. The top of many of these old horns often measured seven inches in diameter, and some even more than that according to the accounts of some old-time cowmen.

Figure 3 shows the so-called gourd horn often mentioned in the Section entitled "Saddles." It is a type of horn popular among Mexican *vaqueros* and has been used by them for nearly a century. This type of horn is still to be seen on the great majority of their saddles today. It was evolved directly from the first or original horn shown in Figure 2.

PLATE 60 *Horns & Forks*

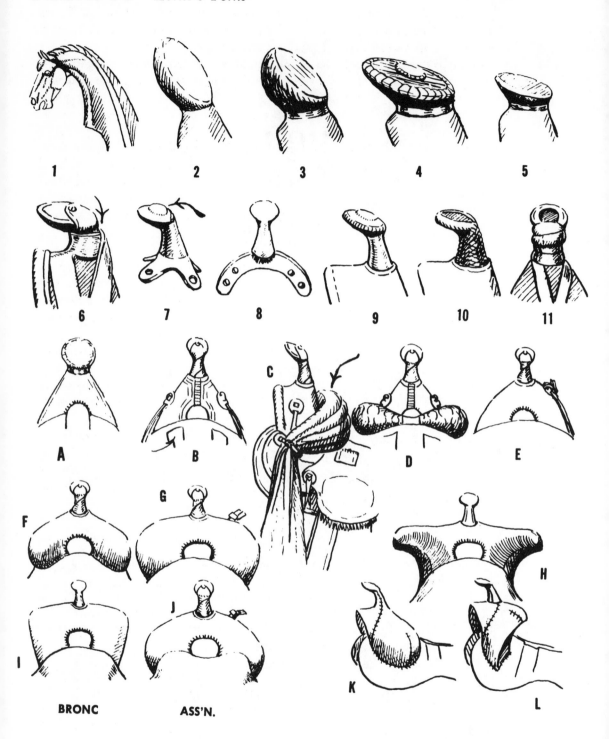

1   2   3   4   5

6   7   8   9   10   11

A   B   C   D   E

F   G   H

I   J   K   L

BRONC   ASS'N.

Figure 5 shows a small type of horn very similar to the one shown in Figure 4. It was evolved just prior to the introduction of the metal or iron horn shown in Figure 6. It had a short life and was never widely used.

Figure 6 depicts the original Texas iron horn as it looks when covered. This drawing shows the top of the fork on the old iron-horn Texas saddle that was shown in Figure 6 of Plate 56. The head is large, about four inches in diameter; the neck is short and thick. It is practically the same horn as that shown in Figure 7 except that it is much heavier.

Figure 7 shows the standard type of steel horn and is practically the same as the original iron horn of Figure 6, except that it is made with a small head about two inches in diameter. The neck is small and well proportioned. This style of horn is always covered. It is attached to the tree with long screws, so long, in fact, that they very seldom work loose. It is the horn used on the great majority of stock saddles.

Figure 8: This is the nickel or combination-metal horn very popular in the northwest. It came into use at the turn of the century. It is not covered and comes in brass, bronze and gun metal, but the nickel variety is the most popular. The base of the horn is set down in a slot cut into the top of the fork and is bolted to the fork. It is known as the Samson horn (if the author's memory of it is correct) and has the modern type of anchorage used on many saddles.

Figure 9: This is a nickel horn with a beveled head extending back to make an offset. This offset is designed to prevent a rope from slipping up over the top. The edge of the top is scored to give it an artistic finish. This horn is sometimes used on high-priced saddles but is not in as general use as the one shown in Figure 8.

Figure 10 depicts a rawhide-covered horn. Here you can see how some horns are covered by plaiting rawhide around them. This type of covering is put over nickel horns as well as over the regular steel horns. The steel horns are always covered with the rawhide that is on the tree, but they are often covered with this type of plaiting instead of the regular rawhide covering.

Figure 11 shows a rawhide- or leather-wrapped horn. The wrapping is often put over the regular leather-covered horn in order to make the neck large and to provide more surface for a dally rope. This is a popular style of horn covering used on the Oregon, Nevada and California saddles favored by dally-welta riders. It is also popular with many cowhands in the northwest. The ends of the string (wrapping) are fastened in under the opening of the gullet in the back of the fork.

The evolution of the saddle fork is shown at the bottom of Plate 60; these illustrate the development of the modern swell-fork so popular with present-day cowhands no less than with other riders. The word "pommel" was often used in the very early days of the range-stock industry and is still used by folks who are not familiar with things typically western. The present-day cowhand never refers to the front of his saddle as the pommel but always calls it the fork.

Figure A on Plate 60 shows the fork of the Mexican saddle and is the type of fork on which the original saddlehorn was formed. It is the style used on the early-day saddles and continued in use up until the iron-horn Texas saddle tree came into being. This Mexican saddle fork is practically the same style of fork as the one used on the old Texas tree.

Figure B shows the style of fork used on the old style of Texas and California saddle trees on which the iron horn was first used. This style of fork is known as a narrow fork because it did not have any bulge on the side. It was also called a straight fork.

Figure C: In this drawing the author has attempted to show the beginnings of the swell-fork idea. It depicts an old-style narrow or straight fork of a saddle to which a slicker slung across the front of the saddle seat has been tied; the slicker is tied to the front saddle strings. The bronc riders in the northwest were the first to do this. The slicker became a sort of bumper and leg hold for the bronc rider to bump against while a horse was bucking or pitching. The slicker also helped to prevent the rider from being thrown over the front of the saddle. When a bronc rider had a hard horse to ride, he generally tied his slicker across the back of the saddle fork and *rode 'em.* This practice of tying a slicker or coat across the fork inspired the idea of using other things to take its place. Round sticks and sacks with some sort of padding in each end were tied onto the fork to enable the rider to set above a hard-bucking horse.

Figure D on Plate 60 shows bucking rolls attached to the straight saddle fork; these are also shown in Figure 10 on Plate 56. These bucking rolls were designed to take the place of the slicker mentioned above and became very popular with bronc riders and cowhands. They were an excellent substitute for the slicker and naturally the demand for them inspired the idea of building a saddle fork that would embody in its construction this same principle and would itself take the form of the bucking rolls.

Figure E shows the first or original swell-fork. It was designed to eliminate the use of bucking rolls and was about fourteen inches wide at the base but did not have a cut-under. It was merely widened out and the surface was rounded. It became popular at once but it did not replace the bucking rolls. Instead, the bucking rolls were still used on this type of fork which really offered a better foundation for them to be attached to. This fork made its initial appearance just prior to the beginning of the twentieth century. In rapid succession, thereafter, many different styles of swell-forks with oddly shaped bulges were developed and the fork of the stock saddle soon lost its original shape.

Figures F and K show the Billings swell-fork which has a bulge that extends back towards the rider. From this type of fork the bull-moose type of fork was evolved. The latter had a distinct cut-under very similar to that shown in Figure L, but not so deep. The bull-moose is a more highly developed type of fork; it allows the rider to get his leg under the fork.

Figure G shows the Curtis swell-fork which was high and at times extremely wide, often measuring eighteen inches across. Such large forks were heavy and naturally increased the weight of the saddle. This greater weight sometimes caused the saddle to hurt a horse's withers.

Figure H shows an extremely wide, cut-under swell-fork, the bear-trap type of fork which is an elaboration of the old bull-moose type. The bear-trap forks were often made up to twenty inches in width, and the tree was often shortened to twelve inches so the rider would be placed up close to the fork. This enabled him to get his legs well in under the fork. It was sure difficult for a bucking horse to jar his pack loose from such a bear trap, so naturally this type of fork became very popular with the amateur cowhand and bronc rider. There were many times when the owner of such a freak, as bear traps were generally called, found it securely wired or tied up to a tree or piled with pieces of salt to prevent it from doing any damage to the scenery or to livestock. Such tricks were a favorite pastime of old cowhands who would not let themselves sink so low as to be seen riding one of these monstrosities; to have been caught riding with one of them would have ruined their reputations as clean sitters. A side view of this fork is shown in Figure L.

The craze for wide swell-forks reached its zenith about 1920. Since then the swelling has been gradually going down till it has finally reached normal proportions in the saddles of today.

The standard type of swell-fork is very similar to that shown in Figures 22 and 24 on Plate 57. The forks shown in these drawings are much like the Association style of fork shown in Figure J on Plate 60, but they are sloped forward much more than the Association forks.

Figure I on Plate 60 shows a style of fork popular with bronc riders because it is especially designed for bronc riding. It was a type used in contest riding by many bronc riders when the Association saddle was not used. It was created in 1914 by the author and was known as the Ward Special tree. The fork is high and is built with shoulders much like those of a man. The sides of the fork gradually slope towards the base, which gives the fork a slight cut-under. The long sides afford the rider's legs a good leverage on the fork when riding without stirrups. (Riding without stirrups was a common practice at the time this fork was designed.) The rider had plenty of play to work with on a horse's neck or shoulders, and he could keep in close contact with the fork. The latter was most generally made fourteen inches wide across the shoulders. It is still being used by many bronc riders and is listed by some saddle makers as a "contest bronc tree."

Figure J illustrates the famous Association fork which is becoming more popular among professional bronc riders because it is the official type of fork used on the Association bronc-riding saddles adopted as the standard style to be rode under the rules of the Rodeo Association of America. It is a sensibly-shaped affair and is turned out in regular fourteen-inch width but can be made to suit the individual's personal needs. The width of the present-day swell-fork averages about fourteen and a half inches, which is a reasonable width for general or all-around riding purposes. It is very apt to remain the normal width.

23

CINCHES

Cincha, meaning "girth," is the Spanish word for cinch. A cinch is actually the same as a saddle girth, but it is not a surcingle.* The cinch is the wide band that goes under the horse's belly to hold the saddle in position. There are cinches designed especially for use on single-rig and double-rig saddles; the single-rig cinch is generally wider than those used on double-rig outfits. (In connection with this Section, refer also to the Section entitled "Trees and Riggings.")

The cinch shown in Figure 1 on Plate 61 is one designed for use on a single-rig saddle and is the type used on a center-fire too. The widths vary from 4 inches to 9 inches. The average width for the center-fire-rig cinch is 6 inches; for the three-quarter-rig cinch, 5 inches; for the Spanish-rig cinch, 4 inches. The widest cinches are those used on center-fire-rig saddles. It would never do to use a wide cinch as a front cinch on a double-rig saddle; such a wide cinch would extend too far forward and the foreleg of the horse would be constantly rubbing against it, which would result in chafing and eventually in sores on the foreleg hide. The wide cinches are often made of horse tail or mane hair and some have a hair tassel attached to the center of the cinch underneath, as shown in Figure 1.

The cross bars, or cinch bars (at A and B), are designed to hold the strands together and to keep the cinch straight. Cinch-ring leathers (under the cinch rings at C and D) are often used on the cinches of the single-rig California and

* A surcingle is a single strap, usually of cloth, to hold the saddle blanket on. A leather surcingle is used in bareback riding to give the rider a hand hold.

Nevada type of saddle, but they are very seldom used in the other range states. The chief reason for this is that riders believe they get in the way when a latigo (saddle strap) is placed in the cinch ring and that they have a tendency to grip the horse's hide, causing it to wrinkle up ahead of the ring when a rider is cinching up. Otherwise they are all right and help to eliminate ring sores.

Figure 2 illustrates the old-style double cinch which consists of a front and a flank (rear) cinch. The front cinch is made of hair and the flank cinch of canvas webbing. The two are connected by a strap which is often referred to as a cinch hobble. Figure 3 illustrates a more modern type of double-cinch outfit.

Two California types of single-rig cinches are shown in Figures 4 and 5. They are made of hair and you will note that the rings have rollers which make it easier for a rider to cinch up a horse. Figure 5 depicts a split cinch especially designed for a center-fire rig; it is strong enough to hold an elephant if the rider should happen to rope one. There is no danger of this cinch slipping if it is properly fastened. Figure 6 shows the modern type of flank-rig cinch. This consists of two short latigos attached to the rigging rings of a saddle and of the cinch strap which is buckled into the latigos. A front cinch like the one shown in Figure 7 is made of strong fish cord and is about 4 inches wide. It is used in conjunction with the Figure 6 flank strap on the majority of double-rig saddles today. Figure 8 shows a cinch designed for heavy roping and used in contests and rodeo work. Figure 9 shows a cinch equipped with center-bar rings which are finding favor with many riders, as they help to eliminate ring sores and are more easily buckled.

Figure 10 represents the bronc-riding cinch designed by the author. It is a good cinch for bronc riding or for contest roping. In Figure 11 you have a woven cinch that is made by some Indians, but it is not a popular type.

Figure 13 shows a cinch-release hook. This contraption is useful to a rider who is riding a steer or horse in bareback events during rodeo work. This rigging permits him to remove his riding rigging (bull rigging) before he quits the animal. A string is attached to the end of the trigger and the other end is placed in under the rigging where the rider can get ahold of it and jerk it when he is ready to get off. This will cause the trigger to kick the cinch ring out and release the rigging. This device was originated by the author.

Figure 14 shows a tackaberry buckle. This buckle is attached to the long latigo of a saddle and then is hooked into the cinch ring. Its use eliminates the need to unwrap the latigo when releasing the cinch. It saves time in saddling and unsaddling a horse. It is used in the northwest more than other parts of the cow country.

How to build a cinch is shown in the diagrams lettered from A to F on Plate 61. Figure A shows how the cinch rings are held by attaching them to a board with staples; this is one way to hold them. The arrow indicates how the center of the cinch cord is attached with a cinch knot to the ring when starting to build the cinch. The two strands are then cinch-looped in the same manner to

PLATE 61 *Cinches*

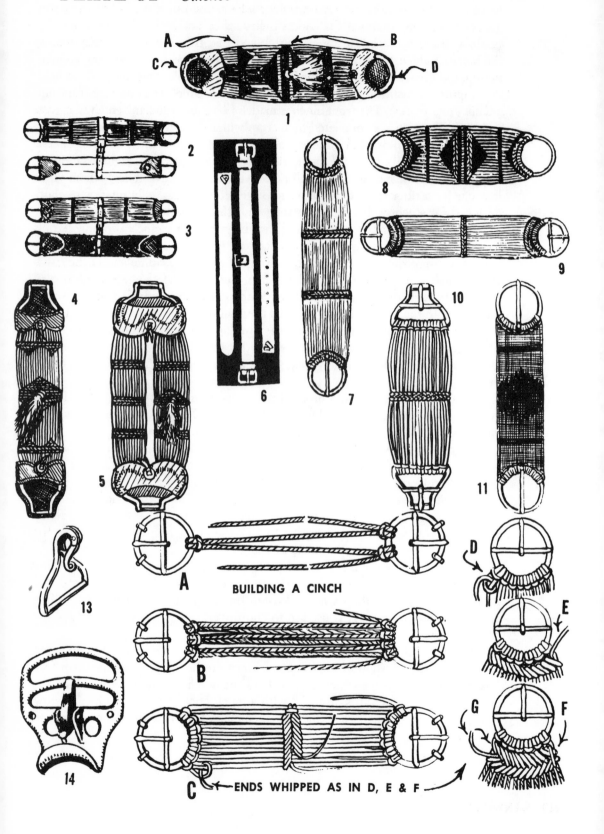

BUILDING A CINCH

ENDS WHIPPED AS IN D, E & F

the other ring and are worked back and forth from one ring to the other, as shown in Figure B, until the cinch is about fifteen strands wide. In Figure C can be seen how the cinch is being completed. The center bar, made by a half-hitching technique, is shown nearly completed. In completing the center bar, the ends of the string are run back in under the hitches a short ways, so that they will be held in place. The ends of the cinch cord itself are whipped or half-hitched around each strand, as shown at the arrows D and E. At the arrows F and G is shown how the end is turned back and worked over to the starting point and how the end is then run in under the hitches to hold it in place. When the end and center bars are properly built into a cinch, the strands are kept in place and the cinch is spread out. A little practice will enable the reader to build a good, serviceable cinch. There are several other ways of building cinches, but the method described here is the one most generally used by the average cowhand.

The material most generally used in building a cinch is cotton fish cord or angora mohair. The mohair is soft and will not chafe or rub a horse the way a hard cord like fish cord will, but the fish cord is more generally used because it is stronger and will last longer. Brass cinch rings with a flat surface are better than the common iron ring since they are stronger and do not rust out.

24

STIRRUPS

AND

TAPADEROS

The history of the stirrup follows pretty closely that of the saddle. To avoid a lot of cuttin' sign and back trackin' we refer the reader to Figure 1 of Plate 62 which shows the type of stirrup used by the conquistadors in the sixteenth century. The other diagrams on this same Plate will suffice to outline the subsequent evolution of this saddle accessory. Also, the stirrups portrayed should give the reader a pretty good idea of which type to use for any specific purpose.

The parts of a stirrup are indicated in Figure 12 as follows: A is the roller; B, the bolt; C, the metal binding; and D is the tread, which is leathered. Stirrups are often covered with rawhide by wrapping a strip of hide about one inch wide around the sides. This prevents the metal binding from breaking and the tread from wearing out.

The stirrup shown in Figure 1 was only one of the various types used by the conquistadors. It was of bronze inlaid with silver and no doubt was part of the equipment of a high officer in the invading army under the leadership of Cortes. In Figure 2 is seen a one-piece wooden stirrup; this was another model brought by the Spanish to Mexico. Eventually it was superseded by the box stirrup shown in Figure 3, which also was made of one piece of wood. This was a wide stirrup averaging about five inches in width. The steel-box stirrup shown in Figure 4 is inlaid with silver and is to be seen in Mexico to this day on the higher-priced saddles of the rancheros.

The old California stirrup illustrated in Figure 5 is made of wood and is bound with metal strips with a bolt through the top part to hold it together. It was a wide stirrup, is still to be found in some sections of the States and is popular in Mexico. Figure 7 is a Visalia stirrup made of wood but metal-bound; this type of stirrup is one of the most popular in use today for all-around riding purposes. It has full leather covering. The average width of tread used is about two inches. This is a type which will remain popular for a long time to come. Wood stirrups are far more popular than the metal variety because they are lighter and not so hard on a rider's shins when the stirrup bumps against them.

Figure 8 shows an oxbow, or round-bottom, steel stirrup, leather-covered. It is difficult to ride with the ball of the foot in a round-tread stirrup and those who use that style generally ride with the greater part of the foot in the stirrup. The flat-tread stirrup, like the Visalia in Figure 7, permits the rider to ride on the ball of his foot or with a full grip, whichever suits him best. That is why it is such a popular style of stirrup.

Figure 9 shows the Texas Number 2 iron stirrup made of cast iron with an oxidized tin finish to prevent rust. It is of the same type as the stirrups shown in Figures 13 and 14, all iron stirrups with round treads; although they were popular when first introduced back in the early 90's, they have lost favor among cowhands and though they were seldom ever broken, the drawbacks of their weight and shape counterbalance their good points and put 'em out of the race.

Oxbow stirrups like the one shown in Figure 12 are popular with bronc breakers and others who ride with a full grip on the stirrup. Their average width is about one and three quarters inches. Because this type of stirrup sets close to the rider's foot, it is more easily held when riding a bucking or pitching horse. Figure 20 shows a forged-steel stirrup especially designed for a bronc stirrup; it is a ring type with a narrow tread.

In Figure 22 is shown a cast-metal stirrup so designed that a rider can place his foot in it easily while mounting. It has a flat tread; the illustration shows the stirrup with a leather cover. Figure 15 depicts an oxbow stirrup similar to the one shown in Figure 12, only the Figure 15 stirrup is cut down so that it has a very narrow tread; this will enable a rider to hold it because he can take a deep grip. Also, it is lighter in weight. It is designed for rodeo-contest purposes and is the type generally used by professional bronc riders. In Figure 17 you have a brass, tubular-ring stirrup intended for bronc riding. It is used by some riders and is made of the same material as the stirrup in Figure 16. This stirrup finds favor with a few riders who like a ring. There are good, sound points to a ring: if a horse should fall, the stirrup will not be mashed or crushed onto the rider's foot because the round surface will make the stirrup turn, there being no flat surface to catch and hold it. Another good point, being tubular the ring is much lighter than it looks and is always in the right position. On the other hand, when mounting or dismounting, it is pretty difficult to hold the ball of the foot in the stirrup because the tread is round. The foot is very apt to slip in or out of the stirrup just at the wrong moment, and this is likely to cause some inconveniences. Nevertheless, it is easier to get a foot out of a ring than out of the ordinary type of stirrup.

PLATE 62 *Stirrups*

Figure 21 shows a forged-steel stirrup overlaid with silver and with filigreed openwork. It has a very wide tread and is shown here as an example of a fancy silver-mounted type. Figure 18 depicts another type of steel stirrup; it is silver inlaid and is designed along the lines of the ring stirrup used for bronc riding. It can also be used for general work if so desired.

Figure 19 depicts a specially designed bronc-riding stirrup; it embodies the good points of both the ring and regular stirrups. It is the lightest in weight with the narrowest tread and will follow a rider's foot when other types of stirrups will slip off and cause a rider to disqualify. Its round surface prevents it from being mashed on the rider's foot when a horse falls; because of the crossbar it will not swing as far away from the foot as others if it should come off and it is always in place. The tread is three-quarters of an inch wide and the surface is flattened so that the ball of the foot will stay put when mounting, etc. Note the side view, indicated by the arrow, of this safety bronc stirrup.

In Figure 23 you have a metal or brass stirrup made on the ring principle, with safety bar to prevent the stirrup from swinging forward; consequently, it will always be easy for the rider to catch the stirrup if it should come off his foot. It has a narrow tread which makes it easy to hold when riding a bronc.

Undoubtedly tapaderos are a Spanish innovation developed about the same time as *chaparreras* (chaps). The term "taps" is an abbreviation of the Spanish *tapaderas* (toe fenders). They are, as can be seen from the illustrations on Plate 63, a pointed piece of leather covering the stirrup on all sides except in back. They are a great protection against brush and thorns, bad weather, storms and cold in northern climates. The reason they are not used more in the northwest during the winter months is no doubt because of the extra weight they add to a saddle. But the protection they offer should outweigh this objection. The "winds," or points, of some taps are made long to satisfy the whims of some riders and have been known to measure up to thirty inches in length. A pair of long taps looks good on a saddle and the weight of a tap on a stirrup makes it easier for a rider, if he keeps his feet down, to hold a stirrup when making a bronc ride. But if he goes scratching back (kicking back with his spurs against the bronc's sides), he is apt to lose the stirrups and then things are likely to happen! Taps are riveted onto the stirrups; they have a tendency to hold a rider's feet down because of their weight. The pair of taps is fastened together by a

PLATE 63   *Tapaderos (Taps)*

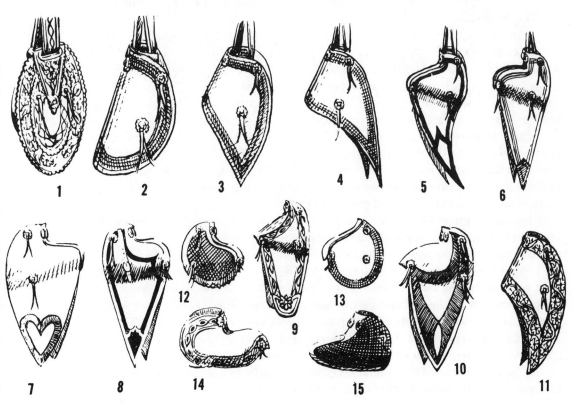

strap or rope running under the horse's body when a rider wants to play safe when riding a bad one. This arrangement is known as "hobbled" stirrups. When a rider spurs the animal while using taps, he naturally hits the horse harder and can punish him more effectively when necessary than he can without taps.

In riding with taps the rider should not place the foot full in the stirrup when mounting; and when dismounting, he should make sure that only the ball of the foot is in the stirrup so he can remove the foot as quickly as necessary. If this advice is not heeded, it may happen that a foot will become hung up or caught in the toe of the tap and the owner of the foot may be dragged to death. Such tragedies actually have occurred and can occur again no matter how gentle the horse may be.

The tapadero shown in Figure 1 of Plate 63 is the granddaddy of present-day tap styles. It was brought over from Spain by the early *hacendados* of Mexico, together with the rest of their riding equipment. The tapadero consisted of a couple of pieces of leather which originally were just attached to the front of the stirrup by strings and suspended from the stirrup leathers. Through being used, the taps were gradually bent backwards. But since these taps also tended to get bent out of shape, the tap shown in Figure 2, that could be riveted to the stirrup, was developed. This type of tap was current in the early California days on old-type saddles.

Figure 3 is the next type of tap developed—the original bull-nose style. Figure 4 shows the old Texas style of tap which was used during the early trail days. In Figure 5 you see the sabre-point style of tap which is an old-timer and is a bull-nose type. It is a three-piece tap with points of a style seldom seen these days. Figure 6 shows an eagle-bill style of nose and one used by many riders. Figure 7 shows a monkey-nose tap made of three pieces of leather. Figure 8 illustrates what is known as the Hamley toe-room style of tap designed by Hamley to prevent the rider's toe from getting caught in the top of the nose of the tap when mounting and dismounting. Note the stirrup strap on the side of the tap; it goes around the stirrup to hold the tap to the stirrup more firmly and is often used on modern types of outfits. Figure 9 shows a one-piece type of bull-nose tap, and Figure 10 shows a one-piece type of monkey-nose tap. Figure 11 depicts a Mexican bull-nose tap often seen on fine Mexican saddles.

Bulldog taps are shown in the last four numbered Figures on Plate 63. They are used in brushy country. The long-wing, or tip, taps are all right when used in open country, but in thickly timbered territory they are in the way because they hang up on the brush and become a nuisance to the rider. Figure 12 shows a monkey-nose bulldog tap; it is laced at the bottom and is a type commonly used. Figure 13 represents a bull-nose style open at the bottom. Figure 14 represents a Chihuahua Mexico type of bulldog tap made of one piece of leather and laced on the bottom. Figure 15 shows the Visalia Excelsior tap made of one piece of leather; an extra piece of leather protects the toe nose.

25

CHAPARRERAS,
OR CHAPS

The word "chaps" is derived from the Spanish *chaparreras* (chapa-re-ras). These leggings ("leg armor," to refer again to the Spanish) have a long history. In order to give the reader an idea of their origin and development, the author can do no better than to quote the brief history of chaps as set down by "Shorty" Shope, the cowboy arist:

"Somewhere back in old Spain the riders gathering cattle in brushy and thorny areas discovered that a hide laid on the saddle and extending forward, then folded back over the rider's legs when mounted, saved many a good pair of breeches from getting torn, many a leg from bruise and scratch, and it also kept the knees dry and warm no matter what the weather. These were the first chaps, or *chaparreras*. Gradually these hides were cut and shaped into a more comfortable piece of equipment. Some were short, of very heavy leather or hide, reaching just below the knee; others were longer and of lighter weight. Some were made with the hair still on them and some without.

"When the Spanish brought their herds and flocks with them to Mexico, they also found use for these leather leg guards. The early Anglo settlers in the southwest were quick to see the advantage of leather chaps and the ones worn today by the cowboys are much the same as those worn by the first stockmen in the southwest."

Figure 1 on Plate 64 shows how the cowhide was placed over the rider's legs, and also how a piece of material was placed over the breast of the horse to

PLATE 64   *Chaparreras (Chaps)*

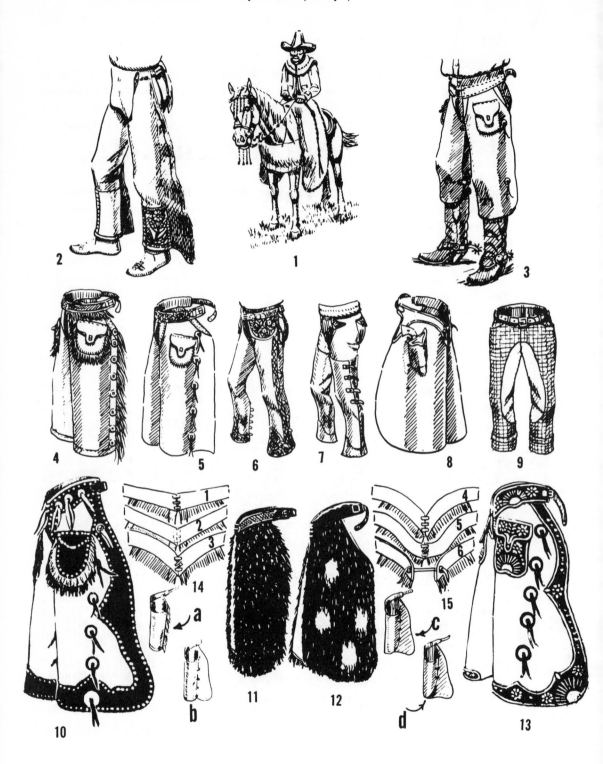

protect it from thorns, in the original Mexican type of *chaparreras*. The leg covering is called *armas,* meaning armor, and is still in use in some parts of South America and Mexico.

The closed-leg chap shown in Figure 4, with the long fringe at the outside seam, is not as popular as it once was, but it is the most practical of all leather chaps according to old cowmen. Because there is no superfluous leather except the fringe, this type of chap is light in weight as well as warm and rainproof. The fringe was added in America, copied perhaps from the Indian leggings in Figure 2. The Indian legging no doubt has had some influence in the designing of the modern chap.

Leather, if it is waterproofed by oiling, becomes stiff and uncomfortable in cold weather. Therefore the fur chaps shown in Figures 11 and 12, which will shed rain without being oiled, became the choice of many riders who lived in damp or cold climates. Such chaps were made of different materials and furs. Angora goatskin became, and still is, the most practical material because its thick hair will shed any amount of water and at the same time act as a good windbreak. Bearskin chaps were common in the early days. Hair chaps also afford protection from bruises when, for instance, riding broncs in a corral. A mean horse may try to throw his rider against the pole fence, or he may go mad and ram the fence in his frenzy.

The bat-wing or flap chaps shown in Figure 5, which have open legs that are snapped together back of the wing, have been worn ever since the earliest times.

The *armitas* (small leg armor) shown in Figure 3 is a type of chap once popular in Nevada and California because of its light weight and because it was cooler in hot weather. These chaps were often referred to as "chinks."

The style of the inside of the leg of the chaps depicted in Figures 4 and 5 is shown in the small drawings of chap legs near the bottom of the plate. The closed leg, which is often called the shotgun chap, is shown in drawing A. Various styles of leg fastenings for bat-wing chaps are shown in B, C, and D: B, known as the California style, has five snaps and rings; C, the Texas style, has four snaps and rings; and D, the Cheyenne style, has three snaps and rings.

Figure 6 shows the tight-leg Mexican chaps fastened on the outside of the leg with leather buttons and loops, but sometimes also buckled on. Figure 7 shows the Mexican, close-fitting legging; its lower half is fastened with a long spring-steel fastener, while the top half is buckled. This is a popular type of legging in Mexico and is much cheaper than regular chaps. Figure 8 shows a modern type of bat-wing chap designed by the author and called the "New Mexico." Note the one-piece belt and the specially designed six-shooter pocket. Many a present-day cowhand packs his gun in his chap pocket which has a regular gun holster built into it. This eliminates the need for a belt and extra weight.

Figure 9 illustrates a pair of California pants foxed (reinforced) with buckskin, a style popular in the early days but seldom seen now. The foxed pants gave the rider a good grip on the saddle and eliminated the necessity for chaps. In hot weather they were much cooler than wearing both pants and chaps. They were a type of equipment used in the northwest which is predominantly prairie country and not nearly so hard on clothing as the brushy or timbered regions of some of the southwest cow ranges.

In Figure 10 you have a pair of fancy bat-wing chaps such as are used mostly by rodeo and wild-west show riders. Figures 11 and 12 show the angora-hair chaps mentioned above and used only in the northwest in prairie country. Figure 13 is the ultimate in a fancy chap; it is trimmed with silver *conchas* and spots and has a fancy carved border. Chaps like these make a hundred-dollar bill look like thirty cents if you're going to buy 'em. You can bet that they are not used for everyday cow work but for show or rodeo purposes.

Chap belts are shown in Figures 14 and 15. The straight belts illustrated were the kind used with old-style chaps. The curved, full-dip styles (2 and 3 in Figure 14, and 4, 5 and 6 in Figure 15) are most popular at this writing. The one-string belt (6 in Figure 15) is the style most generally favored today because this type of belt is seldom, if ever, pulled tight. The other belts shown in Figures 14 and 15 have to be pulled tight together, otherwise the saddlehorn might get under them and cause the rider a lot of grief. The one-string is now generally used in the other types of belts shown as well. The belt sets on the outside of the chap leg to make it hang better and to throw the chap wing back where it should be. The string itself will be in close to the rider's body and the saddlehorn cannot easily get in under it; if it does, it will quickly break the string and release the rider. This is the principal reason why the string is used. It should be light and narrow so it will break when any considerable strain is put on it.

The styles of belts shown in Figures 14 and 15 are: 1, the regular straight belt; 2, the full-dip straight belt; 3, the regular curved belt; 4, the full-dip curved belt; 5, the low-cut curved type; and 6, the regular curved, one-string style, now the one most generally used on chaps.

26

SPURS

AND

SPUR STRAPS

It so happens that the author is able to show the evolution of the *espuelas,* or spurs, a little better than some other parts of the cowhand's equipment. The parts of a spur, as indicated in Figure 5 on Plate 65, are as follows: A, the chap hook; B, the rowel; C, the shank; D, the spur button; E, the heel band; and F, the heel chains. Straps over the ankles hold the spurs on the foot. Sometimes there is a heel strap to hold the spur down, as shown in Figure 17.

The spur, or pryck, is the great-granddaddy of the cowhand's spurs, as can be seen in Figure 1. From this ancient prod the spur rowel was developed. Figure 2 is an old English spur with an extremely long shank often measuring ten inches in length. It shows that the raised spur button is not a modern development. Figure 3 is a drawing of an old Spanish spur of the sixteenth century, the type worn by some of the conquistadors. It is typical of the spurs used by the early *hacendados* of Mexico. This spur had extremely large rowels, often as much as eight inches in diameter. The spurs were seldom worn when the rider was off his horse and were put on his heels by a servant after he had mounted; they were generally removed before or immediately after the rider dismounted. Such large rowels would be extremely difficult to walk with. The heel chains were so long that they served mostly to make noise by striking against the stirrup. A couple of jinglebobs (pendants) were also attached to the rowel pin on the outside of the shank; these were constantly striking against the rowel with a lively ringing sound. Modern developments have eliminated these various accessories as well as the long chains attached to the old Spanish bits, but all these gadgets jingling together must have set up a mighty fine music.

The Chihuahua shown in Figure 4 is a good representative of the present-day Mexican spur. The majority of Chihuahua spurs are silver inlaid in beautiful designs and are far cheaper than their American-made counterparts. They are very heavy and are generally equipped with large rowels averaging about three inches in diameter. The famous OK spur is shown in Figure 16. Many an old-time cowhand broke out with a pair of spurs like this. They were introduced in the early 80's but were superseded by the California type of spur shown in Figure 5. This is a two-piece spur; the shank is riveted into the heel band. (Present-day spurs are generally made of one solid piece of metal, which has eliminated the possibility of the shank working loose.) The heel chains of the California-style spur (Figure 5) served but one purpose, and that was to make a noise when they struck against a stirrup or a rider's boot heel. These spurs did not fit up close to the boot as has been generally supposed. The majority of California spurs had one-half- to full-drop shanks like the one shown.

Figure 8 shows a spur that has a round shank and a barrel-shaped chap hook useful in preventing the back of the chap leg from becoming fouled with the rowel. Most California spurs of this type are silver inlaid. The heel band is straight and this is often referred to as a straight-button spur. Straight-button spurs do not set as well on a rider's boot heel as the raised-button ones illustrated further along on this same Plate. The leverage on the raised button prevents the shank from hanging down and dragging the way the old-style, straight heel band did. The great majority of spurs used by cowhands today are raised-button spurs, and the wide heel band is becoming more popular because it sets more firmly on the boot and does not cut into the counter (part of the foot above the heel) the way a narrow heel band does. The wide heel band is popular for bronc riding also, because it is heavier and easier on a rider's heel. The average width of the wide heel bands is about one and a quarter inches. The split-heel-band, double-button spur shown in Figure 8 has a type of heel band which is good to hold a spur in place: A heel strap is attached to the two lower buttons; this anchors the spur firmly so it cannot slip up and down on the rider's heel. The spur in this Figure is silver mounted and is made of one piece of steel.

Figure 7 illustrates an example of a fine silver-mounted and raised-button spur. The buttons are solid, that is, stationary, like the buttons shown in Figure 13. The spurs shown in Figures 6, 9, 10, 12 and 14 have wide heel bands and swinging buttons which seem to be more popular than the stationary raised-button style. This is because they do not press against the rider's ankle as does the solid-button type. Note the different types of swinging buttons.

Figure 17 shows how the modern rodeo, bronc-riding spur is attached to the boot of the rider. This type of spur is also shown in Figure 10. The small button on the heel band serves to attach the heel strap too; this holds the spur securely in place. Note the dull, round-pointed star rowel which eliminates the possibility of cutting a horse while riding him. The spur is made of stainless

PLATE 65 *Spurs*

SPUR SHANKS

ROWELS

5-P.
6-P.
9-P.
20-P.
16-P.
SAWTOOTH
10-P.
7-P. STAR
5-P. STAR

steel and is mighty serviceable. Figure 15 shows a tapered-heel-band spur of good design. Figure 14 shows the forerunner of the modern wide-heel-band type of spur. Figure 6 shows a silver-overlaid spur, handsomely engraved. The illustrations of the other spurs on this Plate are of one-piece spurs and are self-explanatory.

Spur shanks are shown on the left side of Plate 65 and demonstrate the varying degree of drop in each. The gal-leg (Figure F) was once a very popular type of spur shank. It was mounted with a silver stocking and a gold slipper and garter. This spur also has a lock rowel. This type of rowel was thoroughly experimented with but soon went out of use as it done more damage than good. The goose-neck shank (Figure G) was a popular type with long-legged riders and is still in use. The long-legged rider generally uses a raised-shank spur because it is easier for him to reach a horse with that type of spur. A short-legged rider generally prefers a drop-shank spur to keep from hitting the horse too quick and this type of spur makes it easier for him to get ahold of a horse. The average rider uses a quarter-drop-shank spur which is like the majority of those shown on the spurs on this Plate.

Types of spur shanks are shown in Figures A through G: A is a straight shank; B, a quarter-drop shank; C, a half-drop shank; D, a three-quarter drop shank; E, a full-drop shank; F, a gal-leg shank (with lock rowel); G, a goose-neck shank.

The spur shown in Figure 13 is a good all-around spur and the spurs shown in Figures 11 and 12 are one and the same spur. This is the latest thing in a bronc-riding spur and is made by Crockett. In Figure 11 is shown a bottom view of the right-foot spur showing how the shank is set so that it is turned in to make it easy for the rider to reach the horse without turning his toes out while scratching. Figure 12 is similar to Figure 10.

There are nine different kinds of spur rowels shown in the lower right-hand corner of Plate 65. The eight- and ten-point rowels are the ones most generally used. The star rowels are also popular types, but the twenty-point and saw-tooth rowels have lost their popularity, though there are some riders who still use them. The wide-point, blunt rowel is the type in demand.

It is seldom that one can find a rider wearing a pair of spurs with small, sharp-spoke rowels. The first thing a rider does when he gets ahold of a pair of spurs with sharp-spoke rowels is to get a file and file off the points so that they will be difficult to cut a horse with. As a general rule spurs are more often used to threaten a horse with than actually to spur him. A cowhand knows how to handle a pair of spurs and he knows that if he wants to hold a job with an outfit he has got to use them spurs according to Hoyle. Most cowmen will tell a rider that the part of the horse in front of the cinch belongs to the cowman, but from the cinches back is for the rider to work on whenever this becomes necessary. But the rider who puts bear tracks or panther sign on a horse is apt to find himself looking for another job.

The drawings of spur straps (which hold the spurs in place on the boot)

PLATE 66 *Spur Straps*

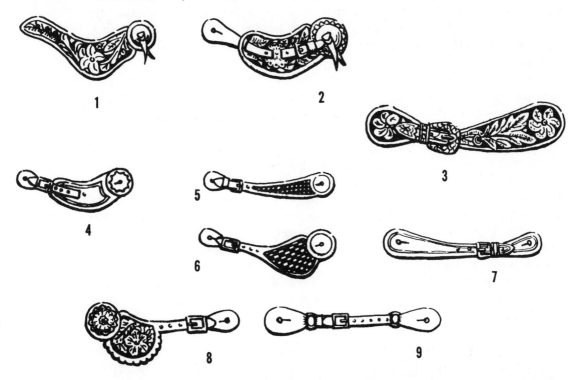

shown on Plate 66 are practically self-explanatory and the style or shape of the straps is clearly indicated. Spur straps are always made in pairs but only one of each type is shown here. The button-spur strap shown in Figure 1 is the oldest type of strap used and was worn by the early Spanish riders. It has been popular in Mexico for many years but is seldom if ever used in the United States. This type of strap cannot be adjusted as well as one fitted with a buckle. All the other spur straps shown on Plate 66 are popular styles and it is a matter of personal preference as to which style a rider will choose.

Figure 3 shows a narrow strap, finely hand-carved and fitted with a silver buckle set (see "Cowboy Jewelry"), which makes it a classy outfit. The narrower style of strap is popular in the southwest and wider ones are worn in the northwest.

Figure 9 shows a strap made on the cinch ring order; it is not used as much as the other styles, since it is a comparatively new style of strap and seems to be much too narrow for comfort.

Button straps like the one shown in Figure 1 are not practical on spurs with large buttons because they are difficult to put on and take off. Nickel or silver *conchas* are often worn on the wide straps, as shown in Figures 1 and 2. *Conchas* (shell designs—see "Cowboy Jewelry") always look good on a pair of wide spur straps.

27

COWBOY BOOTS
AND HATS

The history of the high-heeled boot worn by the American cowhand is a trail that is pretty dim and hard to backtrack to its beginning, but it is known that the horseman of the Mongolian steppes in Asia have for centuries worn a boot with a high, painted, wooden heel and that this heel was regarded by them as a mark of distinction. The wearer of this kind of boot was classed as a cavalier, higher in the social scale than those who plodded afoot. There is no doubt but what the cowhand's boot south of the Rio Bravo (the original name of the Rio Grande) was developed to its present state of perfection by the cowhand, as were other parts of the equipment used by the riders of today.

A typical old-time boot used by the old trail drivers is shown in Figure 1 on Plate 67. These boots had high tops with long mule-ear bootstraps and were generally *low* heeled. In time the fancy top was created and the red-top, lone-star boot made its appearance (see Figure 2). It is the grandpappy of the modern, fancy inlaid boot top and is well remembered by old-time cowmen. Brass or copper toe caps were devised to keep the toe of the boot from wearing out; these were used mostly on boots worn by youngsters and did not find favor with the cowhand.

The high front of the boot top was the forerunner of the scallop-top boot; the latter represents the next step in a shaped top. The scalloped boot shown in Figure 4 is easily recognized; it is a boot made by C. H. Hyer, of Olathe, and the author ventures to state that there were more Hyer boots of this type worn than any other style made in the early days. The design of the stitching on the boot top always identified the Hyer boot and distinguished it from other makes. This firm is still making boots for cowhands.

Figure 5 shows a conservative type of boot, one worn by a great many cowmen. It is well constructed and the heel is well set under. (This boot is similar to the one shown in Figure 4 which has a common-sense heel.) The scallop top is much deeper than the tops on the other boots described in this section and it is the style in general use.

Figure 9 depicts a popular type of boot with a high heel that is well set under. The top of this boot is inlaid with pieces of leather in contrasting colors and is fancy-stitched. This is a good boot, built like a boot should be. Note the shape of the heel and the general structure of the boot which has a strong shank and a well-shaped foot. Note also the fancy wing tip on the toe at I.

In Figure 12 are shown the different parts of a boot: A indicates the bootstraps; B, the scallop top; C, the top; D indicates the tongue counter which is constructed like the tongue of the vamp at H, but is seldom put on a boot unless specially ordered. A tongue counter is superior to the ordinary counter because a spur will not wear out the threads at the top of the counter and cause the boot top to become detached from the counter. E indicates the counter itself; F, the shank; and G, the vamp. Note the stitching on the vamp, which is, of course, a special feature and seldom seen on the general run of boots; it is fancy work that adds to the cost. The shank shown at F is a strongly constructed one and resembles the shank shown in D of Figure 3. No danger of a shank built like this one ever breaking down. Except for the stitching on the vamp, this (Figure 12) is a typical cowboy boot.

Figure 10 shows a full-flower-stamped boot top made of tan calfskin and hand-carved in a style similar to that of a fancy stamped saddle. This kind of top is more expensive than the other styles of tops illustrated on Plate 67. It is made of one piece of leather sewed together in the back. The boot is shown with a square box toe popular in the southwest.

Cowboy shoes are shown in Figures 8 and 11; these drawings will give the reader an idea as to what they are like. They are made of the same materials as the boots and the last and heels are built like those of a boot. Figure 8 shows a Congress type of shoe with elastic on the sides. It has a square box toe. Figure 11 shows an oxford, a type of shoe which is becoming more popular. Shoes cost nearly as much as boots and, like them, are usually made to order.

Boot heels are diagrammed in Figure 3 to show the difference between the good kind and the unshapely ones put on boots by shoe factories that do not understand how to build a real cowboy boot. The factory-made boot is easily distinguishable from the shop-made boot, that is, the locally-made boot of good workmanship. Perhaps a factory-made boot should have been given in an illustration at this point to show the contrast between the two varieties of footgear. But on second thought such an illustration was omitted as possibly doing more harm than good. Nevertheless, in C of Figure 3, certain bad features in the factory-made product are indicated.

The drawings A, B, C and D of Figure 3 show the different types of boot heels. The seam on the side of the boot, indicated by the arrow, should be noted; it will help you to determine whether or not the boot heel is correctly placed. The old-time boots had heels set like those in A and B, that is to say they were set back of the side seam and were built like those shown in these two drawings. The modern boot heel is set ahead of the side seam, as shown in D; this shortens the distance between the heel and the ball of the foot and naturally strengthens the shank. This shank is made much heavier and deeper than the ones in A and B. The old type of shank had a tendency to break down and the heels to run over like those shown in Figures 6 and 7. The old-style shanks were too long and too lightly reinforced compared to the modern shop-made boot. They were much harded for a rider to walk in and would not hold their shape the way the shop-made modern boots will. With the heel well set under as shown in D, the rider's foot cannot go into the stirrup as far as it would if he were wearing the old-style boots. When the rider's foot pushes too far into the stirrup, the stirrup leather tends to rub the front of the ankle, which causes the front of the boot to wear out. The heel shown in D makes the boot more comfortable and the foot of the boot will hold its shape and wear longer than in the old style of footgear, or in the factory-made product shown in C. Note in Figure C the shape of the block-like heel and the flat, shallow shank and how the heel is set back of the side seam. The counters are weak and not properly shaped to hold a spur; they will break down, as will the rest of the boot. Of course, such boots do not cost as much as the shop-made boots, but neither do they give the service per dollar invested that the shop-made article does.

Boot heels that are extremely under-shot have a tendency to cause the wearer to walk on the back of the heel and to throw the boot backward. If it is not strongly reinforced, as shown in D, the shank will arch upward and let the heel go too far forward.

Small heel taps were once the style. The spike heel, the end of which could be covered with a dime, was about three inches high. This type of heel was once thought to be the proper thing, but it finally lost prestige largely because the shanks were too weak to support the foot and therefore broke down.

The leather used in boots is generally French calf, morocco or kid. The vamps are of French box calf, kangaroo and vici kid. French calf is used for boots subjected to hard service, and the kangaroo and vici kid are mostly for dress boots, since these leathers will not stand up under rough work and will peel and become ragged when used in brush and rocky country. Alligator leather, once utilized for vamps, was eventually given up because of the scarcity of this material.

Run-over heels are shown in Figures 6 and 7. With the help of these diagrams the reader can, when ordering a pair of boots, specify how he runs his boot heels so that the bootmaker can build the kind of heels that will be right for him. The majority of riders naturally run their heels out, as illustrated in Figure 6. A rider generally does this because he has become slightly bowlegged

PLATE 67 *Boots*

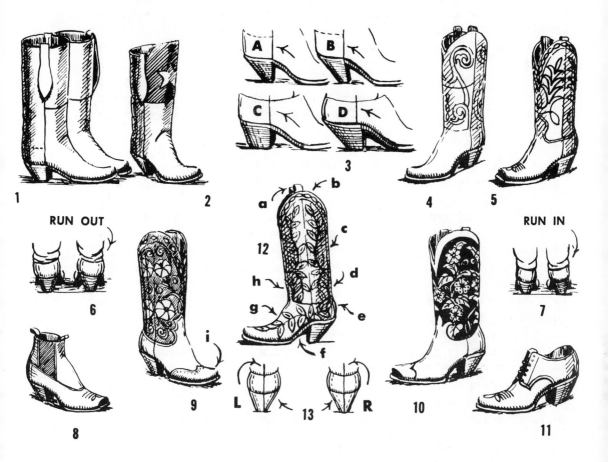

from setting above a horse so much. On the other hand, the average person who works on foot instead of from a horse generally runs his heels in, as shown in Figure 7.

The height of heels depends on the wearer's requirements and the size of the bottom tap depends on what he chooses in the way of a heel. A two-inch heel is a high heel, and the height generally favored is about one and three-quarters inches. The one-and-a-half-inch heel is considered a medium-height heel and is much in demand too. The low, common-sense heel is one inch high—about the height of the average shoe heel.

Boot toes come in two general styles—the square-box and the round-coin toes. Of the two, the round-coin is the most popular as it does not wear out like the sharp-edged, square-box toe. Using the catalogues of the leading cowboy bootmakers which show the various types of heels and styles of toes, the reader will be able to order the kind of boot he wants.

How boot heels should be set is shown in Figure 13 on Plate 67. A line running vertically down the center of diagram L (the left foot), and indicated by the arrow, shows how the heel is set towards the outside to help prevent the cowhand from running the heel over as already explained. An experienced rider is inclined to bow his legs out and would naturally run his boots out, as is indicated in Figure 6. At R in Figure 13, the heel is shown set in the center of the boot; this is done by a lot of bootmakers who do not understand how to make a pair of cowboy boots. Once in a while a hand who does not do much walking may be able to get along without running the heels over when they are set as shown here, but such hands are few and far between.

It appears that the high-crown, wide-brim hat of the American cowboy can be indirectly traced to the large hats worn by Mongol horsemen many ages back. The Spanish and Mexican sombreros are very similar to the headgear worn by the followers of Ghengis Khan, and out of the sombrero evolved the cowhand's head covering. Like many other articles of his working outfit, his hats can be traced back to the equipment brought over to Mexico by the Spanish. It is certain, however, that the modern cowboy hat is a considerable improvement and it can be said that the hat worn by the American cowhand is superior to any hat of its type anywhere in the world. That's sure 'nuff covering a lot of territory, but look 'em over and you will find the statement is correct.

The styles and sizes of the hats worn by cowhands vary considerably because of the differences in climate in the different sections of the cow country. The northwestern cowhand wears a much smaller hat than the rider in the southwest, and the Mexican *vaquero* wears an even larger hat than his American counterpart north of the border. Contrary to general belief, the typical cowboy hat is not worn for display to satisfy the vanity of its owner. It is a product of necessity and is worn for the protection of a rider who is in the saddle every day in all kinds of weather. The big hat is a great protection against wind, rain and sun. Its uses are many, it is subjected to much more abuse than any other kind of head covering, and it must be made of good material to take the punishment it gets. The hats shown on Plate 68 are representative of the many different styles worn by the cowhand of yesterday and today.

The Spanish sombrero shown in Figure 1 was generally decorated with gold and silver ornaments and with a heavy gold or silver braid. The crown was low and flat and the brim was straight and stiff; all in all, it was much the same sombrero as is still worn in Spain today. The Mexican sombrero with its high, pointed crown and wide, upturned brim (see Figure 2) is also highly decorated with braid and ornaments made of gold and silver thread. These sombreros are very heavy, no doubt in order to support such wide brims. They do not set down on the wearer's head like the ordinary hat, but are more or less balanced on top of the head. A neckin' string, or chin cord, is generally attached to this headgear to keep it from making its getaway in windy weather.

Figure 3 shows the old-time Texas hat generally worn during the old trail days; this is the same type of hat as the one illustrated in Figure 1. It was

PLATE 68 *Hats*

1

2

3

6 (5½" X 3½")

7 (5½" X 3½")

8 (6¼" X 4")

9 (7" X 4½")

10 (7½" X 5")

11 (6½" X 4")

12 (7" X 4")

13 (7" X 4½")

14 (7½" X 5")

15 (7" X 4½")

American-made, but of such poor quality that it would not hold its shape and the brim would soon become soft. It was often necessary for the wearer to hold up the drooping brim by perforating the edge and running a leather string through the holes; the ends were tied together over the top of the brim. This string worked on the same principle as a puckering string in a sack and kept the brim from hanging down over one's eyes. Sometimes the brim was pinned to the crown of the hat to keep it out of the way. It is said that the material used in this early Texas hat was wool—which is not used in the modern cowhand hats.

The style or shape of the hats depicted on Plate 68 varies according to the height of the crowns and the width of the brims. These measurements are given under each drawing. Most of the hats illustrated are made by the famous Stetson hat builders and are recognized as the best. The Figure 6 hat is in a style similar to that of the old Texas hat, with a low crown and a straight brim. Figures 7 and 8, known as the Dakota and Big Four, respectively, are two styles most generally worn in the northern states. They have narrower brims and lower crowns than the hats popular in the southwest that are shown at the bottom of the Plate. The style in brims varies greatly. Some brims are straight and others are shaped and have curled edges. Some have a binding around the edge. Hatbands also vary a good deal. Some leather hatbands are often worn around the crown next to the brim to prevent the hat from stretching and to hold it in place, but such bands are not always necessary.

Very few riders know much about the quality of hats or can distinguish one from another in respect to quality. The quality specifications given here are those submitted by the Stetson hat company: number-one quality; clear nutria; real nutria; 3X beaver; 4X beaver; 5X beaver; and 7X beaver, which is the finest quality of hat made. It should be borne in mind that the qualities listed run in the order given. (There is no 6X beaver quality.) In order to give the reader an idea as to the price range for hats in the different quality categories, the Laloo shown in Figure 6 is selected and the prices are given for this hat in the following qualities: number-one quality—$14.50; nutria—$17.00; 3X beaver—$20.00; 4X beaver—$35.00. If this Laloo were made with a lower crown or a narrower brim, it would cost less; and if it were made with a wider brim or a higher crown, it would cost more. Naturally, the larger the hat, the more it will cost. The beavers are made of beaver fur and the others are made of imported English and Belgian hare skins which are blended in different grades. It takes about two weeks to make a hat of the kind referred to above and a lot of hand work goes into it, which accounts for the high price.

The various names of the styles of hats illustrated on Plate 68 are as follows: Figure 6, the Laloo, 5½″ crown and 3½″ brim; Figure 7, the Dakota, 5½″ crown and 3½″ brim; Figure 8, the Big Four, 6¼″ crown and 4″ brim; Figure 9, the Carp, 7″ crown and 4½″ brim; Figure 10, the *El Tavor,* 7½″ crown and 5″ brim; Figure 11, the Jolan, 6½″ crown and 4″ brim; Figure 12, the Carlsbad, 7″ crown and 4″ brim; Figure 13, the Calgary, 7″ crown and 4½″ brim; Figure 14, the Kalispell, 7½″ crown and 5″ brim; and Figure 15, the Champie, 7″ crown and 4½″ brim.

28

COWBOY GARB
AND
MISCELLANEOUS
EQUIPMENT

The clothing shown in the illustrations on Plate 69 is, naturally, designed for riding purposes and is built for service and comfort. No attempt is made here to keep abreast of modern fashion trends displayed by the man on the street. Improvements in cowboy clothes have been made, of course, as time has drifted down the trail of years, but the good basic lines have remained the same as they were in the beginning. The material used in cowboy garb is of the best and therefore costs more than the ordinary run of this kind of clothing. Fine check plaids are the dominating patterns and the colors are generally a neutral brown; this is characteristic of the California make of garments shown in the illustrations. Most of the articles illustrated on Plate 69 are made of pure virgin wool of close heavy texture that will protect the rider against the elements. The need for freedom of action is always taken into account in the design of all the different articles of clothing worn by the range rider.

Heavy clothing is worn more in the northwest than in the southern parts of the cow country. In the southwest a two-piece suit of Mexican serge (blue denim) is the type of garment most popular with the majority of riders. This kind of suit is also worn by many hands in other parts of the range. The suits consist of a pair of overalls like those shown in Figure 15 and a brush jacket of the same material. Two different styles of riding coats are shown in Figures 1 and 5. They are of heavy mackinaw material and are well built. Figures 2 and 4 show California makes of pants. Note the top pockets which are like those on the overalls in Figure 15. These are old-style pants, but they will always be the style used by the cowhand in his work. The legs have medium-width bottoms, a sensible width because there isn't any surplus material—such as the fashionable balloon bottoms or peg-top styles have—to whip around in the atmosphere. The wide type of pants were supposed to be the proper thing in the past.

The special feature of the pants in Figure 4 is the dark leather trimming on the pockets and belt loops. In other respects these pants are identical with those shown in Figure 2. The suit of ducking shown in Figure 3 is a popular garment in the southwest. It is made of brown canvas material and is trimmed in light-colored corduroy. It is made for use in brushy country and is sure serviceable. This suit comes in two styles known as the rodeo and the booger-red, but actually the two are very much the same in build and material.

The rider shown in the picture (Figure 3) is Tom Threepersons, a famous peace officer and a sure-'nuff clean setter in the earlier days.

Figures 6 and 12 illustrate examples of calfskin vests sometimes worn by riders; they are fine in cold weather. Figure 11 shows a vest of the same material as the other California garments. The cowhand of the northwest generally wears a vest, a garment that is seldom seen in southern cow country. Figures 7 and 8 show styles of shirts generally worn in winter. Ordinary shirts are worn in summer and, in many cases, the year around as well in the parts of the cow country that have a warm climate. Figures 9 and 10 illustrate two styles of California jackets or blazers made of the same material as the California pants. A new pattern, in stripes, is shown in Figure 10. In the pants shown in Figure 13 the stripes are there too, but they are less noticeable. The color is a lighter brown, with the stripes in contrasting shades. It is a neat pattern and liked much better than the check by a lot of riders. The pants are built the same as the other Californias.

Gloves made of the best buckskin, like those shown in Figure 17, are also worn by the northwestern stockhand but are very seldom used in the southwest. The gauntlet glove shown in the lower left-hand corner of Plate 69 was popular during the trail days; it was generally made with a long fringe attached to the lower side of the cuff. These gloves were first introduced by the cavalry and Indian scouts during the Indian campaigns of the 70's and were then adopted by the old-time cowhands.

Figure 14 shows a silk muffler, or handkerchief, which is worn around the neck. The muffler is a very handy article at times and is not worn merely for display purposes. When working or driving cattle the dust is sometimes so thick that it is difficult for a rider to breathe without inhaling a great quantity of it. On such occasions the neck scarf placed over the nose and mouth acts as a sort of filter. In very cold weather the muffler is tied around the rider's head to protect his ears. Used in this way it is far more effective than a pair of ear muffs. The northern cowhand generally wears his hat the year round and uses his neck scarf over his ears when there is a possibility that they might freeze. The neck scarf is carried tied around the rider's neck with the knotted ends in the back,

PLATE 69 *Cowboy Garb*

1 HUB-BACK JACKET

2 CALIFORNIA PANTS

3 A SUIT OF DUCKING

4 NEW-STYLE CALIFORNIAS

5 RIDER STAGG COAT

6 CALFSKIN VEST

7 PLAID WOOL SHIRTS

8 CALIFORNIA SHIRT

9 PENDLETON OR CALIFORNIA BLAZER

10 NEW CALIFORNIA STRIPE-DESIGN BLAZER

11 CALIFORNIA VEST

12 CALFSKIN VEST

13 GAUNTLET OR GLOVE

14 CALIFORNIA STRIPED PANTS

15 OVERALLS

16 SADDLE SLICKER

17 BUCK GLOVE

hanging down. It is not tied so it hangs loosely over one shoulder in the manner shown in so many illustrations, but is tied just loose enough for comfort.

Figure 16 depicts a saddle slicker, or raincoat, especially designed for riding. It is made so that it will cover the rider and the saddle and is a great protection in stormy weather. The northwestern cowhand generally carries his slicker tied behind his saddle in order to have it handy. It is a necessary part of his equipment. A slicker is seldom carried by southwestern stockhands and the majority of them do not even own one. The mild climate makes a slicker unnecessary.

The fact is that differences in climate to a great extent dictate cowboy fashions in different sections of the cow country. Climate also dictates pretty much the type of equipment used in various areas. As a general rule an experienced cowhand can tell the country a rider is from by the outfit he wears.

On Plate 70 is shown a collection of many different articles that are sometimes used by riders and are considered part of his equipment.

Figure 1: Cuffs. Two different styles of stamping are shown here. Cuffs like these are sometimes used by brush hands to protect the arms when knocking limbs off brush, etc. They were popular in the early days, especially in the southwest, but are seldom used by riders today.

Figure 2: Belt. This drawing shows a fine, hand-carved design and a style of belt worn by many riders. It is often equipped with a fine silver buckle set.

Figure 3: Body or bronc-riding belt. This item is finely hand carved and is shaped to fit a rider comfortably. These belts are made in five- to eight-inch widths and are a great protection and support to a rider when riding hard-pitching or bucking stock.

Figure 4: Hatbands. A shows a narrow, half-round leather band which is very popular. B shows a wide band, fancy-stamped, which has cinch-tie fasteners. C shows a woven horsehair band with silver ornaments on one side. These hatbands are made in a combination of colors and are very attractive. They are worn more in the northwest than in the south.

Figure 5: Hair saddle pockets. These are made to be attached to the back of a saddle and the hair used to cover them is generally angora goat hair, but sometimes bearskin or sealskin is used. Such saddle pockets were popular in the northwest in the 90's but are not often used today because of their extra weight on a saddle; in these times a cowhand likes his outfit light.

Figures 11 and 12 show other types of saddle pockets that are handy to pack things in and are still used by some riders; they are more popular in the northwest than in southern territory.

Figures 6 and 7: Mexican quirts. These are shot-loaded and differ considerably from those described in the Section of this book entitled "Building a Quirt."

Figure 8: Cantle pocket. This is designed to fit on the back of the saddle's cantle (see Section entitled "Saddles") and is handy because it is out of the way and light in weight.

PLATE 70 *Miscellaneous Cowboy Equipment*

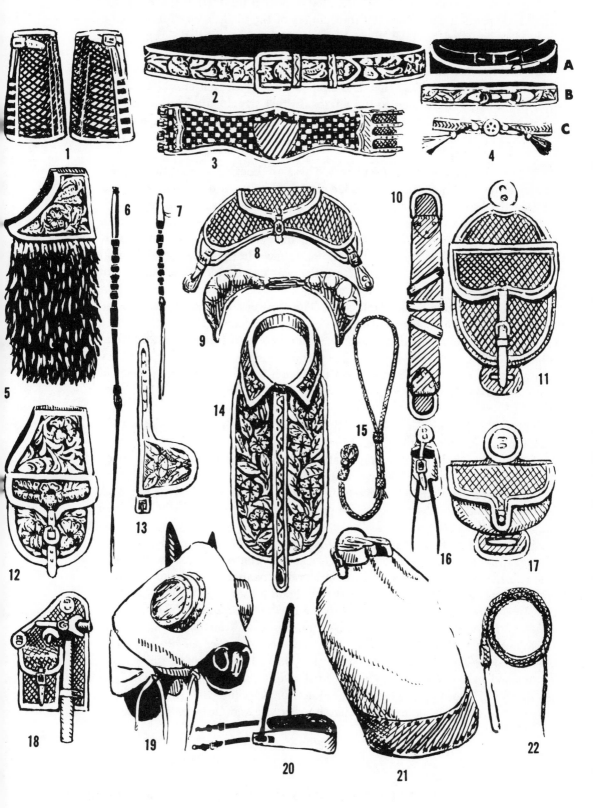

Figure 9: Bucking rolls. These are used to widen the fork of the old-style, narrow-fork saddles; they were the forerunners of the modern swell-fork saddle which was designed to take their place (see Section entitled "Horns and Forks").

Figure 10: Back band of a riding surcingle or bull rigging (see p. 140). A latigo is attached to the D's (metal, D-shaped pieces) in each end of the back band, and a cinch is attached to the latigos, so that the rigging can be cinched on a steer or a horse that is to be rode bareback. Three handholds (at the center of the band) are shown so the rider can either ride with two handholds or with one center hold alone.

Figure 13: Stirrup-leather protectors. These are buckled around the leathers just above the stirrup so that the fender piece will be next to a rider's boot and will keep the boot from rubbing against the leathers and wearing them.

Figure 14: Leather shirt front and collar. The shirt front was made to take the place of the old-time, hard-boiled, white shirt front popular in the 80's. It was generally fancy hand-carved, like the one shown in the drawing, and could be worn over any kind of a shirt. The collar was detachable. Such collars can still be bought today but are seldom worn.

Figure 15: Leather neck watch chain. This type of chain was popular in the 90's and was sometimes made of hair in contrasting colors. These chains were also made of fine plaited calfskin and were adorned with tassels and sometimes with silver and gold sliding ferrules. The main objection to them was that they often got caught over a saddlehorn and the watch to which they were attached would be jerked out of the pocket and broken; otherwise they were quite decorative.

Figure 16: Wire-plyer holder. This is attached to the front saddle string and is a handy holder for the plyers when riding fence.

Figure 17: Staple pocket. This is attached to a front or back saddle string and is used to pack wire staples when riding fence.

Figure 18: Combination fence-riding outfit. This is attached to the back end of the saddle; it has a pocket for packing wire staples and a holder for a hammer.

Figure 19: Horse hood and goggles. These are used to protect a horse's eyes from dust, flying stones and splinters of rock. This contraption is also put on a horse's head while he is being hauled in a trailer behind an automobile. Many rodeo ropers and bulldoggers transport their rope horses and dogging horses in specially constructed trailers attached to the rear of their automobiles, and it is necessary to protect the horses' eyes from injuries while traveling.

Figure 20: Saddle breast collar. This piece of equipment is often used by ropers on their rope horses in contest roping work. The ends of the two straps are attached to the front rigging rings of the saddle (see Section entitled "Trees and Rigging") in order to prevent the saddle from slipping back while the horse is pulling on the rope after a steer has been roped and thrown. These collars are also used by brush hands in mountain work to prevent the saddle slipping back when going up steep mountains.

Figure 21: Saddle bag for shipping a saddle. These bags are used when a rider is doing a lot of traveling while playing rodeos, etc. The bag is made of heavy canvas reinforced with leather and is securely fastened at the top with a padlock.

Figure 22: Cow whip. This is the old-style, hand-made whip popular in the 80's and early 90's. It was used by many riders while trailing cattle. In the hands of a cowboy who knew how to handle a whip it was very effective and one rider wielding it expertly could do as much work as two riders without whips; but cow whips are seldom seen these days.

PLATE 71 *Cowboy Jewelry*

29

COWBOY JEWELRY

Gold and silver buckles and *conchas* (Spanish for "shells") are generally the only type of ornament worn by the cowhand and are often referred to as horse jewelry by the riders. It will be found that as a rule the majority of such articles of adornment are attached to a piece of leather equipment—a pair of spur straps, a belt, a hatband, or perhaps a bridle, etc. The cowhand finds as much satisfaction in the possession of a fine pair of *conchas* or a belt-buckle set as the person who sports a diamond ring. The most popular article of personal adornment is a fine belt-buckle set like the ones in Figures 2 and 4 on Plate 71. They consist of a buckle, loop and tip. Those shown used at one time to range in price from $8.50 to $28.25. Prices of cowboy jewelry quoted herein are, of course, subject to fluctuation. The flowers on the buckle shown in Figure 2 are of gold with rubies set in their centers. The sets themselves are made of fine sterling silver and are beautifully engraved. Figure 1 is a flat-plate buckle made of silver; the steer head is of gold with ruby eyes. Figure 5 shows a flat double buckle of sterling silver.

A scarf holder is shown in Figure 7. Figure 8 represents a silver cuff link in the form of *conchas;* these are often overlaid with gold initials or the head of a horse or steer. Figures 3 and 15 show tie pins, usually either gold or silver with rubies set in the heads for eyes. A hatband buckle set, in practically the same design as the belt-buckle set shown in Figures 2 and 4, is made for small hatbands. Figures 10, 11, 14 and 16 are ornaments of silver used on saddles,

PLATE 72 *Cowboy Jewelry (Cont.)*

bridles, breast straps and standing martingales, or on any other part of a cowhand's equipment that can possibly be decorated. The ornaments are graduated in size; spur-strap buckle sets are made like belt-buckle sets, only they are much smaller.

Conchas like those shown in Figures 12 and 13 are made with a loop or a button attached to the back to fasten them to the article on which they are to be worn. These are excellent examples of high-grade *conchas* and the horse head is of overlaid goldwork, as are initials when they are ordered. These *conchas* come in different sizes and are used on bridles, chaps, spur straps, saddles, etc. Such *conchas* used at one time to cost from $12.00 to $15.00 per pair, but much less if they were made of sterling silver only. Figure 18 is a drawing of a fancy saddle-horn cap with an overlaid gold brand. These ornaments are used on fine saddles. Figure 17, a string *concha*, is used for saddle-string buttons and is also used on chaps and bridles.

It is not the intention to give the idea that the average cowhand's equipment is ablaze with gold and silver mountings. Such ornaments are not for everyday range work. The fancy mounted outfits are generally awarded for prizes or used for show purposes; they are too expensive for general riding purposes. A pair of silver-mounted spurs, or a silver-mounted bridle bit, or a pair of *conchas* on his spur straps are about all the ornaments that the average cowhand displays.

In Figures 6 and 9 you have silver mountings used on high-priced fancy saddles. In Figure 6 are shown engraved silver fork plates and a silver-inlaid saddlehorn. Figure 9 is a drawing of a silver cantle rim with engraved silver name plate. Silver ornaments are also used on the saddle skirts and are engraved to match the other silver ornaments used on the saddle. A look at the saddles shown in Figures 17, 20 and 23 on Plate 57 will give the reader some idea of how fancy a saddle can be made. Further details in this connection are given in the Section entitled "Saddles." For other types of ornaments used on the various parts of the cowboy's equipment—buckles, spurs, taps, etc.—see Plate 72.

30

WORKING
RAWHIDE AND
LEATHER—
ROPE KNOTS—
HOBBLES

There are many different ways of plaiting, or braiding, knots, quirts, ropes, whips, nosebands for hackamores and so forth. Only the methods in general use are shown in this work. The reader will be able to get an over-all idea of how to proceed in building the items mentioned out of rawhide. In working this material, much depends on its original condition and on how it is prepared. The rawhide generally used for plaiting purposes is cowhide and it should be clarified (see below) to put it in proper condition and give it life.

The northwestern cowhand's method for preparing rawhide is to stretch and stake down a green (fresh-skinned) cowhide flesh side up (Indian-style), and then to sprinkle salt on the top side. This will tend to draw out the blood and other foreign matter and cause the hide to become transparent. Rawhide work is generally done in the winter months which are favorable to the conditioning of rawhide. The salt on the hide will melt any snow that might fall on the hide; this is beneficial to the skin which is moistened and kept from becoming dry and flinty. An old, sun-dried, flinty cowhide will not provide good material for plaiting purposes.

In handling rawhide in the southwest, the hide should also be staked down on the ground with the flesh side up and salted thoroughly to clarify it; then the moisture must be removed; about a week's exposure to the sun will suffice to do this pretty thoroughly. Then the hide should be placed where it will be in the shade.

When a fresh-skinned hide is first staked down, it should be fleshed; that is, the surplus flesh should be scraped off it so the salt will do an even job of clarifying.

The rawhide worker's tool kit contains three items, namely: a good sharp knife, a marlinspike, and a leather gauge—generally a notched stick used in conjunction with the knife. A pitchfork tine or an ice pick is often used in place of the marlinspike; it is used as an awl to make openings under the plaiting strands when other strands are to be run through them.

In selecting a piece of rawhide to be worked, do not take one showing deep cuts, burns or brands. Such blemishes will tend to weaken the material. If the rawhide is dry when a piece to be worked is cut out of it, soak it in water until it is thoroughly pliable. Rawhide, however, should *not* be left in water any longer than is necessary to soften it, for it will rot if soaked too long. When the rawhide is sufficiently softened, it is removed from the water and the hair is scraped off the outside with a sharp knife; the worker should be careful while scraping not to cut the hide. This hair-removing process is known as graining; the grain (the thin outer layer of hide) is removed as the hair is scraped off. This prevents the outside of the rawhide from drawing up more than the under (or flesh) side and this in turn makes the material more pliable—not only while it is being worked, but also after it has been worked up into the article wanted.

In cutting an endless, or very long, strand such as the strands that are required in building a *reata* rope, an oval or round piece of material is used so that there will be no sharp turns to be made by the cutting tool. The worker starts on the outside of the material by cutting a strand, or string, of the width wanted. When the desired length has been cut the strand is sheared off. The thickness of the strings should be made uniform by trimming the thick places down. The outside, or top, edges should be lightly beveled to remove the sharp edge; this makes the surfaces of the articles constructed smoother when they are rolled. Any surplus flesh left on the flesh side of the rawhide should be peeled off. If the material should become too dry while it is being worked, it should be dampened to keep it in good workable condition. When an unfinished piece of rawhide work is laid away for a short period, it should be kept moist by rolling it up in a damp cloth.

In plaiting work the strands should be drawn down close and taut so that there will not be any space left between them when the material is dry. A rawhide strand or string should be one continuous piece to avoid the need for splicing. It is often a good idea when working a piece of rawhide to pull the material back and forth across the edge of a board to break the stiffness in the material. This is a good way to soften up the rawhide to be used in building a pair of hobbles (see diagrams on Plate 76). To preserve a rawhide article you have made, you should lubricate it by rubbing tallow into its surface. If the rawhide becomes too dry it will lose its life, will deteriorate through dry-rot and will eventually go to pieces. Rawhide ropes should be well lubricated at least twice each year if they are exposed to the weather. Rawhide hobbles should also be treated with tallow to keep them from becoming too stiff and hard and injuring an animal's legs.

All the plaited knots that are described below may be made of rawhide and also of tanned calfskin leather:

On Plate 73 the first diagrams 1 through 6, the "6-Plait, One-String Knot" series, show the style of knot which appears also in the upper end of the quirt body shown in Figure 7 on Plate 77; there you have the knot in its completed stage. (The body knot on the quirt just referred to is also made with a *three*-string, *six*-plait knot, illustrated in Figures 12 through 16 on Plate 78; this is the same style of plaited knot as that put on the handle of a quirt—see Section entitled "Building a Quirt.") The one-string, six-plait knot is held to a length of about 2 inches and is therefore used for short knots.

The six-plait, one-string knot is shown step by step on Plate 73: The lower end of the strand shown in Figure 1 is stationary, while the end indicated at A is carried around to start forming the knot. Figure 3 shows how the end follows the arrow, and in Figure 4 the marlinspike shows how the end is carried in under the strand indicated. In Figure 5 the marlinspike indicates how the end is brought around to follow the stationary strand. When the A strand has followed the string around until it is a double strand throughout, as shown in Figure 6, the knot is completed. The ends are lapped over each other under a strand.

The four-plait, one-string knot (see at the middle of Plate 73) is a two-turn knot (two turns at each end of the knot) which can be made any length desired. It is used for long knots such as those on the front of hackamore nosebands (see B in Figure 1 on Plate 35). In Figure 1 of the series of four-plait knot diagrams, the end is carried around to form the knot, as indicated at B. In Figure 3, the arrow indicates how the end of the string is carried in under and over the other strands; and in Figure 4 is shown how the end B is brought around and in under the end of the stationary strand. It now proceeds to follow around until it meets the end of the stationary strand, as shown in Figure 5; here the knot is completed by lapping the ends of the two strands in under a set of other strands and the protruding ends are cut off.

The four-plait, two-string knot is shown in three diagrams at the bottom of Plate 73. The strands are numbered to enable the reader to follow them in proper order. Number 1 strand is the first to be carried around the object and over number 4, as indicated by the arrow. In Figure 2 the number 3 strand is carried around to the left and in under number 2, and over number 1. Figure 3 shows how the plaiting looks. The ends of the strings can be turned back to form a double-strand plait by carrying numbers 1 and 2 around so they will follow numbers 3 and 4 back, and then by carrying numbers 3 and 4 around so that they will follow numbers 1 and 2 back. When the knot is completed it will look like the four-plait knot shown in Figure 5, immediately to the left of the three Figures just described.

The eight-plait, four-string knot is shown in four phases in Figures 1 and 2 in the lower right-hand corner of Plate 73 and Figures 3 and 4 at the top of Plate 74. The strands in Figure 1 are numbered and the arrows on numbers 1 and 5 indicate how the strands are turned. Number 1 turns down over number 2 and number 5 turns down over number 6. In Figure 2 the arrows indicate how numbers 2 and 6 are carried around the object and how they are carried in under and over the strands indicated, in proper sequence: Number 6 strand is carried over 1 and under 3 and over 4; number 2 strand is carried under 5 and over 7, and under 8 and over 6, as indicated by the arrow. The order in which numbers 2 and 6 cross each other on the back side of the object is: 6 goes in under 2. Figure 3 on Plate 74 shows how the strings have been handled, and in Figure 4 the knot is seen completed by carrying numbers 1, 2, 3 and 4 strands around so they will follow numbers 5, 6, 7 and 8 strands when they are turned back; numbers 5, 6, 7 and 8 strands are carried around so they will follow numbers 1, 2, 3 and 4 strands when *they* are turned back. The end of each string is generally lapped over the strand it meets when it has completed a full circuit at the opposite end of the knot, and it is held in place by the strand which it has last passed under.

The one-string, three-plait knot illustrated on Plate 74 is a narrow knot generally used as a guard knot on each side of a strap to hold the strap in place. This type of knot is often used on hackamore nosebands (see B in Figure 1 on Plate 35). There are six diagrams pertaining to this knot: In Figure 1 in the upper right-hand corner of Plate 74, the end which is carried around to start the knot is indicated by the letter C; in Figure 4 is shown how the knot is made in single strand; Figure 5 shows the completed single-strand knot; and in Figure 6 can be seen the knot made double-strand when the strand indicated at C is made to follow the single strand around until it meets the stationary end. The knot is almost always made double-strand, as shown in Figure 6. When the knot is completed, it should be rolled or hammered down to make it smooth.

The techniques in plaiting lengths of rope, whips, nosebands, quirts, hatbands, watch chains, bridle reins and other plaited articles are those indicated in the diagrams with the headings "4-Plait," "6-Plait" and "8-Plait" on Plate 74. All the strands are numbered and arrows indicate the direction and route they travel.

Four-strand plait: In Figures 1, 2 and 3 on Plate 74, under the heading "4-Plait," the strands are numbered 1, 2, 3 and 4. In Figure 1 the two center strands are crossed in straightening the plait. Figure 2 shows strand number 1

PLATE 73 *Working Rawhide & Leather*

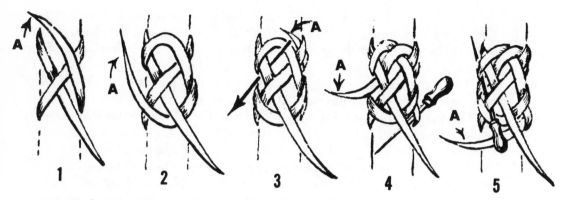

1 2 3 4 5

6-PLAIT, ONE-STRING KNOT—FIGURES NUMBERED 1 TO 6

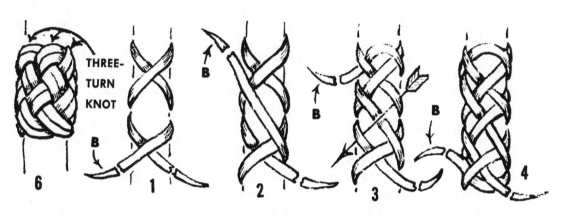

THREE-TURN KNOT

6 1 2 3 4

4-PLAIT, ONE-STRING KNOT—FIGURES NUMBERED 1 TO 5

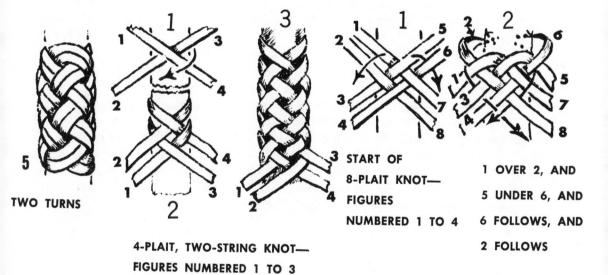

5

TWO TURNS

4-PLAIT, TWO-STRING KNOT—
FIGURES NUMBERED 1 TO 3

START OF
8-PLAIT KNOT—
FIGURES
NUMBERED 1 TO 4

1 OVER 2, AND

5 UNDER 6, AND

6 FOLLOWS, AND

2 FOLLOWS

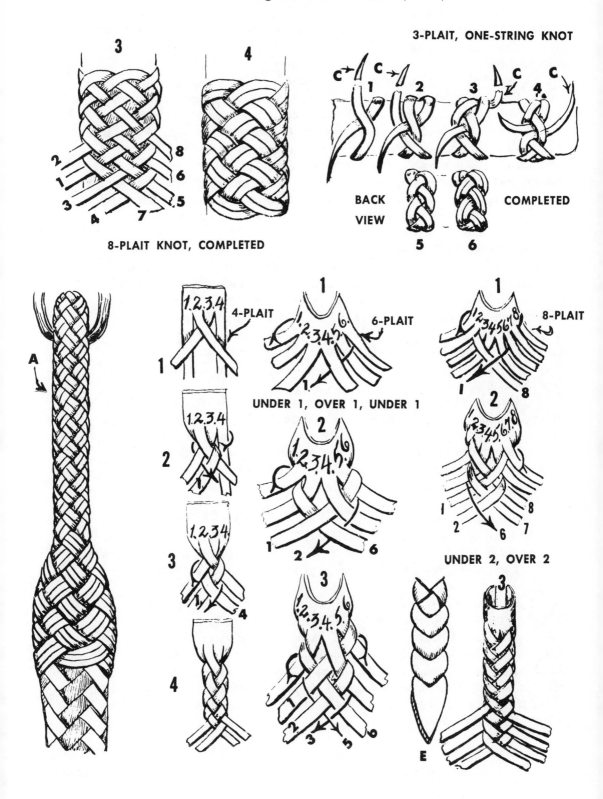

PLATE 74 *Working Rawhide & Leather (Cont.)*

3-PLAIT, ONE-STRING KNOT

8-PLAIT KNOT, COMPLETED

BACK VIEW — 5

COMPLETED — 6

4-PLAIT

6-PLAIT

UNDER 1, OVER 1, UNDER 1

8-PLAIT

UNDER 2, OVER 2

carried around and in under number 4 and over number 2. In Figure 3 strand number 4 is carried around and in under number 3 and over number 1. In Figure 4 the plaiting is well started and the general order of plaiting is: over once and under once, etc.

Six-strand plait: This is the plait of six strands which is used in plaiting the body of the quirt shown on Plate 77. In Figure 1 on Plate 74, under the heading "6-Plait," the arrow shows how strand 1 is carried around in under 6 and over 5 and under 4. The general plaiting order is: under once and over once and under once. Figure 2 shows how strand 6 is carried around and in under 2 and over 3 and under 1. The number 2 strand follows the arrow, in under 5 and over 4 and under 6. In Figure 3 the number 5 strand is carried around and in under 3 and over 1 and under 2. The number 3 strand is brought around and in under 4 and over 6 and under 5. The strings are now all properly started and all that is necessary is to continue the order.

Eight-strand plait: The number 8 strand in Figure 1 on Plate 74, under the heading "8-Plait," is carried around and in under 1 and 2, and over 3 and 4. The arrow shows the course followed by the number 1 strand which is carried around and in under 7 and 6, and over 5 and 8. In Figure 2 the number 7 strand is carried around in under 2 and 3, and then over 4 and 1. The number 2 strand is brought around and in under 6 and 5, and over 8 and 7. The arrow shows the number 6 strand brought around and in under 3 and 4, and then over 1 and 2. By following the general order of under two and over two, the plaiting will assume the form shown in Figure 3.

Knots in the ends of plaited work: There are several different ways of building knots in the ends of plaited work. The Spanish knot (see below) shown in Figures 1 through 6 on Plate 75 is the one most generally used. The free end of a *reata* is generally interlaced, as shown in the drawing at E in the lower right-hand corner of Plate 74. Knots in the ends of plaited work should be drawn down close and tight to keep them from slipping.

The rope knots and hitches described below are the ones in general use in the cow country. If they seem a puzzle to the green hand, this is because no matter how clearly they are explained, it takes some practice with a rope to see how they are built. This is true, of course, of the leatherwork described herein, also.

The Spanish knot is one often used on the ends of catch ropes and is illustrated in Figures 1 through 6 on Plate 75. It is necessary to untwist about six inches of the end of the rope in order to have the strands long enough to work with, as shown in Figure 1. Figure 2 shows how the ends of each strand are run under the adjoining strand, as is shown also in Figures 3 and 4. The ends of the strands are carried in under the crossed strands and brought up through the center of the knot, as shown in Figures 5 and 6. Figure 6 shows the knot completed when pulled down.

PLATE 75 *Rope Knots*

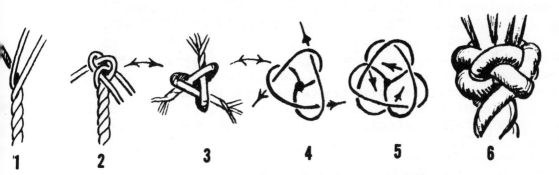

SHOWING HOW THE SPANISH KNOT IS MADE—FIGURES 1 TO 6

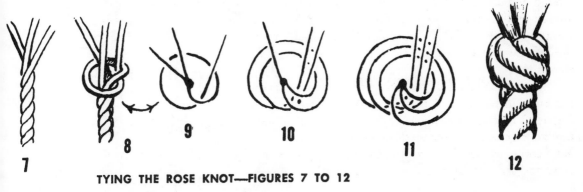

TYING THE ROSE KNOT—FIGURES 7 TO 12

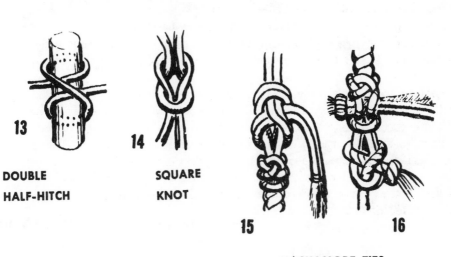

**DOUBLE
HALF-HITCH**

**SQUARE
KNOT**

HACKAMORE TIES

PLATE 76 *How to Make Rawhide Hobbles*

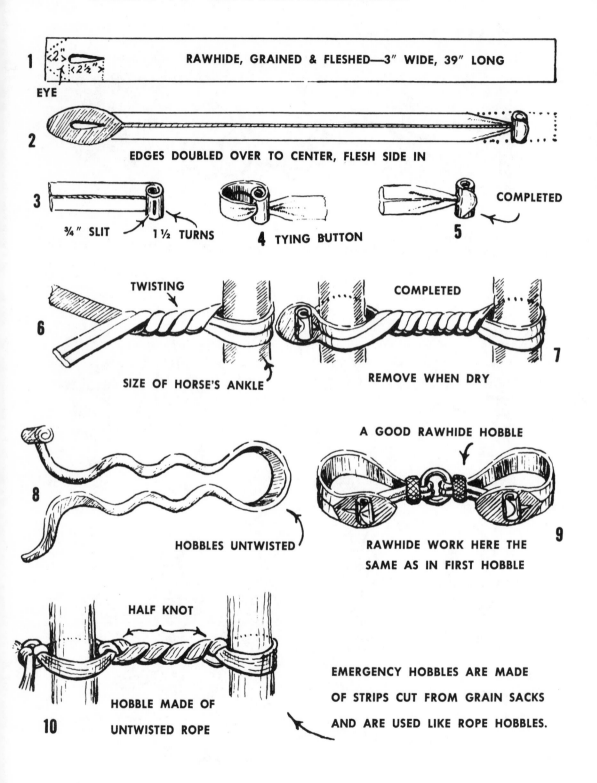

1 EYE <2" <2½">

RAWHIDE, GRAINED & FLESHED—3" WIDE, 39" LONG

2 EDGES DOUBLED OVER TO CENTER, FLESH SIDE IN

3 ¾" SLIT 1½ TURNS

4 TYING BUTTON

5 COMPLETED

6 TWISTING SIZE OF HORSE'S ANKLE

7 COMPLETED REMOVE WHEN DRY

8 HOBBLES UNTWISTED

9 A GOOD RAWHIDE HOBBLE RAWHIDE WORK HERE THE SAME AS IN FIRST HOBBLE

10 HALF KNOT HOBBLE MADE OF UNTWISTED ROPE

EMERGENCY HOBBLES ARE MADE OF STRIPS CUT FROM GRAIN SACKS AND ARE USED LIKE ROPE HOBBLES.

Figures 7 through 12 show how the rose knot is tied. Figure 7 shows the untwisted strands and Figure 8 shows how a simple granny knot is tied in strand 1, encircling the other strands. In Figure 9 is shown the same situation, only in a simpler form. The ends are numbered so the reader will be able to keep track of the work. In Figure 10 strand 2 is carried around in the same manner as strand 1, and the end is brought up through the center of the loop formed by strands 1 and 2. In Figure 11 can be seen how strand 3 is carried around and is brought up through the center of the three granny knots formed by the other strands. In Figure 12 is shown the completed knot when the strands have been tightened. This rose knot is a popular type of knot often employed in the ends of catch ropes and other ropes used by cowhands and packers.

Figure 13 is the well-known clove hitch, or the double half-hitch. It is often used by cowhands in tying a horse to an object and in securing or fastening a rope to a post or pole. It is easily untied and a very effective hitch to use.

Figure 14 shows the square knot or reef knot which is one that can be easily untied. It is often used in tying the ends of rope hobbles and in tying a wild ox up to a tree, as was shown in the Section entitled "Handling Wild Stock."

Figure 15 shows how the two ends of the feador rope on a hackamore or hackalea are tied in double loops (see p. 144 and Figure 21 on Plate 30). This is the hitch known by sailors as a sheet bend. It is easy to untie and holds the rope securely. Figure 16 shows how the end of the *mecate*, or hackamore tie rope, is tied into the double-loop end of the feador of the hackamore; this is the same procedure as that shown in Figure 15.

On Plate 76 are shown three different types of hobbles. The first diagrams, from Figures 1 through 8, show how to build a pair of hobbles. In Figure 1 is shown a piece of rawhide 3 inches wide and 39 inches long which has been grained and fleshed. An eye 2½ inches long has been cut in the form shown; this eye is rounded at the outer end to prevent it from tearing out. Note that this end of the eye is located 2 inches from the very end of the material; this is to give a handhold and keep the rawhide from tearing out.

Figure 2 illustrates how the edges of the piece of rawhide are folded over to make the material double. Note that the flesh side of the rawhide is on the inside. The way the button knot in the end is made is shown in Figures 3, 4, and 5. The end of the rawhide is turned back one and a half turns and a slit ¾ inch long is made through the three thicknesses of material; then the other end of the raw-hide is drawn through the slit to complete the knot. Two stakes, about the size of the forelegs of a horse, or 3¼ inches in diameter, are used to shape and twist the hobbles, as indicated in Figures 6 and 7. The stakes are drove into the ground about 9 inches apart and the hobbles are placed on them as shown in Figure 7. In twisting the hobbles between the stakes, the material should be twisted in opposite directions, on the same principle as that of twisting a rope. This will round the two pieces and make them look like the diagram in Figure 8 when they are untwisted.

The rawhide hobbles with ring centers in Figure 9 are made in much the same way as those just described, only they are connected with a ring. The material is doubled and the ends are made in the same way as in the other hobbles.

Rope hobbles are made from the untwisted strands of a hemp rope and are put on in the manner shown in Figure 10. When the rope is first placed around the leg of the horse, a half-knot is tied and the two parts are twisted together; then a half-twist is tied at the end of the twist. Then the two ends are placed around the other leg of the horse and are tied in a square knot.

Emergency hobbles are made from strips cut from a grain sack. They are about 6 inches wide and are placed on the horse's legs in the manner shown for the hobbles in Figure 10.

The regular, or common, chain hobble (not shown) has a swivel in the center of the chain. This hobble is used a great deal by those who do not know how to make the other hobbles described above.

The "figure-eight" hobble is a good leather hobble made by saddle makers. This hobble places the horse's feet closer together than the other styles described and so prevents a horse from grazing very far from camp.

31

BUILDING A QUIRT

The word "quirt" is derived from the Spanish *cuarta de cordon*, meaning whip of cord. The *cuarta* is a cowboy's whip and is of many designs. The majority of quirts are made in Mexico. The short handle is loaded with shot or lead to give it weight. At one end of the whip are the lashes (tail) and at the other end (the head or handle) is a loop by which the cowboy hangs the quirt from his wrist or saddlehorn when he is not using it. The handle of a loaded quirt is flexible, whereas the type of quirt shown in this work is known as a stiff-handled quirt and is not flexible. The stiff-handled quirt is the kind most generally used by cowhands because it handles better. The material used in making a quirt is mostly rawhide and tanned calfskin. The diagrams on Plates 77 and 78 are pretty much self-explanatory and if the reader will follow closely the directions given below he ought to get to be able to build a fair sample of a quirt such as is described in these pages.

Figure 1 on Plate 77 shows a strip of rawhide 1½ inches wide and 46 inches long which has been properly prepared for working. This is the material from which the outside of the quirt body is built.

Figure 2 shows how the strings, which measure approximately 40 inches in length, are cut, leaving 6 inches uncut for the handle of the quirt. The material should be placed on a board and tacked down to hold it in place while the strings are being cut. A straight edge, or ruler, should be used as a guide to assure that the strings will be cut accurately; they are ¼ inch wide at each end but are tapered down to ⅛ of an inch in the center.

Figure 3 shows the material used in making the filler, or center, of the quirt body. A piece of rawhide 2 inches wide and 21½ inches long is cut into four strands. This rawhide is also tacked down on a board so it will be held in place while the strands (strings) are being cut. A space 1½ inches long is left uncut at the base; this will be wrapped around the 7-inch iron handle (shown in the drawing at the right of Figure 3). The strings are ½ inch wide at the base and are cut to a point, as indicated in the drawing, at the spot where the awl is stuck in the end of the rawhide to hold it in place while it is being cut. The strings, when they have been cut, will turn out to be about 20 inches long.

A piece of steel about 7 inches long is used for the filler of the handle. A pitchfork tine is often used as the steel filler; the tine is straightened out and the large end is flattened to a width of ⅝ of an inch. A hole ⅜ of an inch in diameter is drilled through the metal about ¾ of an inch from the end, as indicated in the drawing at the right of Figure 3.

Figure 4 shows the rawhide filler of the quirt body plaited and completed. Before the filler (which was prepared in Figure 3) is plaited, the uncut base end is wrapped around the small, or lower, end of the metal handle filler. A length of cord is then tightly wrapped over this base end of the rawhide to keep it and the handle filler together and firmly in place. About 5 inches of the steel handle piece is left showing after this is done. The four rawhide strands are then plaited out to their ends (by the "4-Plait" method shown on Plate 74 and described on p. 257) and a cord is tied around the end of the plaiting to hold it together.

A piece of saddle string 12 inches long and ½ inch wide is then run through the hole in the top of the metal handle piece and the two ends of the saddle string are either interlaced or tied together, as shown in Figure 4. This string becomes the loop of the quirt by which the latter is hung on the cowhand's wrist. The plaited rawhide filler is then dipped in boiling water to stiffen it. The next step is to hang the filler up on a nail by the saddle-string handle loop, with a weight attached to the end of the plaiting to stretch it. Now the rawhide filler is left to dry.

Figure 5 shows the quirt body about half completed with the filler almost covered. In starting to cover the filler of the quirt, the uncut end of the covering (which was prepared in Figure 2) is tightly wrapped around the metal handle, between the handle loop and the beginning of the filler plaiting; it is then wrapped with a piece of cord to hold it firmly in place, as is indicated in Figure 5. Then the six strings of the quirt cover are plaited down to the point where they are the narrowest, which is about midway; the plaiting method used is the "6-Plait" shown on Plate 74 and described on p. 258. The strands of the quirt cover are now ready to be "turned back." The strings are drawn fairly tight when they are first plaited, but they are not laid as close as they will be when they are run back; at the point that has now been reached, they will appear as shown at the bottom of Plate 77 in the detail drawings numbered 1 through 4 under the heading "6-Plait Turned Back," etc. The technique for turning the strings back is described immediately after the four paragraphs below which concern Figures 6 and 7 on Plate 77.

Figure 6 shows the body of the quirt nearly finished. The turning-back process to be explained below has been completed and then extra, decorative filler strings—the black strings running about two-thirds the length of the body of the quirt—have also been run in place. (Figure 11 on Plate 78 is a detail drawing showing how these decorative filler strings, six in number, may be made to follow any six strands of the quirt cover that all run in the same direction; see also p. 269.) The lower ends of the decorative strings are left loose and about 3 inches long to form a sort of tassel.

To the right of Figure 6 on Plate 77 is shown the pattern for the quirt tail, a piece of leather about 24 inches long and about ½ inch wide across the center. A slot, or split, is made in the center, large enough to slip over the end of the quirt, yet be held on tight. The ends of the tail are pointed, as shown. The tail is put on by slipping the slotted center over the end of the quirt; then the two ends of the tail are brought out together through the center of the end of the quirt. This is done by first making two holes, one on each side, just above the end of the quirt; one end of the tail is run into each hole. Then the ends are pulled out and down together through one central hole in the very bottom of the end of the quirt. This can be understood if the reader will note how the finished tail is arranged in Figure 7.

Figure 7 shows the completed quirt, with its handle and with a one-string knot tied on the upper end of the quirt body. This knot is shown in Figures 1 through 6 at the top of Plate 73; it is a three-turn, six-plait knot made with one string and is described on p. 254. It is tied *after* the handle knot (see below) is tied.

The handle knot is a twelve-plait knot (the same number of plaits seen in the body of the quirt) and the end of it is turned back in exactly the same way as is done for the end of the quirt (see below). The knot is made with three strings, as shown in Figures 12 through 16 on Plate 78 and described on p. 269, and is not started at the end of the handle, but down next to the top of the body of the quirt. It is plaited down to the other end of the handle and then turned back. Before starting the handle knot, the wrist loop strap is removed; it is replaced when the knot is completed.

"Turning back" the end of a quirt is difficult to explain—in fact, it was said that it could not be done—but here it is! The quirt ready to have the end turned back is shown in Figure 5 on Plate 77. The ten detail diagrams used to illustrate this subject are Figures 1 through 4 at the bottom of Plate 77 and Figures 5 through 10 on Plate 78. These should enable the reader to do a good job of turning back the six strands of the outside covering of the quirt without much trouble.

First, the ends of the long, hanging strands seen in Figure 5 on Plate 77 are sharpened, or pointed. A round, sharp-pointed instrument, such as an ice pick,

PLATE 77 *Building a Quirt*

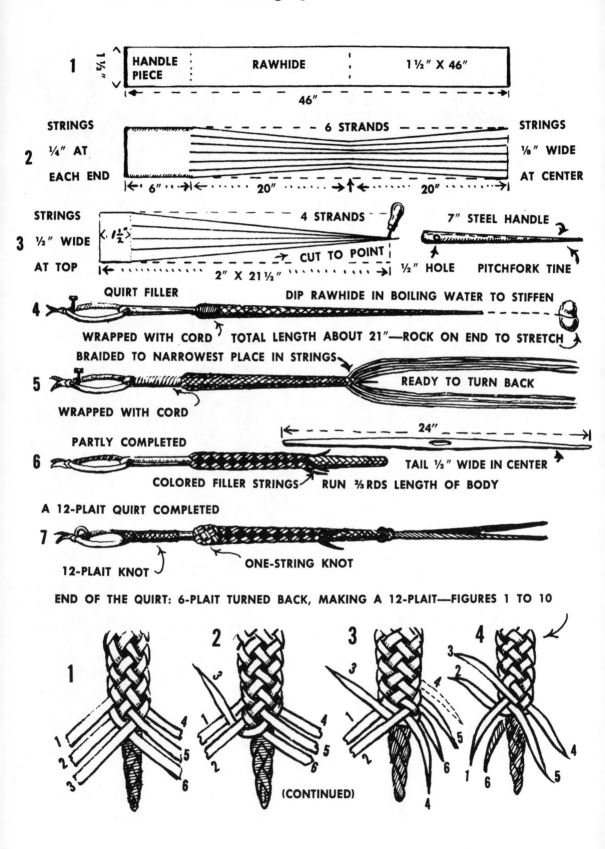

1 1½" — HANDLE PIECE — RAWHIDE — 1½" X 46" — 46"

2 STRINGS ¼" AT EACH END — 6 STRANDS — STRINGS ⅛" WIDE AT CENTER — 6" — 20" — 20"

3 STRINGS ½" WIDE AT TOP — 1½" — 4 STRANDS — CUT TO POINT — 2" X 21½" — 7" STEEL HANDLE — ½" HOLE — PITCHFORK TINE

4 QUIRT FILLER — DIP RAWHIDE IN BOILING WATER TO STIFFEN — WRAPPED WITH CORD — TOTAL LENGTH ABOUT 21"—ROCK ON END TO STRETCH

5 BRAIDED TO NARROWEST PLACE IN STRINGS — READY TO TURN BACK — WRAPPED WITH CORD

6 PARTLY COMPLETED — 24" — COLORED FILLER STRINGS — RUN ⅔RDS LENGTH OF BODY — TAIL ½" WIDE IN CENTER

A 12-PLAIT QUIRT COMPLETED

7 12-PLAIT KNOT — ONE-STRING KNOT

END OF THE QUIRT: 6-PLAIT TURNED BACK, MAKING A 12-PLAIT—FIGURES 1 TO 10

1 — 1 2 3 4 5 6

2 — 3 1 2 4 5 6 (CONTINUED)

3 — 3 1 2 4 5 6 4

4 — 3 2 1 6 5 4

PLATE 78 *Building a Quirt (Cont.)*

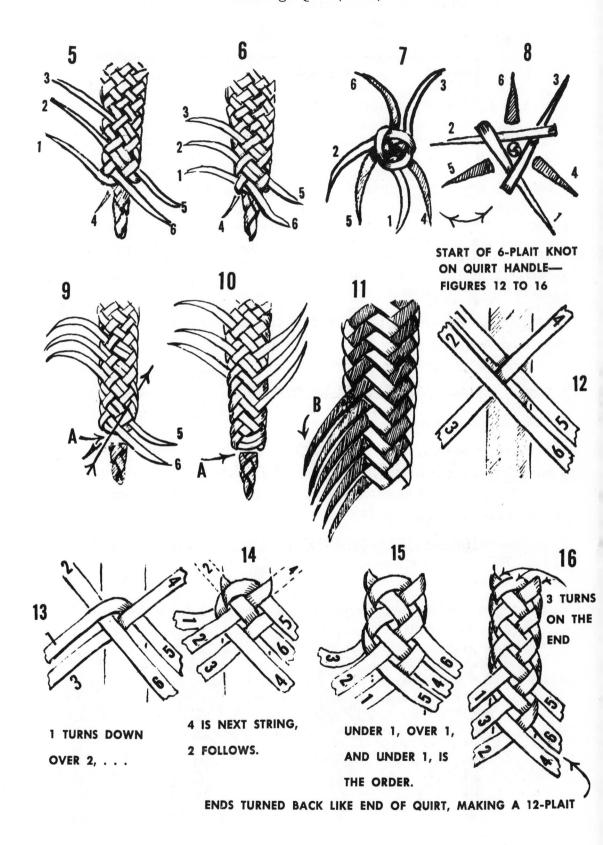

5

6

7

8

START OF 6-PLAIT KNOT
ON QUIRT HANDLE—
FIGURES 12 TO 16

9

10

11

12

13

1 TURNS DOWN
OVER 2, . . .

14

4 IS NEXT STRING,
2 FOLLOWS.

15

UNDER 1, OVER 1,
AND UNDER 1, IS
THE ORDER.

16

3 TURNS
ON THE
END

ENDS TURNED BACK LIKE END OF QUIRT, MAKING A 12-PLAIT

is used for a marlinspike to punch holes under the plaited part of the strands—holes through which the pointed free ends of the strands will be drawn.

It will be noted that the end of the rawhide quirt filler (see the four Figures at the bottom of Plate 77) is not quite covered before starting to turn the ends of the strands back; this is as it should be, because the filler is made temporarily longer than the quirt body and helps to hold the strands in place while they are being turned back. As soon as the first three strands of the quirt body are turned back, the end of the filler is cut off, as indicated at A in Figure 9 on Plate 78.

The strands of the quirt body are numbered in their proper order for turning back in Figure 1 at the bottom of Plate 77. Strands 1, 2 and 3 on the left side are the first to be turned back: 3 is the first strand turned back, 2 is the second one, and 1 is turned back third. As each strand is turned back, the quirt is revolve-turned toward the right by one-third of a revolution in order to present a different view of the work as it progresses. There is really no need to describe the movements made in turning the strands back, as the diagrams should suffice to explain the whole in detail. If the reader will watch the six numbered strands closely in Figures 1 through 10, everything will work out all right.

Figure 6 on Plate 78 shows how the first three strands have been turned back, with number 3 at the top and number 1 at the bottom. Figure 7 shows the end view of the quirt after these first three strands have been turned. The three strands numbered 4, 5 and 6 are in proper position and are the next to be turned back. Figure 8 is a simplified diagram showing the end already shown in Figure 7; Figure 8 will give the reader a clearer idea as to how the end of the quirt will look with the first three strands turned back.

Figure 9 on Plate 78 shows the start of turning the last three strands back. The end of the outside plaiting work is pushed back on the filler in order to be able to cut the end of the filler off close up under the covering; the outside strands will then cover the end of the filler (see at A of Figures 9 and 10).

The arrow shows the course taken by number 6 strand, the first strand to be turned back in this direction. In turning the last three strands back, it is necessary for each strand to jump (pass) over either one or three strands; this is to break the double-strand appearance of the plaiting created by the first three strands. This double-strand look was caused by the under-and-over method of plaiting that was employed. This jump-over procedure is necessary in order to finish up with a correct twelve-plait job. The order which these last strands follow while being worked back is: Over three, under two, over two, and then under and over two strands all the rest of the way back. Number 6 is the first strand of the three to be turned back, then number 5, and then number 4.

Figure 10 on Plate 78 shows all six of the strands turned back. The end shows the three complete double turns. The strands should be drawn tight so the plaiting will be tightly laid and make a neat-looking job.

When a piece of plaiting work is completed, it should be placed on a smooth hard surface and then rolled; this is done in order to round the work and make the strands lie flat and smooth.

Figure 11 shows body filler strings; these strings are for decorative purposes and to give weight and balance to the quirt as a whole (see the finished quirt in Figure 7 on Plate 77). The strings are of tanned calfskin and of different colors; tan and black are the colors most generally used for filler work and for plaited knots. The filler strings indicated at B in Figure 11 are not left in the order shown when the work is completed, but are in this order in the illustration to show how they are carried while they are being worked into the body of the quirt. When the operator starts a string, he proceeds to work it through to its destination before starting another string. Sometimes, when six strings are being worked into the body of the quirt, three of the strands are carried only one-third of the length of the body and the other three are carried on until they have reached two-thirds of the length of the body and are then stopped. There are several different ways to work the strings, each giving the quirt a different decorative design.

Figures 12 through 16 on Plate 78 illustrate the six-plait knot which, when it is turned back, becomes the twelve-plait knot mentioned above for making the quirt handle shown in Figure 7 on Plate 77. (A variation of this handle is also shown in detail at A on the left-hand side of Plate 74; see below.) The three-strand, six-plait knot can also be built on the front part of a hackamore noseband such as is shown in Figure 2 on Plate 35, or on any other piece of plaited work.

Note how the three strands are arranged in Figure 12 on Plate 78 to start the six-plait knot. The strands are numbered from 1 to 6 so the reader will be able to keep track of each strand as it is being worked. The next four Figures, through Figure 16, are self-explanatory. If the knot is being started on the handle of a quirt, the base is always on the *lower* part of the handle, as was explained above. The knot is worked towards the upper end of the handle, then the strings are turned back over the end as in turning back the end of the quirt body, as was also explained above. When the strings have been worked back to the base, they must again be turned back to finish the knot and they are then cut off.

The quirt-handle knot shown at A on the right-hand side of Plate 74 is not in the regular twelve-plait style of braiding, but it would have been if, in turning it back, the last three strings had been made to jump one or three strands instead of two. The procedure shown here makes six double strands; where the strands have been turned back again at the base of the handle, the knot has become a triple-strand piece of work. This style of handle knot is a good one and makes a neat job.

PLATE 79 *Guns & Equipment*

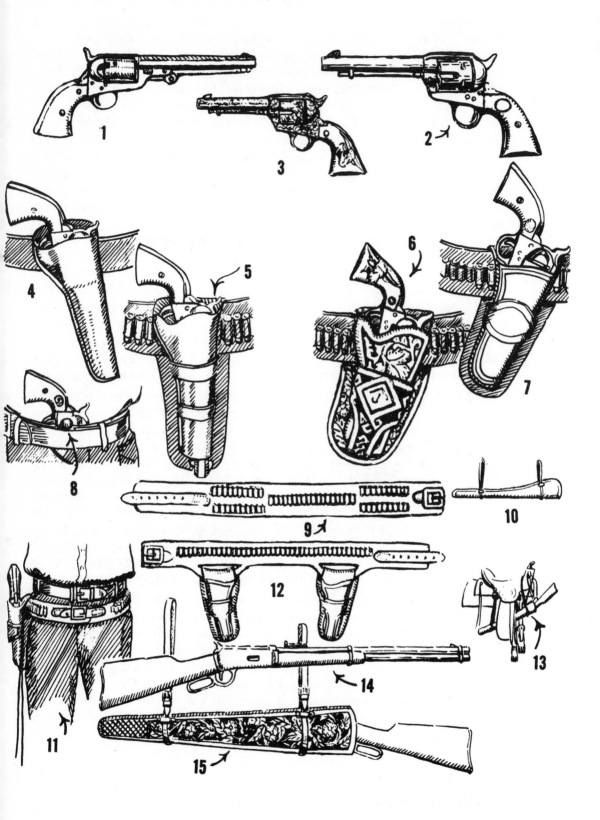

32

GUNS

AND

EQUIPMENT

The Colt six-shooter (so called because it can fire six shots without reloading) has played an important part in the making of Western history and has ever since its development been a part of the cowhand's equipment. Samuel Colt whittled out his model in 1830 and patented his revolver in 1835. The Patterson Colt was made in 1836, and two years later the famous "Texas pistol," or six-shooter, came into being (see Figure 1 on Plate 79). This is the celebrated .36-caliber, cap and ball gun, equipped with a tamper* located underneath the long octagonal barrel. In 1873 the .45-caliber, single-action "frontier model" six-shooter was built to shoot the new .45 center-fire metallic cartridges. It was known as the "Peacemaker" and was the first big-bore gun to use the new center-fire cartridges. In 1875 the gun was chambered to shoot the famous .44-40 cartridges which were being used in the Winchester 1873-model rifle. Figure 2 shows this renowned gun which is chambered to shoot the .32-20, .38-40 ammunition as well as the .44-40's and .45's. The stirring history of the cow country has been written to a great extent in the smoke of the .44; no other caliber of gun used in the early days made as much history. Figure 3 shows a silver-plated .45 Colt, highly engraved and equipped with carved ivory handles.

Types of holsters are shown in Figures 4 through 7 on Plate 79. Figure 4 depicts the old-style holster used during the Civil War and before. It had a small loop attached to the back for the belt to pass through. It was difficult to draw

* A tamper is a rod that works on a swivel to tamp the ball down on the cap.

this gun quickly. Some holsters were made with a flap that buttoned down over the handle of the gun, similar to the style of holster used by army officers and cavalrymen in the early days. Later came the Texas holster shown in Figure 5. It hung straighter and was held more firmly against the side of the individual carrying the gun, enabling him to get faster action. The end of the holster was often tied down to the side of the rider's leg with a leather string. This prevented its slipping up when the gun was drawn, permitting still faster work in getting the gun into action. Some of the holsters were open at the bottom and the long-barrel gun generally protruded a few inches. Some claim that this was for the purpose of tilting and firing the gun from the holster by the old hip-shooting technique; actually this would be highly impractical. The explanation for the short open holster is that saddlers made holsters mostly for short-barrelled guns, so that the rider who owned a long-barrelled gun made the shorter holster useable simply by cutting off the end.

Cartridge belts are worn in the position shown in Figure 11 and *not*, as is sometimes shown in illustrations, so loosely that the gun hangs far below the hips. Tie-down strings shown in this Figure, attached to a holster to tie the latter to the leg, are seldom seen today but when they are used, the holster is in the position shown.

Figure 6 shows the modern manner in which a six-shooter is carried by the range rider. This holster is a very practical one made by Myers.

Figure 7 shows a style often used by peace officers. It permits of a very rapid draw since the gun rides high and less time is required to draw the gun out of the holster than in the case of the holster in Figure 6. The holster shown in Figure 7 facilitates placing the finger on the trigger and the thumb on the hammer because there is nothing to interfere with these motions. The gun is tilted far ahead so that it responds to the draw freely.

Carrying a gun in the waistband is quite customary when a rider has removed his cartridge belt and holster (see Figure 8). The cylinder gate is opened so it will catch on the belt and prevent the gun from slipping down. A gun can be carried this way under a coat or jacket, or even under the wearer's shirt, if desired. It is a favorite way of packing a gun not being carried in a holster and permits a quick draw.

In Figure 9 the four short rows of cartridge loops shown are for six-shooter cartridges and the long row is for rifle cartridges. This is a very popular type of rifle-revolver cartridge belt used by Rangers who carry a rifle and a six-shooter at the same time. The belt is made of calfskin or horsehide and is folded double. An opening slit is made in the end under the buckle so that the belt can also be used as a money belt.

Figure 12 shows a buscadero,* a two-gun belt used by some peace officers but more by movie gunmen than by any other set of individuals. Two holster loops are located to the right and left at the lower edge of the belt; the holsters

* From the Spanish, *buscar*, to search; used in southern cow country to designate an intrepid law officer.

are swung from these. This type of belt places the holsters lower than they would naturally be if attached to the ordinary type of cartridge belt. Guns placed low make for easier drawing as the arm has freer action.

Figure 10 depicts an old-style rifle scabbard still popular with riders. Figure 13 shows how a rifle is carried on a saddle by the majority of cowhands.

Figure 14 represents a Winchester model-1894 carbine or saddle gun. This is the most popular style of rifle used in the cow country and is carried by the majority of cowhands and peace officers. It is made in several different calibers, but the .30-30 is most generally used. This is a high-powered cartridge, powerful enough to kill any type of game. This rifle has a twenty-inch, round barrel and is light in weight, which makes it adaptable for carrying on a saddle.

Figure 15 is a drawing of the Ranger type of rifle scabbard. It is designed so that the rifle can be carried with the stock turned up or down. This scabbard is attached to a saddle like the one shown in Figure 13, or it can be reversed so that the stock will be at the back of the saddle. The majority of riders carry it with the stock in front.

Of guns and equipment, "Coteau" Gene Stebbings has this to say:

"Trick gun stuff and trick knife stuff have been my hobbies from infancy and often they have been the means of catching the honorable eats. One of the first things I noticed was that the gun-toters packed their weapons in various ways. I wondered why somebody didn't figure out the *one best way* and everybody pack their gun or guns that way. I hear about 'secret' ways and 'mysterious' ways but, though I began to ramble and meet hundreds, yes, thousands of gunmen— some very famous and some very notorious ones—I discovered no 'secret' and no 'mysterious' stuff. In fact, even many of the famous and notorious gunmen packed their irons in what I considered very slow and awkward ways. Though fifty years have passed, I still think so.

"I now consider that less ingenuity and less horse sense have been used in toting short guns [six-shooters] than in anything else man has done. There are no secret draws, or mysterious draws. Not one! And, outside of my own trick guns and trick-gun harnesses, there has never been one thing of the kind unearthed that shows more than a modicum of ingenuity. That may sound egotistical but, after fifty years of digging into the matter, I believe it to be the actual fact. No one would be more pleased than I if I can be proved wrong.

"Years ago I developed my 'all ways' gun harness for two purposes. First to have a harness with which I could test thoroughly every possible way to tote a gun or two. Second to have just one harness that I could arrange so it would be convenient for any work or play I might engage in, and, incidentally, to have it so I could draw my gun or guns with the least number of movements possible to the position. Now, guessing isn't a safe method for a gunman to follow. He may guess he is very fast but have another guess coming when it is too late. The Boot Hills of the west, yes, of the world, are well planted with gunmen who guessed

"The way to find out whether you are really fast is to time yourself and to do that right takes well-designed timing equipment. There are and have been many such machines rigged; they range all the way from a stop watch to an electric device.

"Long ago I found by test that the easiest, fastest draw was from a low-hung pocket, if, however, that gun pocket was hung just right. In the upper left-hand picture I am rigged with my 'all ways' gun harness and the pockets *just right* [see Plate 80].

"The most natural way for a man to carry his arms is hanging down by his sides. Every man carries his arms in this fashion more than he does in any other way. Therefore I place my gun butts right where my hands can close over them when my arms are hanging by my sides either when I am walking or riding a horse. This eliminates to a great extent the motion, or more likely, the motions, of going for your gun. Now every motion eliminated tends to shorten the time it takes to draw and fire a short gun. Further, the easier the motions can be performed, the shorter is the time required. Again, if the arm, hand, or even the trigger finger has come to a complete stop, a new order must be sent from the brain to start the arm, hand, or finger again. Dr. Snively, using a very delicate timing machine, made many tests and found that it takes the average person approximately one-tenth of a second to transmit such an order and have the part ordered start moving to perform the order.

"Now hanging the gun pocket and holding it where put, in just the right way for the arm to draw the gun in the fastest and easiest possible manner, is very essential to a fast draw. Let me say right here that mere fast movements do not mean a fast draw.

"The upper left-hand picture [Plate 80] shows the fastest possible position and way to pack a short gun. Further, after the gun is drawn, the gunman is in the best position to direct that gun anywhere. His arm and body are free and relaxed.

"Now another thing about making a fast draw: Suppose the gun in the picture was to be carried higher, and the draw arm was in some other position. In place of the arm's being swung fast and easily its full length and coming down squarely on the gun's butt, it must be crooked at the elbow just the right amount to shorten the arm so the hand will come on the gun butt. If you crook the arm just a fraction of an inch too much or too little you miss making a good grip, may have to feel around, and that's slow, even if it's fast. Again, a crooked arm is tensed, muscles are hard, stiff and slow to start in some other bending of the arm movement.

"But there is no use to hang a gun low unless it is held firmly to a position where the arm and hand can, by practise, learn to find it instantly. A sagging belt or any other arrangement that allows the gun pocket to swing or flap or twist will confuse the drawing. By placing the pocket down as shown in the picture it can be held there easily by one or a pair of straps, held horizontally by the pocket, around the leg above the knee. These need not be very tight because

PLATE 80

"COTEAU"

GENE STEBBINGS

"ALL WAYS" GUN HARNESS,
SHOWING FIVE WAYS TO
CARRY A GUN FOR A FAST DRAW

the leg increases in diameter so rapidly that the straps tighten with the slightest upward pull at one side. The wide straps do not cut or chaff like narrow leather strings, nor do they stretch or loosen easily—in fact, not at all.

"Note the way the gun pocket is made. It consists of a rather large base piece which lies flat against the leg or body, taking the curve of leg or body; and in the case of the low-hung position, the leg being larger near the gun's butt than at its muzzle, throws the gun's butt out away from the leg to afford a good clear grip.

"The 'all ways' is made with a snug-fitting belt two and a half inches wide and of fine quality leather. Such a belt is much more comfortable than a sagging, loose belt. The sagging belt causes a feeling like one's breeches slipping down and it does cause that embarrassing trouble. The pockets are hung on a pair of adjustable hanger straps. These straps loop through metal D's in the bottom of leather slip-loops on the belt. These slip-loops may be slipped on the belt to any position desired and then tied in place by means of latigos, *i.e.*, leather strings. The hanger straps and their belt loops allow the pocket to be placed to suit the gunman so he can reach his gun butts easily and quickly, and so his gun will follow the line of his draw. It makes a great deal of difference whether the gun can come out with the easiest way to raise the arm or whether the arm has to humor the gun. The positions show a pair of shoulder straps to help hold up the heavy guns and harness. They may be removed if not wanted, but if a man must wear one or two heavy guns for long stretches at a time, it is better to use the shoulder straps.

"Now let us look at the lower right-hand picture. This illustrates the fastest cross-belly draw. To the amateur gunman this may appear to be the same as the way in which most policemen pack their guns, but *it is far from being the same,* though it is the way they *should* pack their guns if they want to use a belt pocket. Now glance at the lower left-hand picture. This is the two-gun, cross-belly draw. Note that my hands are gripping the gun butts which are exactly where my hands come when I swing my arms across my belly *without hunching my shoulders down and around* in a reach. My shoulders are *back* and I am standing quite straight. Now those gun butts, or one gun butt as in the other picture at the right, are grippable, firmly, with just one fast flap of my arm or arms. I don't have to guess whether my hands are going to find the gun butts. I *know* they will. Further, those gun butts are not down under the curve of my belly, not where the belt may catch on the guns when I draw, but *up* clear of all interference. Again, note the lean of the pockets on a line with my gun arm shoulder. The instant my hand or hands close over the butts I can jerk straight back and my gun clears. Now, if that pocket hung perpendicularly or slanted the other way, I'd have to first lift the gun straight up while holding it at arm's length and then level the barrel. This would involve several very difficult and slow movements in place of one, easy and very fast.

"In the forming of this cross-belly position, the top part of the base piece is folded back and laced with a leg strap to form a *wide* belt loop for the pocket. Note that the gun butt comes above the belt to afford a good grip. Now that wide loop serves a valuable purpose. It is so wide it curves with the curve of the body on the inside of the belt. This causes the pocket to remain in any position the gunman places it in. If he wishes to make a fine adjustment he just draws in his belly where it needs to be to allow a slick, clean, fast draw, then lets out his slack and the adjustment is perfect. Further, that curving of the base piece tends to stiffen it, so that with the wide grip on the belt, the pocket and gun are held from swinging, flapping or twisting, yet it is very comfortable and gives the gunman a feeling of confidence which is half the battle.

"Now look at the picture in the upper right-hand corner. Here I am repping for 'Little 7 Up,' the notorious gunman John Wesley Hardin, who beat some forty men to the shot. This is his favorite position. By position I do not mean harness or holster, but that the gun is in a certain position, no matter what means is used to put it there.

"The guns shown are 45-caliber S.A. Colts with 7½-in. barrels, about as heavy and long as any pistols in use these last fifty years. You can see easily just how the gun is held in this picture. The position is similar to the cross-belly draw, but the draw arm must be bent at the elbow more, yet the lean of the gun allows a very fast draw. The gun can be carried out of sight, though I would not call it concealed. This is a very fine way to carry a gun when doing many kinds of work, as the arms, legs and seat are free.

"The central picture illustrates one way of arranging the harness for an under-the-arm position. This is not a fast draw position, but it is as concealed as possible with such a big gun. In both of these last two positions the shoulder straps and leg straps are used. The central picture also illustrates the use of my quick-reload cartridge pocket. I do not use belt loops for my cartridges for several reasons. I am not a contortionist, so it is difficult for me to remove all of the cartridges from belt loops. And I am particular about my ammunition. I do not like it to corrode so the shells stick in the cylinders and I don't want the lubrication worn off. So I make a supply pocket large enough to hold a box of cartridges (fifty) for the gun or guns used. Then I place a round, counted at my leisure, into the top of the quick-reload pocket. Then, if I am in a hurry to reload I swing one hand under the pocket, flip the bottom flap over with my thumb and the counted round drops into my palm. I can be firing one gun with one hand and arm and getting a round of cartridges ready with the other.

"Ambidextrous? Yes, somewhat; only because of some practice. I am rather right-handed, but it is all hooey about it being difficult to shoot a short gun with either hand. I know hundreds of fine and fast gunmen, and the only one I know who cannot shoot with both hands very well is my old friend J. D. O'Meara, Chief of Guards of the Great Homestake Mines at Lead, South Dakota. And the reason J.D. can shoot with only one arm is he *has* only one arm to shoot with! There was a time when he could shoot two guns at the same time, but years ago when Lead was red hot, J.D. lost one arm. A big Norsky miner bit him and caused blood poisoning so that arm had to be amputated. He can draw fast and point a wicked gun to this very day. He has joined Ed McGivern, 'the fastest living gunman,' in saying: 'The "all ways" gun harness is the finest I have ever seen.' "

"Coteau" Gene is dead—but the interest in the fast draw and straight shot goes on. Today's experts have perfected the art beyond anything the old-timers knew. And in books, movies, TV, and rodeos the cowboy is more popular than ever. The old-time cowboy might be hard put to match some of the stunts that are done today, but he's the one that taught 'em the right way to handle a rope or a bronc or a bunch of cattle in the first place. This book has been about the old-timer's know-how on the range, and without that the modern rider wouldn't be what he is today.

INDEX